BROAD
INFLUENCE

BROAD INFLUENCE

How  Are

Changing the Way

America Works

JAY NEWTON-SMALL

WASHINGTON CORRESPONDENT
TIME MAGAZINE

TIME
Books

Published by Time Books, an imprint of Time Inc. Books
1271 Avenue of the Americas, 6th floor • New York, NY 10020

ISBN 10: 1-61893-155-5
ISBN 13: 978-1-61893-155-9
Library of Congress Control Number: 2015949929

We welcome your comments and suggestions about Time Inc. Books.
Please write to us at:
Time Inc. Books
Attention: Book Editors
P.O. Box 361095
Des Moines, IA 50336-1095
If you would like to order any of our hardcover Collector's Edition books, please
call us at 800-327-6388, Monday through Friday, 7 a.m.–9 p.m. Central Time.

For my mother.

TABLE OF CONTENTS

GETTING TO
CRITICAL MASS

My mother was a tiny Asian woman—5'3" and less than 100 pounds—but she filled up every room she entered. She was usually the smartest person there; she spoke seven languages and had graduated from Cambridge, Oxford and Columbia, where she got her degree in international law. These credentials brought her into the United Nations at a high level, one of a handful of women at the top of the organization. My parents, both U.N. professionals, met in Zambia, where my father was deputy chief of mission and my mother went to work on international development in 1972. My father gave her a tour of the office, which evolved into a tour of the town. When the afternoon became dinner and cocktails, my mother understood that my father had more than a professional interest in seeing her properly settled in. I bet it was easy for her to fall for him: a gregarious Australian, so different from her. My mother was blunt and bold but socially awkward, while my jocular father, a real guy's guy, had a way of putting everyone around him at ease. Their marriage in Malawi two years later created a bureaucratic dilemma: it was against the rules for couples inside the U.N. to marry. In every previous instance, the bride immediately had resigned her post to follow her husband's career. But my mother outranked my father, and always would. In order to keep my mother on, the U.N. had to make an exception.

They led impossibly glamorous lives. Though my father came from a modest Australian family, my mother was born to a prominent Chinese one with huge construction interests in Hong Kong and Malaysia. We traveled so much, my father called us global gypsies. They hunted in Africa, danced in Tahiti, skied in Switzerland and sailed in Sydney Harbor. For much of my childhood they were stationed in separate countries: him in Bangkok while she worked in Geneva, or her in Phnom Penh while he was in New York. Some years I saw my mother only when we all met up to celebrate Christmas or take a vacation. No matter what city we were in, my memories have a common feature: dinner parties where my father had everyone roaring over his stories about Winston Churchill or tall tales of African exploration. But every holiday visit also included a darker scene. There would be at least one night, after they put me to bed, when my mother collapsed crying as she described the brutal way she was treated by the men she faced at work.

This same scene took place in Paris, London, Singapore, Kuala Lumpur and Windhoek, but it happened most often in Greenwich, Conn., where we lived when my parents worked at headquarters in New York. I remember waking up late at night to the sound of her sobbing. I picture my 10-year-old self coming around the corner into a kitchen thick with cigarette smoke—Dunhill Reds—and empty wineglasses and cups of decaf coffee scattered on the kitchen table. The overhead light illuminated just my mother and father, him with his hand on her arm, rubbing softly back and forth. He was so engrossed in trying to soothe her that neither of them noticed me enter the room. When she saw me, my mother pulled in the sobs, detached from my dad and straightened up. She never wanted anyone to see her that way; she never wanted to be seen as weak or complaining. By the time I asked if there was anything I could do for her, she was fully upright. She assured me nothing was wrong, and my father scooped me up and put me back in bed.

Only much later did I understand how tough it was for her. Back then, and arguably today, there were only about 20 countries that endorsed the equality of women, and not just on paper. The fact that my mother outranked most of the men she encountered didn't matter to them. Africans ignored her. South American men thought it was part of a woman's job description to sleep with them, my mother would say only half-jokingly. Middle Eastern men were the worst. Once she had a Palestinian subordinate who refused to look her in the eye or shake her hand and constantly appealed her directives to her Syrian boss. At U.N. headquarters in New York the assault was sexual. When my father moved to Thailand on assignment when I was 10, one of my mother's peers, an Argentine friend of my father's, groped her every time they were alone, continually inviting her to a hotel nearby. My father gave up his promotion to be transferred back to New York, hoping that his presence in the U.N. building would prevent his colleague from insulting my mother this way.

Despite these assaults and insults, my mother loved her work. In Geneva, she worked on high-level international finance and business development treaties. After the Khmer Rouge fell in 1991, my mother was part of the U.N. peacekeeping mission to restore the Cambodian government. The U.N. appointed her governor of Kandal Province, where the capital, Phnom Penh, is located. She advised on the drafting of the country's new constitution and helped supervise its first democratic elections.

So you can imagine my surprise when, as I was graduating from college, my fierce, career-driven mom very strongly advised me against going to graduate school for journalism at one of her alma maters, Columbia University. Over many phone calls, she tried to persuade me to use the classes I'd taken in art history to get a job in a museum or a gallery, find a husband and start a family. She so disapproved of my life direction that she said she wouldn't attend my graduation from Columbia. She kept her word.

At the time, it was hard to see that as an act of love, but I understand now things that I could not then. My mother's profound wish was for me to be happy and not have to fight as hard as she had. But our experiences working with men were so different. I had come up after substantial progress in women's equality, the result of battles fought by pioneering women like my mom. Plus I was in the United States; my encounters with overt sexism were comparatively mild. I was one of the first girls to integrate the previously all-boys Deerfield Academy boarding school in Massachusetts. Not everyone there was happy about the arrival of girls. Some of the legacy students were especially boorish, trying to intimidate us by singing the old lyrics to the school songs, the ones that referred to an exclusively male environment, while looking pointedly at the girls. I had a teacher who refused to call on female students, from time to time barking, "Women should be seen and not heard!" I think he was asked to retire after our second year. While this was infuriating, I never felt unsafe, as my mom often had.

When I went to D.C. as a Capitol reporter, my mentors were men; they had to be, since I was usually one of the few women in the bureau, first at Agence France-Presse, then at Bloomberg, and later when I started at TIME. The atmosphere was a lot more civilized than what my mom had encountered. I never felt slighted because of my gender; I covered politics and received assignments in hot spots like Iraq and Iran. During my time in Washington the female ranks in the White House press corps have swelled; there are so many that at a news conference in 2014 President Obama made a point to call on only women. That would've been a very brief event when I first started covering the White House.

When there were more women alongside me at work, we went out to dinner together and had drinks after work, supporting each other and gaining confidence that helped us to be bolder. I had peers who understood how it felt as a woman when a congressman handed you the key to a room at a nearby hotel or made a clumsy pass at you during a convention. When one of us told the story of some drunken lout of a lobbyist calling late at night with sloppy propositions entangled in every one of his sentences, we could all laugh at him instead of feeling isolated and vulnerable. I had always felt comfortable and confident at work, but with more women as peers, I felt more supported and validated. My workplace had achieved what sociology refers to as critical mass.

The theory of critical mass is originally from science, when a reaction reaches an inflection point and cannot be stopped, like a nuclear explosion. In sociology, it has come to mean the point at which a minority begins to change the tone and policies of the institution it has begun to integrate. When schools were desegregated in the South, for example, the government mandated a minimum "critical mass" of 20 percent. At Deerfield, when less than 20 percent of the student body was female, we were considered odd, outsiders and decidedly second class. But when we became a third of the students, we were no longer an exception, an experiment or an afterthought. With more girls around, we got more comfortable. We began asserting our right to be included, to be heard and to lead. I had always imagined that it would take decades—beyond the scope of my lifetime—to reach parity. Turns out, women don't need parity to change the culture and influence outcomes. My own experience demonstrated that while parity was the ideal, if women reached more than 20 percent of a group, life improved dramatically for us.

Early in 2012, Michael Duffy, my boss at TIME, asked me to embark on an in-depth story on the women of the Senate. At first, I rolled my eyes at the predictability of assigning a woman to cover the women. When I thought about it a bit, though, I became intrigued, partly because I'd just started to look into research that validated my personal experience of critical mass. Substantial research—sociological, political, economic—showed that whether it was a legislative body, a corporate board, an appellate court or a Navy ship, if numbers of women were lower than 20 percent, women's voices weren't heard: either they didn't speak up or men didn't listen. If somewhere between 20 and 30 percent of women were included in the mix—the proportion depends on the institution or group—outcomes were better, sometimes dramatically. In 2012, women had finally reached 20 percent of the Senate. Some of the female senators who had been around for decades were just attaining seniority and coming into their power; at the time, women sat atop half the Senate's 20 committees. In fact, that's a key factor: if you have powerful critical actors and leaders like chairs, military officers or chief executives, the percentage needed to reach that tipping point is lower. The Senate women were at the cutting edge of change. I suspected I was seeing another female turning point.

In the story I wrote, "Women Are the Only Adults Left in Washington," I described how the female senators of both parties led the negotiations to reopen the government during the shutdown when the men were frozen in an ideological standoff. The cross-party alliances that the women had built over years of monthly dinners made it easy for them to communicate effectively and quickly to find common ground. The story got more attention than any other I'd ever written. I was most touched by the handwritten note I received from an 80-year-old woman in North Carolina who said she'd never before written to a journalist but had mustered up the courage to write to me. She felt compelled to thank me for letting her know that women were finally making a difference. I'm sure there were many other women around the country who were also heartened by the news. In their 2014 campaigns, female candidates on both sides of the aisle cited that story as Exhibit A on why it was important to elect more women.

Soon after the story was published, friends, acquaintances and complete strangers began alerting me to other places where women had recently reached critical mass. Turns out that all three branches of the federal government were reaching it at about the same time. Every woman I spoke with had a story about how their work lives changed when more women were added, from miners in Australia and doctors in Baltimore to high-powered executives in London. The stories I found were too numerous to put into this book: it is a truly enormous universe of firsthand experience.

Writing the story about the women of Congress raised more questions for me about how women, achieving this tipping point in so many arenas simultaneously, potentially change the way we govern, manage, rule and command. The struggle for women of my mother's era was to prove that they were as good as men and capable of leading and wielding power. For women of my age, our competence is not in dispute. The question is, what difference do we make? Does the presence of women in the boardroom, on the police force and in the judiciary change what issues are focused on or how things are done? Do outcomes change when women are in charge? And if so, do they change for the better?

Women are not monolithic, but studies show that they tend to be more collaborative, more empathetic and less interested in grandstanding than men. Having more women on police forces improves community outreach; women are also less confrontational, which helps to curb police violence—a valuable benefit in the age of Ferguson. As of 2014, women in the military have begun to be allowed to fight on the front lines, the final brass ceiling to women's attempts to permeate every area of the armed forces. The Navy found long ago that putting only a handful of women on a ship created misery for everyone involved; trial and study found that 20 percent was the magic number, with a mix of officers and enlisted, at which gender issues disappeared and people began working as teams. Women also tend to be more cautious and consider issues differently than men do; for example, women generally won't make big decisions, such as running for office or accepting a big promotion, until they've read all the research and examined every angle. Study after study shows that including more women at the executive level is good for bottom lines. Companies with more women on their boards earned higher profits, took fewer crazy risks, restated their earnings less often and were better at dealing with crises.

Yet the country still wrestles with the idea of a woman in power. Women's traits—such as consensus building and a willingness to see the other side—are often seen as assets when they are running for Congress or serving as judges, but they can hinder those seeking to rule or lead: the ultimate glass ceiling. We've never had a female president and have seen only a few women elected governors or chosen as CEOs of major corporations. Most of the more than 150 high-powered women I interviewed for this book shared stories about being left out of the room or brought in almost too late to have an impact, or finding that they lacked the confidence to speak up or take a seat at the table.

In this book I'll examine the steadily rising influence of women as they achieve, and in some cases surpass, critical mass. In the public sector, I'll tell the stories of the women in the West Wing of the White House, in Congress, in the judiciary and in law enforcement. In each circumstance I'll show how women have used a variety of unique approaches to find common ground, negotiate compromises and advance issues that were previously neglected. For example, having more women on the judicial bench has changed how family issues are handled, with a greater focus on intervention and problem solving. The book reaches a turning point in the sixth chapter, looking at how the public sector has succeeded while the private sector has stalled. The private sector, which once led the way in the advancement of women in leadership, has lagged behind in recent years, and I'll show the cost that we all paid for having fewer women governing the financial markets. The last part of the book looks at the areas in which women haven't yet reached critical mass and why it's important for our nation's future that they do. With the retirement of the baby boomer generation, the U.S. faces a shortfall of 26 million workers over the next 20 years, a gap that can be bridged only by either increasing immigration or bringing women to full employment and much closer to parity.

In many ways, it's amazing how far we've come in just a generation. Twenty years ago, women couldn't wear pants to work. Fifteen years ago, they were still excluded from many caucuses, clubs and meetings. Ten years ago, Senate women were often mistaken for wives and staffers: how else could a woman enter the halls of power? Five years ago, there was still no bathroom for women off the House floor. And it wasn't until recent years that women breached both the West Wing's inner circle and the armed services' front lines. And still, much work remains to be done.

My mother was never far from my mind as I wrote this book. Women like her often went unheard. As one of a handful of powerful female diplomats, my mother was an aberration, easily dismissed by powerful men as a token hire or an attempt at diversity. This casual bias seemed so cruel in the face of my mother's fierce analytic mind, acute attention to detail and astute sense of politics, both internal and global. The men were right. She was not their equal. She was so much better than most of them. Alone, though, she fought a daily battle for respect and significance. In one way I wanted to write this book for my mom, who died in 2011. I think of her often when I'm the only woman in the room, moments that are blessedly fewer these days. I wonder what she would say about the idea of a critical mass of powerful women and how it affects policy and the course of world affairs, the world she struggled so hard to influence. I wonder too if she would agree that when the numbers of women become too big to ignore, women begin to exert a broad influence.

Although women now hold only a small portion of leadership posts, their influence is already broad, which is why I chose the title *Broad Influence*. "Broad" was a disparaging term derived from the undeniable physical fact that women have broader hips than men. Of course we do; we have to in order to bear children. As it was used before it fell out of favor in the 1960s, "broad" implied a coarse, vulgar woman and was frequently used as an insult. The term was so much despised by women, particularly second-wave feminists, that in the late 1960s the U.S. Olympic Committee renamed the "broad jump" the "long jump." Fifty years later, I hope we can reclaim the word with pride: yes, women bear children, but the contribution they make to the world is so much more than that, as the pioneering women I feature in this book demonstrate. They have studied hard, made sacrifices, forged alliances and entered the halls of power in every aspect of society. But that's just the first part of the battle. The story I tell in this book is one in which women are beginning to be taken seriously for their contributions, celebrated for the unique benefits they bring and, at last, being treated as full equals as we move from critical mass to broad influence.

— 1 —

THE

WEST WING

One of the oldest boys' clubs in the country resides in the West Wing of 1600 Pennsylvania Avenue, a bastion of male power so obdurate that it has been among the slowest to open to women. In the 216 years from the country's founding until 1992, just 14 women served in the Cabinet; in the next 23 years, there's been some acceleration, with 20 women in Cabinet positions. When President Obama took office in January 2009, his secretaries of state, labor, homeland security and health and human services and the director of the Environmental Protection Agency were all women, as was his United Nations ambassador.

The new president, who was raised by a strong and independent single mom and is the father of two daughters with his formidable spouse, promised to promote women's voices and views in ways previous administrations had not. Thirty-nine percent of Obama's West Wing staff was female, a 10-percentage-point increase over the end of the Bush administration. His top communications adviser was Stephanie Cutter, who managed the messaging; Valerie Jarrett, a close friend of the president and the first lady, was one of the president's most important confidants; eight other women held vital senior staff positions. At last women had reached critical mass in all corners of the West Wing.

Yet even without the smoky back rooms of a bygone era, where men cut deals over cigars and whiskey, these savvy and supremely qualified women quickly found that they had a tough time being included in rooms where decisions were being made.

Almost immediately they noticed that some key male staff bypassed women or outright blocked them from major initiatives. When Obama took office, ushered in by the economic collapse in late 2008, the financial crisis was the top focus. The economy was flagging, and it desperately needed an infusion of capital from the government. The only question was: how big? Some argued that if it were too small, not only would the economy take longer to recover but the U.S. risked a limping decade marred by deflation, as Japan had suffered in the 1990s. But too big and the massive government borrowing would risk further inflating the nation's debt and crowd out private investment, stunting private-sector growth.

Obama's inner circle on the issue—Larry Summers, the director of the president's National Economic Council; Rahm Emanuel, chief of staff; and Budget Director Peter Orszag—seemed to have little interest in the women's point of view. Summers shut out Christine Romer, chair of the Council of Economic Advisers to the White House, when she wanted to make a case for a $1.8 trillion stimulus, more than double the size of the one favored by several senior White House officials—a characterization Summers disputes. Orszag took his issues directly to the president. Emanuel had a foul mouth and could be brutal. Though he was an equal-opportunity screamer, he did little to foster team spirit. The women suspected—although these men would deny it if asked—that they were excluded intentionally. Women were in the upper echelons of the West Wing and, for the first time, had achieved critical mass, but they were still having a hard time getting in the room. And while they raised this issue, even expressing their frustrations to the president, the problem persisted to the end of Obama's first term.

Symbolically, Obama started off poorly with the West Wing women. At the president's first address before a joint session of Congress in January 2009, Summers got a seat in the congressional chamber, but the director of the Domestic Policy Council, Melody Barnes, did not, much to the outrage of many of the senior White House women. Then Ellen Moran, a former director of Emily's List, which works to elect pro-choice women to office, quit as White House communications director. She'd lasted just 92 days. Even though senior White House officials begged her to remain, Moran's replacement, Anita Dunn, stayed only seven months, as she promised her family she'd return home. Later, in Ron Suskind's 2011 book *Confidence Men: Wall Street, Washington, and the Education of a President,* Dunn said the atmosphere "fit all of the classic legal requirements for a genuinely hostile workplace to women."

By that fall, the acrimony had become so pronounced—it spawned several newspaper stories full of unhappy quotes about the treatment of women—that the president invited the women to air their grievances at a dinner at his private residence on the second floor of the White House. Obama listened carefully but did not offer to admonish or replace anybody. "He didn't totally defend bad behavior," said a participant, "but he didn't say, 'You're right.' " He explained that Summers, Orszag and Emanuel were playing the roles he wanted them to play, and he advised the women to step up their game.

But which game was it? The game as played in the West Wing was a decidedly male one. It's more than just the chummy way men communicate with one another: men set the standards for the behaviors that broadcast power. The president's chief forms of relaxation were pick-up basketball games and rounds of golf, but nearly a year into his presidency, no woman had joined his teams. At some staff meetings, the men tossed a football around. How could the women be part of his inner circle if they weren't part of the sports play? Almost offhandedly, as the dinner came to a close, the president suggested that the women start getting together regularly. Maybe they could build their own power base.

None of the women had had time to form friendships on the job, and few had known each other well before starting at the White House. The pace was so frenzied, they'd had little opportunity to spend time together outside of work. So they took the president's suggestion of monthly dinners in order to get to know each other and devise a culture of their own.

"The White House is a hard place at times, and being able to talk to someone else, to strategize on an issue, often helped," said Lisa Brown, Obama's staff secretary. They began to form a team where none existed in the White House. "The women were much more about being team players—the president's team," said a high-ranking woman. "The guys, it was about their own agenda."

This is a common difference between women and men. Studies show that women are better at consensus building and less interested in "I" than "we." Some sociologists theorize that this may be because women only recently learned how to compete. Women hardly participated in team sports in school until 1972, after the enactment of Title IX required that women's sports receive funding equal to men's. Until then, women's largely domestic worlds revolved around others and not themselves. "There was a tangible difference after Title IX," said Dunn. "It was like suddenly women learned they didn't have to compete with each other, but they could work together as a team and they were more powerful that way. They also learned to leave their differences on the field. It changed the way women worked in the workforce."

As the women of the West Wing grew closer, they discovered

they'd all had the experience of men talking over them at meetings and ignoring their input until the same idea came from a man's mouth. Barnes advised her female peers to change their communication style and state decisions as declarative sentences. "I've seen this a million times where a woman who's smart, has a great idea, is aggressive professionally" but will pose an idea as a question, Barnes said, as if it needed reinforcement from the men in the room. "It's being comfortable with your very well-reasoned opinions and having it understood that way."

If being heard was the problem, maybe they needed to speak up more often so they were more comfortable expressing themselves. The women encouraged each other to be bolder, to weigh in even in areas outside their expertise. "The self-editing that goes on is huge," said Nancy-Ann DeParle, White House deputy chief of staff. "The women in the room—especially a room that includes the president—would often tend to self-edit, avoid restating an obvious point, and listen more, to ensure they were making an organized contribution in a meeting."

But men didn't play by those rules. "I was spending days thinking about what I wanted to say," said Carol Browner, who served as the director of the White House Office of Energy and Climate Change Policy. "Men, I am sure, spent five minutes before the meeting thinking about what they'd say."

Minorities at the leading edge of critical mass—as the women of the West Wing were—often feel self-conscious about how they should behave or look. They keep their heads down and get business done to display their competence and diligence, rather than speaking up inside the existing power structure. They'd rather stay quiet than risk being seen as a fool.

Some of the women were self-conscious about how they dressed. How much makeup was too much? How long or short should their hemlines be in order to be fashionable and still be taken seriously?

And what about necklines? These were problems the men didn't have to consider, but they were a concern among the women, who eagerly sought one another's advice.

Barnes once shared her simple rules of professional behavior. "One-piece bathing suit, two drinks, conservative dancing," she said, half-joking. But within a month, the offhand tips had spread quickly among mid-level and younger women. "Women were coming up to me and saying, 'I heard your rules. That makes a lot of sense,'" Barnes said. The younger women, Barnes realized, were watching more senior colleagues like herself, Jarrett and DeParle for cues on how to dress and act in order to be taken seriously. Sharing and addressing those concerns helped make it easier for the women of the West Wing to assert themselves.

Their frustration about how to be taken more seriously contrasted sharply with the atmosphere in one policy area that ended up being run almost completely by women: the environment.

In addition to Browner, who was Obama's environment czar, and her deputy, both of Obama's EPA administrators were women: Lisa Jackson, followed by Gina McCarthy. Heather Zichal crafted climate change policy, and the head of Obama's Council on Environmental Quality was Nancy Sutley. Together, the women negotiated a compromise on a critical achievement that had failed four previous administrations: a national automobile fuel efficiency standard.

States can set emissions standards that are tougher than the rest of the country's; California had been doing this for decades, which drove car companies crazy because they had to make cars both for the rest of the country and specifically for California. The Bush administration had enacted new fuel efficiency standards, and the Supreme Court compelled the administration to regulate greenhouse gases, starting with cars. Browner suggested combining all three processes into one national set of standards that would allow automakers to make one car for the entire country.

The talks were marked by a lack of bluster and bluffing, perhaps because the negotiators for California and the car companies were women too. Browner said they were quick to sort the wheat from the chaff: what each party needed versus what they simply wanted. This is a key difference between male and female negotiators: women generally look for ways in which everyone can win a little, even if that means that everyone loses a little. It's not that women don't like to win—they do. But they don't see it as a winner-take-all game. Their lack of blood thirst creates trust and long-term partnerships that are more durable.

"I do feel that [women] problem-solve differently," Browner said. "You've got a complicated problem with a lot of different players, and everyone articulates what is it that they want or need." Women, she notes, are good at distinguishing between want and need—a skill honed through their role as family conciliators. "We're always the one trying to problem-solve, to figure out how we move forward, how we make that happen and what needs to happen for the family, for the workplace and for these complex climate problems," she said.

Yet no triumph could go forward without a man trying to take credit for it. As the deal moved closer to finalization, Larry Summers alerted Browner's staff in a memo that he had decided she should start reporting to him, rather than directly to the president. Browner was nonplussed, sources said. And, indeed, nothing ever happened: Browner continued to report to the president as she always had.

Ultimately, women representing California, the West Wing and automakers negotiated a set of national standards that benefited consumers: by 2025 cars will be required to get 54.5 miles to the gallon on highways, a major leap in efficiency from the previous target under George W. Bush of 35 miles per gallon by 2020. "It was really amazing to watch these women tackle this incredibly complex issue and just sort it out," said Dunn, who was White House communications director when the talks began. In fact, several studies indicate that women are far more likely than men to put ego aside in search of a greater goal, which often makes them much more effective at tackling large, complex issues, as we'll see later on in the House chapter.

Perhaps the most illustrative and impactful female duo in Obama's White House were deputy chiefs of staff DeParle and Alyssa Mastromonaco. Over lunch late in the summer of 2014, I interviewed them together over salads and coffee sitting in the window table at the Peacock Café in Georgetown. Both are petite brunettes. Mastromonaco has a unique fashion style—she's written about it for *Marie Claire* magazine, which she joined after leaving the White House—that is at once laid-back and quirky chic. She is quick with a smile and a quip. DeParle is more reserved, though her affection for Mastromonaco is obvious. Neither knew the other well when they were approached by the president to become deputy chiefs of staff in 2011—the first time there have been two female deputies. The job is daunting: the two deputies basically divvy up the entire world and run interference for the White House chief of staff and, therefore, the president. Mastromonaco was deputy chief for operations, in charge of scheduling, advance work, the administration and its various and enormous departments, and the budget, crunching the numbers on major policy initiatives; and DeParle became deputy chief for policy, in charge of shepherding the president's foreign and domestic policies and seeing his agenda through Congress.

In the past, there have been turf wars and tension between deputy chiefs, with their overlapping and enormous fiefdoms. Mastromonaco and DeParle quickly decided that they would share power and support, rather than try to undermine, each other. "So we marched upstairs together and we're like: we're in!" Mastromonaco said with a laugh. Instead of jockeying for prominence, they took on the responsibilities as a team.

Mastromonaco noted that she never concerned herself about health-care reform, as long as she knew DeParle was in the room.

Why spend time re-creating work that she knew was being handled by DeParle? "We were the least competitive people ever. We just divvied things up and did our own thing," Mastromonaco said.

"We rarely worked together," DeParle echoed. "We coordinated on the president's travel, because one of us always traveled with him. But for the most part, she was doing her thing—operations—and I would do mine—policy."

The two also tried to have some fun along the way. They started a private joke that they were the administration's Smurfettes: the lone female character on the animated *Smurfs* show, created by mistake, in a village of male Smurfs. Both had blue Smurfettes prominently positioned on their desks. "I kept waiting for one of the guys to say something, but no one ever asked," DeParle said.

And instead of keeping their male predecessors' Secret Service names, they chose Popsicle for Mastromonaco and Peaches for DeParle—and delighted in watching the mostly male, macho Secret Service agents announce the arrival of Popsicle or Peaches.

But for all their playfulness, the pair were much more focused on the nitty-gritty of their work than on the politics of the West Wing.

On any given day, something is bound to be spinning out of control in the world: Yazidis stuck on an Iraqi mountaintop surrounded by ISIS, schoolgirls kidnapped by Boko Haram in Africa, an oil spill in the Gulf of Mexico, an avian flu outbreak in Mexico. And in the West Wing, those overseeing the crisis have the president's ear until it's resolved. But there are other incredibly important though not terribly prominent issues to attend to, and the staff has to handle those alongside the crises. The temptation for most men had been to drop everything and jump into the crisis. But if everyone does that, no one is left to do the other work that needs to get done. For example, during the Ebola outbreak, as the White House weighed calls to suspend all direct flights from Africa or to quarantine Dallas when a deadly case popped up there, DeParle was charged with figuring out how to appease environmental groups seeking to preserve the lesser prairie chicken as an endangered species without restricting development of large swaths of Texas.

"Everyone would want to be doing Ebola, and she'd have to come and have a meeting on these prairie chickens," Mastromonaco said. "It'd be so great if we could say, Oh, I'm so interested in [Ebola] right now, I'm just going to take it up, like a hobby. But we never do. Ever. We just did what we could that would make the West Wing productive."

Perhaps the best example of the eagerness to show proximity to power is the night Osama bin Laden was killed, one of the most important moments of Obama's administration. Neither DeParle nor Mastromonaco was in the Situation Room the night of the raid, but many male White House staffers bluster and brag that they either were there or knew about it—when in reality, few did. "I shouldn't have [been there] because that's not my job," Mastromonaco said. "And that's part of the problem . . . if people aren't swimming in their lanes." If everyone in the building were to drop everything to work on a crisis, the work that's critical to running the nation would simply stop. The women were more aware of sticking to their duties and coming in on a crisis only when absolutely needed. They didn't insert themselves into other people's business.

Mastromonaco and DeParle's duties included serving as traveling chief of staff with the president. They would switch off, coordinating schedules around DeParle's nightly tuck-in duties for her two young kids. They both preferred riding in the staff van rather than in the president's limo so that they could get work done.

DeParle and Mastromonaco used to marvel at some of the men who traveled with the president, secretly calling them "moths to a flame." These men loped down the steps of Air Force One and got into the waiting limo, assuming they'd be riding with the president.

If you sat with the president, you had to talk to him—and

Mastromonaco and DeParle both worried that he'd be distracted by whatever relatively mundane task they were tackling.

"We often didn't want him to know [what we were working on] because we didn't want him to be distracted by the daily 'whack-a-mole' of batting down problems that cropped up," DeParle said. "That's one reason I usually rode with the military aide instead of in the limo with the president when we were on the road. He noticed that, and finally he said to me, 'Is there something about me that you don't like sitting with me?' " DeParle said. "And I said, 'No, Mr. President, it's not that. I just thought that you deserved some time to be by yourself.' "

Women breaking into high-level positions often keep their heads down so they don't stand out in a roomful of men, studies show. Those same studies show that men do the opposite: they need to fight to stand out in a sea of similar people. And women more often seek to be rewarded for competence rather than charm, so they often overprepare. For example, almost every woman I interviewed said they wanted to be absolutely accurate before speaking—a challenge in the White House, where "you're operating usually on 40 percent, maybe 30 percent information," said Mona Sutphen, Obama's first deputy chief of staff for policy before DeParle. "You're balancing this nuance and caution with also being confident."

And it's not just what you say but also how you act that conveys authority. In one meeting, a senior White House official was impressed by a young woman leading the meeting. Then an administrative task arose, and the woman leaped up to deal with it. "The minute she did that, she completely changed her relationship with the table. She was no longer the leader. She was the follower. She was no longer an equal," the official said. "I see it all the time. The women jump up to make shit happen. . . . They just wanna get it fixed or keep it moving and keep everyone happy."

Where one sits in a meeting is important too—and Mastromonaco and DeParle led by example, sitting at the table only when they were key to a meeting. "To me, a staffer at the National Economic Council who is doing housing should be at the table if the meeting's on housing," said Mastromonaco. "And then the men would always sit at the table. Relevant, not relevant. . . . It could actually be a meeting about how birth control makes you feel, and they would sit at the table."

As deputy chiefs of staff, DeParle and Mastromonaco encouraged only relevant staff to sit at the table; as a result, junior staffers didn't have to shout from the back, and more senior men were left standing. For the first time, the women of the West Wing had enough numbers and clout to elbow their way in and run things as well as the men—often more efficiently.

But while a woman may not be terribly concerned about riding in the car with the president, men care very much about such symbols. And ceding this territory in a world run by men can make a woman less of a player; it's a far greater compromise than they realize. When the men in power envision which key players they want at the table, they don't see women there, despite the increased presence of women in the West Wing.

Such was the case in July 2011 when President Obama and his staff were trying to strike a Grand Bargain, a sweeping bill to reduce the deficit by raising revenues and cutting spending, with the Republicans. Negotiations had been going on for weeks, always in danger of collapse. The Obama administration wanted to end specific tax breaks for the wealthy, while the GOP instead wanted to cut entitlements.

To satisfy both sides, House Speaker John Boehner and Obama would each have to give up something dear to their supporters, and negotiations were intense, frequent and largely out of view of the press; Boehner would slip through a side door for his meetings with the president. There were also the meetings with White House and congressional staff to strategize the best maneuvers, identify the least-painful budget cuts and assess the politics that stood in the way of selling any deal to their respective parties.

On the table that summer were trillions of dollars of spending and taxes. And women—especially DeParle and Mastromonaco—were doing a lot of the legwork behind the scenes. But they were being excluded from some of the vital negotiations. The men involved would walk into the Oval Office to hold impromptu sessions with the president when ideas struck them, or they'd turn to the topic in an unrelated meeting.

The women shared their frustrations with each other and tried to figure out the best way to be included without an awkward scene or confrontation. So first, they activated their network. Early on, Lisa Brown, the president's staff secretary, made sure that the women were either called into meetings that they'd been left out of or advised on impromptu meetings after the fact. "I could make sure when a policy position was being made, when I saw someone was being excluded . . . that whoever was left out was let back in again," Brown said. "Some of it's sisterhood; some of it's 'That's the right thing . . .' There was a sense of 'We're in this together,' and that's the way it should have been."

Other women picked up Brown's cue. During her tenure, Sutphen took pains to ensure that pertinent women were involved in the right discussions. "There were enough senior women that you can basically all look out for each other's interests," Sutphen said. DeParle and Mastromonaco also did this when they could.

Two years after their dinner with Obama, the West Wing women's network was in place. What they needed was a plan.

They'd half-jokingly proposed just barging into the Oval Office, musing about the looks on the men's faces if they walked in uninvited—but no one really thought it was a good solution.

Then one Sunday they heard that there was a meeting in progress between the president, Chief of Staff Bill Daley and top political adviser David Plouffe. As the women gathered outside the Oval, frustration boiled over and they decided they weren't going to wait to be invited to do their jobs. Mastromonaco, DeParle and Stephanie Cutter did what they had rejected as unthinkable: they opened the portal to world power—the door to the Oval Office—walked in, sat down and began participating.

"The president was like, 'Hi, guys,' " said a person who was present. "Everyone pretended like nothing was amiss. Nobody ever said anything."

But the men, and the president, got the message: the women were never excluded again. Ultimately, the Grand Bargain failed, but for the women in the West Wing, it was a watershed moment: they finally broke into the room. And their voices were just beginning to be heard.

— 2 —

THE

SENATE

Within weeks of being named Budget Committee chair in November 2012, Sen. Patty Murray asked to meet her House Republican counterpart, Paul Ryan, for breakfast in the Senate Dining Room. It was a bit like an awkward first date, she recalled, rather than a business meeting between two political adversaries: Ryan is a conservative, Murray a liberal Democrat who is 20 years his senior. Instead of talking shop, the two, led by Murray, spent over an hour getting to know each other. How did they get started in politics? How did they meet their spouses? Murray and Ryan forged a friendship that ultimately achieved the country's first budget agreement in four years, during an infamously gridlocked congressional session marked by paralyzing partisanship and a government shutdown.

In their first breakfast, the word "budget" never came up. "We talked about his family and my family, what he grew up with. I wanted to know him. I wanted to know what drove him and what is his passion," Murray said.

They both fished, Murray for salmon in her home state of Washington and Ryan for muskie and walleye in Wisconsin. Both their young lives were altered by their fathers' tragedies: Ryan at age 16 found his father's body in the family home, dead of a sudden heart attack, and Murray's father was diagnosed with multiple sclerosis when she was 15, which forced her family onto food stamps. "We know what it's like to be on your own and fight through existence," Murray said.

But perhaps the most important commonality was a shared love of football. Murray was an avid Seahawks fan and Ryan supported the Green Bay Packers. The Seahawks had stunned the Packers in September in a close game featuring a notoriously controversial officiating call at the end. Murray would jibe him about the rivalry to fill awkward pauses during their initial breakfast and later in sometimes heated budget negotiations, particularly over Seahawks quarterback Russell Wilson, who'd attended the University of Wisconsin—home state of Ryan's beloved Packers—and then went to play for Seattle. "I think the reality of that is if you focus on something that makes people human beings . . . if you actually find a way to be friendly with each other and understand where they are coming from, that's how you get an agreement," Murray said. "I think women can do that."

For Ryan, sports became their language. "Basically our staffs had this notion that we'd both start from our 20-yard lines and we'd try to get together in the middle of the field," Ryan said. "With Patty, we were able to dismiss all of the theater . . . and get to a very common understanding so that we could achieve our objective. The key was that we set out from the get-go not to swing for the fences and get a grand-slam budget agreement, which we knew would fail because the prior four times it had failed."

Indeed, that December morning as they laughed over sports, they recognized the scope of the task before them. Murray was determined to do things differently, to break with the system of the past—and she wasn't the only one. For the first time in history, the Senate was 20 percent female. Even more important, the women sat atop half the committees, exerting outsize influence. By the end of this rancorous congressional term, the women produced 75 percent of the major legislation that passed the Senate, showing how different the Senate can be—how much more functional—when women reach a critical mass. Study after study shows that women govern differently than men in legislative bodies. They tend to compromise more and grandstand less. They are better at building consensus. And at a time when bipartisan relationships have all but died in Washington, the 20 women of the Senate also had 20 years of deep friendships and trust to draw upon.

Murray and Ryan's budget deal wasn't the only breakthrough. Sen. Barbara Boxer saw through a $12.5 billion water resources bill and $54 billion transportation legislation; Sen. Debbie Stabenow got a gigantic $955 billion farm bill passed; Sen. Barbara Mikulski shepherded more than a dozen appropriations bills; and all 20 women came together to ensure passage of the Violence Against Women Act.

It wasn't that the women had some special feminine powers. To some degree they took charge because the men had lost the ability to find common ground. In the 1990s, then House Speaker Newt Gingrich raised congressional salaries, and members started traveling home every weekend. Though intended to get members outside the insular Beltway, it also gave them less opportunity to maintain relationships. Bipartisan friendships began to evaporate, and most male members hardly knew people in their own party, let alone those across the aisle. But the women of the Senate made a point through the 2012–13 session to continue holding regular bipartisan dinners that started more than 20 years ago, from which have grown countless baby and bridal showers, dinners with spouses and children—and dozens of pieces of legislation.

The women were hardly monolithic. They ranged in ages between 45 and 80. New Hampshire Republican Kelly Ayotte and New York

Democrat Kirsten Gillibrand, the youngest, sometimes came into the Senate muddied from a run or softball practice. California Democrat Dianne Feinstein, the oldest, had a prim dress code for women on her staff: stockings and skirts of a certain length. Some women were single, some were childless, and some were grandmothers. Some ran for office when their children were grown. Their politics spanned a broad spectrum, from Massachusetts liberal Elizabeth Warren, the scourge of Wall Street, to Tea Partier Deb Fischer from Nebraska. Some found more in common with those on the other side of the aisle. "I'm a moderate, and there've been times where I've disagreed with my caucus," said Missouri Democrat Claire McCaskill, adding that former Maine Republican Olympia Snowe "really took me under her wing and said, 'I know how it feels.'" The amity and collaboration forged by Murray and the other women of the Senate in the 113th session provides a glimpse of what Washington will be like when women cement a critical mass in both houses of Congress.

All rarely agree, which is why when they do it is so powerful. I interviewed nearly all 20 women—some multiple times—and found commonalities amid their diversity. Women aren't necessarily less partisan than men, but they are more inclined to listen and try to understand the other side. All the chairs and ranking members insist on regular meals with their counterparts so they can better get to know those across the aisle. Many have visited their counterparts' home states. They each put stock in personal friendships and bonds: fellow female senators are almost always their first calls when they need partners across the aisle or advice on how to approach other members. They rarely campaign against one another, despite party lines, and have an informal agreement not to criticize one another publicly.

It is ironic that women are the only ones in Washington who still do business the old-fashioned way: by forging relationships and fostering trust. That's what worked with Murray and Ryan. "You need to get to know people in order to deal with them, and there's not a lot of that right now," Ryan said. "For instance, I've only ever spoke to [Senate majority leader] Harry Reid once in my life and that was two minutes talking about Reno, Nevada, at the inauguration. So that doesn't lend itself to working together. Patty and I . . . I've got her cell phone; we text each other."

Murray didn't start out to be a politician; her story embodies how and why the women of the Senate have become so effective and progressed so rapidly in such a relatively short amount of time. Born Patricia Lynn Johns, she and her twin were two of seven children. Her father was a World War II veteran and Purple Heart recipient, and all the kids worked in his five-and-dime on Main Street in Bothell, Wash. Patty went to Washington State University, where she met Rob Murray; they married after they graduated in 1972. They had two kids, and Patty settled into the life of a soccer mom, teaching and carpooling in Bothell. Then, in 1980, Washington State cut funding for preschool programs. Murray was aghast. So she bundled her kids, ages 1 and 3, into the car and drove 75 minutes for her first visit to the state capital, Olympia.

"So I was just going around the hall and finding who I could talk to, and one state legislator just said, 'That's a nice story, but you're just a mom in tennis shoes,' " she recalled. "[It] made me so angry that he thought that moms in tennis shoes shouldn't have a say in public policy. He just dismissed me because I didn't look like what they thought everybody important should look like. So I drove home and started calling all the other moms, and they called the moms they knew—all were mad—and we were back at the state legislature." Their resulting grassroots campaign restored the cuts. Murray knew she could make a difference and went on to win election to her school board and later to the state senate.

Supreme Court Justice Clarence Thomas's televised 1991 Senate confirmation hearings were a watershed for Murray. She watched as Anita Hill testified that she'd been sexually harassed by Thomas, her boss at the Education Department and the Equal Employment Opportunity Commission. And she was incensed when the all-male Judiciary Committee denigrated Hill, forcing her to take a polygraph test and asking if she was simply a bitter, spurned woman seeking revenge. This one hearing galvanized a generation of women into political action.

"It was so stark, watching these men grill this woman in these big chairs and looking down at her," Murray said. She was furious in the same way she'd been when the state legislator told her that she couldn't make a difference as a mom in tennis shoes. At an event that evening, she found that Hill's humiliation was all women wanted to talk about. "And I just said: I am going run for Senate," Murray recalled. "Because they need somebody there who is going to say what I would say if I was there," which would've been to defend Hill and grill Thomas instead.

That year, 1992, Murray and three other women were elected, tripling the number of the female contingent in the Senate to six; seven months later, Republican Kay Bailey Hutchison became number seven when she won a Texas special election. When Murray arrived, there was no family medical leave in America. Federal funding for breast cancer research was a paltry $100,000 a year. There was limited funding for Planned Parenthood and no state medical insurance for poor children; no support for equal pay; and no laws protecting women from their partners' abuse or violence. Murray and her six fellow senators made a difference—certainly more than the two lonely women before them had—and things began to change more and more as the women approached critical mass.

During her first year in office, the Senate was debating the Family

Medical Leave Act, a bill that the women had pushed aggressively. Murray took to the floor and spoke about how a dear friend had been forced to quit her job to take care of her dying son, nearly bankrupting her family. On her way out of the chamber, an older male senator stopped her. "We don't tell personal stories here," he admonished. Murray said that she had every intention of telling personal stories on the Senate floor. "Years later he apologized and thanked me," she recalled. "He realized that highlighting the real impact, that that's how we help people understand what we're doing."

All the women have stories of overcoming sexism and marginalization. Token minorities always face such challenges: they are overlooked, discounted and shut out. Their presence is considered an anomaly and temporary, so there's little effort to accommodate them. The message: Don't get too comfortable; you won't be staying.

Women were kept out of certain caucuses and rooms, and they didn't even get their own bathroom off the Senate floor until the end of 1993. When they spoke on the Senate floor, male senators often interrupted, claiming they lacked knowledge or experience about issues. While California's Dianne Feinstein was debating a ban on assault weapons in the mid-1990s, Idaho Republican Larry Craig piped up. "The senator from California, in her arguments tonight, I must say, was somewhat typical of those who study the issue for the first time," he said. "The senator from California needs to become a little more familiar with firearms and their deadly characteristics."

Feinstein quickly retorted: "They found my assassinated colleague, and you could put a finger through the bullet hole. I proposed gun control legislation in San Francisco. I went through a recall on the basis of it. I was trained in the shooting of a firearm when I had terrorist attacks with a bomb at my house when my husband was dying, when I had windows shot out. Senator, I know something about what firearms can do." Craig never underestimated Feinstein again.

In her early years in office, Murray was on a senators-only elevator with Strom Thurmond, who was notoriously hands-on with women. Female Senate pages were warned not to get within arm's reach of him, even in his waning years, when he was confined to a wheelchair. Murray, trapped in a small elevator, wasn't so lucky. Thurmond groped Murray's breast, according to several staffers who'd served in the Senate at the time.

The women endured men's frequent slights, insults and dismissive behavior. Three months after taking office in 2007, when the number of female senators rose from 14 to 16, Minnesota's Amy Klobuchar was in another senators-only elevator when an older male senator, whom she won't name, wanted to enter. He looked at her and barked: "This elevator is for senators only!" Her aide replied, "She is a senator." The man went bright red and stepped back. On McCaskill's first day that same year, a Senate chamber doorman told her that she couldn't enter the chamber because there would be no floor passes for the public that day. McCaskill then identified herself. "I said, 'I think I earned my floor pass,' " McCaskill recalled. "He was mortified."

During her new-member orientation as the only woman elected in 2010, New Hampshire Republican Kelly Ayotte was in the Capitol with Florida Republican Marco Rubio. An aide approached and reminded Rubio that he and his wife needed to get an ID, gesturing to Ayotte. "I think Marco was more embarrassed than I was," Ayotte said, laughing. Rubio hastened to say that the woman next to him was Sen. Ayotte. Even in 2010 the default assumption was that the rare woman in a sea of male faces had to be either a staff member or a wife.

The women were steadily growing in seniority and in power. With six-year terms, the Senate is a waiting game, and leadership and chairmanships eventually come to those who reach seniority. In the Senate, that takes a very long time. Chairs have incredible power to legislate, hold hearings, investigate and set the agenda in the areas within their jurisdiction.

By 2007, 14 years after she'd first entered the Senate, Murray became the first Democratic woman elected to leadership, chairing the Democratic Caucus, the Senate Democrats' No. 4 leadership position. Yet she wasn't always included in critical negotiations. Her presence in the room, even by 2011, was not always guaranteed. One night in 2011, at the end of the failed attempt to pass a Grand Bargain—a sweeping bill to reduce the deficit by raising revenues and cutting spending—Majority Leader Reid summoned Murray to the Capitol at 11 p.m. She entered a room full of men who'd been up for days trying to avert defaulting on the U.S. debt—yet no one had thought to call her until that moment, and then only because they wanted a woman's perspective, or rather a woman's outrage. They told her that they had a deal on everything except cuts to Planned Parenthood sought by House Republicans.

Murray hit the roof. " 'Absolutely not,' I told them. 'I'd rather default on our debt,' " she recalled. Over the next three days, she organized four press conferences with female members to highlight the importance of Planned Parenthood—not just to provide abortions but for contraception, mammograms and children's health. The funding was saved.

By 2013, Murray was chair of the powerful Budget Committee; that year, for the first time in history, women headed 11 of the 20 Senate committees: California's Barbara Boxer chaired both the Ethics Committee and the Committee on Environment and Public Works, Debbie Stabenow helmed the Agriculture Committee, Barbara Mikulski ruled the powerful Appropriations Committee with an iron fist ("We're all afraid of her," Reid once commented on the Senate floor), Louisiana's Mary Landrieu first chaired the Small Business Committee and then the Energy Committee, Feinstein chaired the Intelligence Committee, Washington's Maria Cantwell helmed the Committee on Indian Affairs, Alaska Republican Lisa

Murkowski was the ranking member on the Energy Committee, and Maine's Susan Collins was the top Republican on the Aging Committee. Now when women gathered on the Senate floor during votes, McCaskill said, the men half-joked that it made them nervous. "They worry that we're scheming, and we are," she laughed. Even at that key tipping point, women were seen as an anomaly and a disruption to normal business.

Murray's negotiations with Ryan in 2013 were the result of the failed Grand Bargain two years earlier. When the Senate didn't reach a deal, it passed what became known as the sequester: $1.2 trillion in automatic, across-the-board cuts to the Pentagon and entitlement programs like Social Security designed to be unacceptable to both parties and intended to force compromise on a real budget. It quickly became evident that the cuts were still easier to live with than the pain of negotiating another deal. Complicating the process was the looming "fiscal cliff," when the U.S. government would either shut down because of a lack of funds or default on its debt. The ensuing two years saw nothing but temporary fixes that bridged budget gaps by weeks and months, creating a perpetual state of fiscal brinkmanship that merely pushed the cliff farther out inch by painful inch.

By the time President Obama won re-election in 2012, the country was thoroughly sick of fiscal cliffs and threatened defaults, and both parties recognized that they needed some breathing room. So in March 2013, they passed a six-month extension, funding the government until the end of the fiscal year in September. The idea was to give Murray and Ryan's budget process some time and to allow Congress to turn to other issues like gun control and immigration. After Murray's breakfast with Ryan, it would be four months before the two spoke again.

In the interim, Murray had to prove her chops by getting the Democrat-controlled Senate to pass a budget, something it had refused to do since the passage of Obamacare in early 2011. The senators were worried that Senate minority leader Mitch McConnell would amend the budget either to strip funding from the Affordable Care Act or to force votes on issues that would be tough on Democrats who were up for re-election. To win her party's support, Murray first had to convince Majority Leader Harry Reid that she could protect both Obamacare and vulnerable Democrats. "I don't think [Ryan] ever believed that I was going to get a budget," Murray said. "He knew that I was going to try."

Murray and many of the women of the Senate tended to employ what's known as the PTA strategy of legislating. Women tackle large, divisive issues more effectively than men by employing what a Vanderbilt University study calls "high-effort, consensus-building" tactics. In other words: they split up the work and delegate tasks. "Women are more likely to say, I can't do all this, but what if I take this and you take that and so-and-so takes another piece," said Blanche Lincoln, a former Arkansas senator and longtime Murray friend who coined the phrase. Debbie Stabenow used it to get the $1 trillion farm bill through; Boxer, to win reauthorization of $300 billion to fund transportation infrastructure.

Women work harder to prove themselves in a male-dominated Congress, and in doing so they increase their understanding of many issues. They also have stamina and are willing to go 10 rounds on a single issue.

So instead of hoarding power as committee chair, Murray distributed it. Murray deputized many of her committee members, particularly Stabenow and freshman Tammy Baldwin, a Wisconsin Democrat, to divvy up and track the hundreds of pending amendments.

The PTA strategy worked well for Murray. After a hard-fought vote-o-rama, in which the Senate tackled 567 amendments, Murray won passage of her budget by a vote of 50–49 on March 23, 2013. Several vulnerable Democrats voted against the measure, which proposed $975 billion in cuts, including $275 billion in new cuts to

Medicare and Medicaid spending. No Republicans voted for it, but McConnell hailed its passage as "one of the Senate's finest days in recent years."

Earlier that same week, Ryan got his budget through the Republican-controlled House. Each house of Congress approves its own version of a bill, but only a single bill, approved by both houses, will reach the president's desk to be signed into law. Ryan and Murray faced obstacles before they could even begin to talk. To iron out the differences between the two, the leaders of both parties must designate members as conferees, who negotiate the compromise version on behalf of both chambers and parties. Democrats named their conferees, but, after four years of clamoring for a budget, the Republicans suddenly grew leery. Texas senator Ted Cruz claimed that the budget conference process was simply a backdoor ploy by Democrats to raise taxes. There was little Ryan could do to move his party along politically. Over the next six months, Murray went to the Senate floor 21 times to publicly demand that Republicans name their conferees and begin negotiating in earnest.

Meanwhile, the women of the Senate were taking advantage of the respite from the fiscal cliff to pass major pieces of legislation, including the reauthorization of the Violence Against Women Act, which expanded protections to Indian tribes; the farm bill that reauthorized a host of farming, agriculture, food and energy programs; several appropriations bills to fund the government; the Water Resources Act, which gave nearly $13 billion to water projects and conservation; and a transportation bill that funded the building and repairs of roads, bridges, runways and other transportation infrastructure. But at the end of September, legislation came to a halt. Murray and Ryan were still stalled, waiting for the Senate Republicans to name conferees, and with no budget in place, funding for the government ran out.

Bomb thrower Cruz, who was already eyeing a 2016 presidential bid, had been encouraging House conservatives to shut down the federal government by refusing to give Republican leaders enough votes to pass a bill funding it unless Democrats defunded Obamacare. The Tea Partiers, itching for a fight, agreed. And thus, despite the best efforts of Republican leaders in both chambers, the government shut down on Oct. 1.

For the next week, senators paraded across the floor talking angrily past one another, and communication between the parties came to a halt—at least among the men. More than a week into the shutdown, over pizza and wine in New Hampshire Democrat Jeanne Shaheen's offices, the women half-joked that if the men weren't finding any good solutions, maybe the women could do a better job. Susan Collins, a Maine Republican, had been pushing the women to step up, and she now encouraged them to leap into the breach. The next day, she went to the floor to propose a simple compromise that would become the basis of the talks to end the shutdown.

"I ask my Democratic and Republican colleagues to come together," Collins said. "We can do it. We can legislate responsibly and in good faith."

Senate Appropriations chair Barbara Mikulski picked up a microphone and joined in. "Let's get to it. Let's get the job done," she said. "I am willing to negotiate. I am willing to compromise." Ten minutes later, a third woman stood. "I am pleased to stand with my friend from Maine, Senator Collins, as she has described a plan which I think is pretty reasonable," said Alaska Republican Lisa Murkowski. "I think it is pretty sensible."

A bipartisan Gang of 14 senators formed, including six women. They began negotiating an end to the impasse—taking their proposals to groups of their colleagues to build consensus. The shutdown ended eight days later. "The women are an incredibly positive force because we like each other," Klobuchar said. "We work together well, and we look for common ground."

The headlines read: "Senate Women Lead in Effort to Find Accord," "Men Got Us into the Shutdown—Women Got Us Out" and "Women Are the Only Adults Left in Washington."

The shutdown came with a silver lining: Republicans dropped their objections to the budget talks, and Murray and Ryan were empowered to move ahead. They had until the end of the year to come to an agreement before funding would yet again run dry. On the day the government resumed normal operations, the two met with Jeff Sessions, the top Republican on the Senate Budget Committee, and Rep. Chris Van Hollen, the top Democrat on the House panel. The Republicans had named their negotiators. Walking into the room, Murray had a moment of satisfaction: finally, after so many months of blockages and hurdles, they were being given this chance to fix things. For the first time in years she felt hope that it could be done.

Sessions wasn't interested in compromise—indeed, he'd go on to vote against the deal. And since the minority isn't usually needed to pass legislation in the House, Murray and Ryan decided to negotiate one-on-one. The six months of talks they'd had leading up to this moment built mutual trust, an essential ingredient missing in previous attempts at a deal.

"We had to spend some time kind of building confidence with each other—that we would hold each other's confidence, that we would not leak [to the press] so that when we would begin negotiating with each other in earnest, we wouldn't undermine those negotiations," Ryan said. Once they'd established that level of trust, "we began to understand each other's limits very well and we knew when each one of us were not bluffing."

Ryan was fresh off the 2012 election in which he had been Mitt Romney's vice presidential nominee. He'd been the top Republican on the House Budget Committee since 2007, and his budgets controversially turned Medicare into a voucher system and slashed entitlements. His "Road Map" to address long-term fiscal shortfalls was even more drastic and was the bible for Tea Party fiscal conservatives. In 2013, he was rated a zero by Americans for Democratic Action; Murray got a zero from the American Conservatives Union.

Right off the bat, Ryan ruled out raising taxes and wanted to keep the entitlement cuts. Murray's bottom line was that no defense spending would be restored without equal increases in entitlement spending. "She was a very tough negotiator. She stood her ground on a number of things. As did I," Ryan said. "Basically, we laid over three budgets [including President Obama's budget] on top of each other and found the common ground between them. It was just basically a smart methodical process that we went through."

A 5'2" blonde with a bob and glasses, Murray is not a poker player. She doesn't bluff. She's as direct as they come. She tells you where her boundaries are and expects the same honesty from you. Murray often recounts how, after she first arrived in Congress in 1993, her seventh-grade daughter wrote an op-ed in her school newspaper criticizing Murray's support of a controversial trade bill. Murray has said her kids have always been harder to convince of anything than anyone in Congress. Talking about her kids played into her soccer-mom persona, which Murray often uses to get people to underestimate her. "She doesn't bluster and she just gets down to business very quickly," Ryan said. "She's not emotional and she's not lying. Some of these folks walk out of the room, and they huff and they huff. She's not like that. She's just even-keeled and very straightforward and pleasant, while very firm."

They spent time together, getting to know each other as Murray strived to discover his boundaries: what he needed and would not compromise. "I knew that he, in order to get down to a compromise, had to have a win," she said. "So I knew him enough to know how we could make a story for his win and how we can make a story for my wins so that we could reach an agreement."

After Congress broke for Halloween, Murray and Ryan conducted their negotiations over the phone, each stepping away from family celebrations to chat or text ideas, lending privacy and intimacy to the talks.

With Murray and Ryan closeted away, the Senate was lurching toward its next quasi-catastrophic showdown. Just before Thanksgiving, Reid, sick of the logjam, moved to limit Republican filibusters, a move considered so antithetical to the Senate that it was dubbed "the nuclear option." The Senate came to an abrupt halt. The Upper Chamber is an institution built to work on agreement. Even without the filibuster, mutual agreement is required on every little thing: the daily prayer, the schedule, permission for staff to enter the chamber, whether bills can be debated. When consensus is lost, the minority can object to literally anything, resulting in time-consuming votes to achieve the simplest of tasks. This is what happened when Reid went nuclear. Boom. Both sides stopped talking once again.

Remarkably, at least one thing emerged from the nuclear winter: Murray and Ryan's budget deal, which passed the Senate on Dec. 18, weeks ahead of the Jan. 1 deadline. Murray and Ryan reached a two-year deal that ended—or at least suspended—the fiscal cliffs. These ideological opposites had achieved what Speaker Boehner, President Obama, Senate Majority Leader Reid, Minority Leader Mitch McConnell and Vice President Joe Biden had failed to do in previous rounds. Both chambers passed the deal in December, and the president signed it into law on Boxing Day, a late Christmas gift to the nation.

To commemorate all the times she'd given Ryan grief over Seahawks quarterback Russell Wilson, Murray got Wilson to sign a jersey. She presented it to Ryan as a gift when their bills passed Congress. Less than two months later, Wilson led the Seahawks to Super Bowl victory, making the jersey very valuable. "I don't know if he has told you this, but he really owes me because he has a signed jersey from the Super Bowl champion," Murray laughed.

Ryan knows: the jersey is framed and hanging on a wall in his home—though not in his study, which is a shrine to the Green Bay Packers. "It was sort of a big deal," he chuckled. When Ryan did the ALS Ice Bucket challenge a year later, he publicly challenged Murray to do it without warning her. A few days later he texted her: "I don't see your ice bucket challenge online." Murray texted back: "You owe me big." She'd donated a hefty sum instead.

The night of the 2014 elections, Murray and Ryan also exchanged congratulatory texts and began work on a joint bill to create a 15-person commission to study "evidence-based policy making," using data to assess the efficacy of certain spending programs and tax credits. As, sources said, Ryan teased Murray at their Super Bowl celebration that February, "Patty, I think this is the beginning of a beautiful friendship."

— 3 —

A CRITICAL ACTOR
IN THE HOUSE

On a gloomy Monday afternoon in September 2008, Speaker Nancy Pelosi took to the floor of the House. She was angry. Her clipped speech and the sharp movements of her head as she stood at the podium showed her barely contained frustration. The economy was teetering on collapse, and she was being asked to save it. Two weeks earlier, Treasury secretary Hank Paulsen had gathered congressional leaders together to ask for what was essentially a $700 billion blank check to bail out Wall Street. Republicans, especially fiscal conservatives, were outraged; so too were Democrats who blamed President George W. Bush's regulatory and economic policies for the financial crisis. The bailout bill simply could not pass unless Pelosi, who controlled the majority of votes in the House, threw her political weight behind it. And she was not happy to support bailing out Wall Street and, by proxy, the Republican Party.

"They claim to be free-market advocates, when it's really an anything-goes mentality. No regulation, no supervision, no discipline," Pelosi railed. "And if you fail, you will have a golden parachute, and the taxpayer will bail you out. Those days are over."

Republicans gathered on the floor before her as she spoke. As her 15-minute speech built to a conclusion, they began to grumble. By the time the vote came up, those grumblings had led to full-on revolt. All day, Republican members were bitter about this vote, about their president and party leaders, about Pelosi and her power. The bailout did not pass; only 65 Republicans, 35 fewer than promised, voted for it. The Dow Jones Industrial Average tanked 778 points.

Republicans rushed into the corridor to face a wall of journalists. Pelosi's "speech cost us votes," charged Rep. Adam Putnam of Florida, the No. 3 House Republican. Her "partisan tone" pushed wavering legislators to the "nay" column, he asserted.

Coming up behind the Republican leaders was a Democrat with a different point of view. House Appropriations chairman Dave Obey barked, "Bullshit! Do they really think it's credible to say that they changed their mind on how they were going to vote because of a speech? If they're that tenderhearted, they don't belong in this place."

Pelosi's speech hadn't been any more or less partisan than those given on the floor during five hours of debate. But Pelosi was a woman whom Republicans had spent years caricaturing as a shrill liberal. With global outrage weighing on them for the clumsy mismanagement of the world's most important economy, they grasped at a pretext to distract from the crisis by vilifying Pelosi.

Pelosi took it in stride. She was used to it by then. Pelosi was at that pivotal moment the most powerful woman in the world; only she could pass the bank bailout that would bring the economy back from the edge of depression. She'd endured a lot more insults and cheap shots than the ones the Republicans were lobbing at her that September afternoon. After her speech, the Democratic leaders gathered in the Speakers Lobby nearby. Pelosi stood stone silent and flushed, her eyes gazing over the journalists and staffers seated before her. Pelosi had had years of experience dealing with attacks. In many ways, she played the game like a man: punching and counterpunching. Four days later, the bank bailout would pass on the votes of 172 Democrats and 91 Republicans. Pelosi got 32 Democrats to switch their votes to support the measure; Republicans never managed to deliver the 100 votes they had pledged.

It wouldn't be the last time that Pelosi saved House Republican leader John Boehner and his party from themselves. Indeed, Pelosi's speakership stands as the most powerful in a generation. Even when her party was in the minority, Pelosi led the most unified caucus in history, rarely losing more than a handful of members in her opposition to President George W. Bush. She averaged 90 percent cohesion through her 11 years as leader from 2003 to 2014. That's compared with 88 percent cohesion for Speaker Boehner during his seven years as House Republican leader. That may not seem like much of a difference, but in the world of lost votes, that 2 percent is enormous.

Were America a parliamentary system, in which the majority party caucus elects the country's leader, Pelosi would've been president a decade ago. Leading the House, she helped oversee the most productive legislative session since Lyndon Johnson's Great Society, passing the 2009 stimulus package for the economy, fair pay for women, tobacco regulation, an expansion of children's health insurance and, most important, the Affordable Care Act. Her victories would ultimately cost her the House in 2010, a price she wasn't afraid to pay. Through a unique mix of shrewd character assessment, personal charm, fiscal acumen, a formidable memory and exacting score-keeping, she has risen higher, and broken through more glass ceilings, than any other contemporary American woman. In the theory of critical mass, the sheer number of women matters, but so too do critical actors, those who first break through and help pull up the rest. Pelosi is such a critical actor, one who wielded power decisively and used it to help other women advance, bringing House Democrats—though not the full House—to critical mass.

While Pelosi could play hardball with the best, her stewardship was a uniquely feminine one. She could be incredibly sweet and incredibly tough depending on what worked best to get their support—a unique combination that ranged outside the traditional narrow arsenal of power levers and often caught members off guard. She was neither a screamer nor a bully, and she was easily and often lampooned as a liberal San Francisco housewife, labels she often turned to her advantage. She played up the softer maternal image that cloaked her steely spine. She was a master at orchestrating theatrical moments. And she remains the best fund-raiser in Congress, raising well over $400 million since 2002—more than $100 million in 2014 alone— more money than any other member in either chamber. As she led House Democrats to critical mass, Pelosi played politics on the men's field and played it better than any of them.

Nancy D'Alessandro was born the Princess of Charm City, the youngest of six and the only girl to Baltimore mayor Thomas D'Alessandro. She had a taste for politics even as a child. On weekends she sat in the foyer of their family home with her father, entering into a ledger the favors people lined up outside to ask. When she was 7 years old her parents took her with them to vote. A Republican poll worker handed her a toy elephant that she promptly handed back. Even then, Nancy had a sense of partisanship. "It was about us versus them," she said. "We didn't know any other life; that's my DNA."

But a life in politics was something neither of her parents imagined for their little girl, who grew up in crinoline skirts and took dance and flute lessons. A deeply devout Catholic Italian, her mother wanted her daughter to become a nun. Some on her staff joke that if she'd gone that route they'd have been working for the first female pope. When it came time for college, Nancy had to beg her parents to allow her to attend Trinity College, 40 miles away in Washington, rather than finishing school. While in Washington she interned for Sen. Daniel Brewster, a Maryland Democrat, in the same office where Steny Hoyer, who would one day become her second in command of the House, happened to be interning. "She's been a politician all of her life, since she was 4 or 5," Maryland's Hoyer said.

Nevertheless, as her brothers grew up and went into the family's political business, Nancy did what was expected of her: she married financier Paul Pelosi right out of college and moved with him to San Francisco, where she spent the next 20 years as a housewife and mother of five. Like many wealthy homemakers of her era, Pelosi had a string of causes she supported, from the Leakey Family Foundation, the group that found the Lucy skeleton in Ethiopia—Pelosi was a closet paleoanthropologist—to the Democratic Party. Politics was never very far from her heart. She rose to chair the Democratic Party of California—a part-time job in those days—where she took a special interest in recruiting and promoting female candidates. In 1985, Sen. George Mitchell asked her to serve as finance chair for the Democratic Senatorial Campaign Committee, which works to elect Democrats to the Senate. "She's an amazing hostess," said John Burton, California Democratic Party chair and a longtime friend. "She makes you feel your comfort and needs are her top priority. You practically expect her to break out the tray of canapés. Don't let her fool you: if she's feeding you a canapé, she wants something from you."

Two years later, she ran to fill retiring Sala Burton's seat in Congress. At some point, her father dispatched her brother Tommy to check on Pelosi's progress. "Tell me how she's doing with the grassroots" were his instructions. Tommy found a legion of Italian-American grandmothers knocking on doors and making calls for Pelosi, which the campaign dubbed the Nana Brigade. "My brother called home and said, 'Dad, I don't know if she's gonna win, but she's [her] father's daughter,' " Pelosi recalled. " 'She knows how to organize.' " Pelosi narrowly won the special election primary in 1987, but she's won re-election by comfortable margins since.

By 2000, Pelosi decided to run for leadership. "She was raising more money than any other member but [House Minority Leader Dick] Gephardt. She decided if she was going to raise so much money, she was going to have some input," Burton said. She took on and beat her old intern buddy Hoyer to become minority whip, the No. 2 position in the House Democratic Caucus. After Gephardt left in 2003, Pelosi rose to minority leader and immediately began plotting to retake the House. In 2006, with Bush's popularity waning, Pelosi got her wish, winning 31 seats to retake the House with a margin of 15 seats. Her one regret on election night? Not enough winners among the women she'd handpicked to run. Only four new female members were added in the election, bringing the total number of women in the House to 94—a marginal increase that Pelosi set about to fix.

"This is what I was striving to do on the issue of gender," she said in an interview in September 2014. "We had a vision of what our purpose was and a plan on how we could advance that cause with that purpose and the support that we would give to candidates to carry that message . . . It was about having vision, having a plan."

Pelosi's plan to increase women's presence was rooted in a sense that women help make Congress more successful and active overall. The most comprehensive study on women in Congress, from the Vanderbilt Center for the Study of Democratic Institutions, detailed how women are pigeonholed into feminine issues like education and health care and ignored on matters of defense and the economy. This forces women to work harder than their male counterparts and become standouts and specialists in their fields to be taken seriously. The study also showed that bills sponsored by women are less likely to be enacted than those sponsored by men. Pelosi wanted to change that mentality and build a stronger coalition of women in the House.

The House has never reached critical mass across both parties, so

Pelosi had to find ways to use her gender to her advantage. Like many powerful women, Pelosi shrewdly cloaked her toughness in a feminine veil. When I interviewed her in her corner office on the second floor of the Capitol overlooking the Library of Congress, Pelosi offered me Ghirardelli chocolates from San Francisco—her favorite, as she tells most visitors. The office was neat as a pin: no clutter, just flowers and a collection of keepsakes from her time in office and, of course, a plethora of family photos.

She spent every available minute in her schedule scribbling thank-you, birthday and condolence notes to legislators, constituents, lobbyists, donors, journalists, national and local officials, prominent labor and businessmen, family and friends. She remembered every birthday, the birth of every child and grandchild, every major milestone from college graduations to deaths. But she also leveraged that information to lobby members, relating a particular passing or graduation to a bill pending before the floor. Pelosi often talked about motherhood and grandmotherhood. She gravitated to any baby in the room. That was partly because she honestly loved kids and partly because it mellowed her tough side. It was a uniquely feminine balancing act: trying not to be perceived as either too tough or too weak. For Pelosi, who tended to be on the tougher edge of the spectrum, her maternal image made her less threatening. Ask members about her, and they're filled with mother references.

"Having raised many children and grandchildren, she has eyes in the back of her head," says Rep. Chris Van Hollen, a Maryland Democrat and a Pelosi deputy.

Rep. Dennis Cardoza, a California Democrat who was on Pelosi's leadership team, noted that, though she didn't support him when he challenged an incumbent Democrat for office, she held no grudges and promoted him to her leadership team when he was elected. "When you disagree with her, you better have good arguments and you better be right or she'll rap your knuckles with a ruler pretty quick. I always got my say, if not my way," he said. "Typically politics has been a man's world. Men have a history—perhaps it's all the team sports—where you can argue today but tomorrow it's back to business. Nancy has learned that. She'll argue very vehemently one day and the next day she's back to her gracious self."

On the House floor, Pelosi once surprised Rep. Ellen Tauscher, a fellow California Democrat, when she remembered a long-ago request from Tauscher to help the daughter of Tauscher's then-fiancé. "She has the ability to personalize things, to draw information out of nowhere; it's very disarming and the key to her success," Tauscher said.

The near-eidetic memory extended also to policy, which made her one of the wonkiest Speakers in history. "She's as good at policy as you get," Rep. Jim Clyburn said. "She disarms people with how thorough she is. She rarely asks a question she doesn't already know the answer to."

Despite the charm, the thank-you notes and the chocolates, Pelosi learned to keep score when she was a little girl waiting in the foyer with the ledger book. She never hesitated to punish those who did not fall into line. Help her and you may find yourself on a powerful, coveted committee; or the House representative to the North Atlantic Treaty Organization, traveling monthly to Europe; or with an extra $10,000 for your re-election just when you most need it. She also exerted an unprecedented grip on the House agenda and who enacted it. "She controls the Steering and Policy Committee," Clyburn, the No. 3 House Democrat, said of the leadership committee that sets policy and determines committee assignments. "Everyone knows that what the Speaker wants, the Speaker gets. She's meticulous—leaves very little to chance. She's very hands-on."

As speaker, Pelosi had a Gulfstream 5 Air Force plane at her disposal, one of the perks of the office, on which she offered rides home to the California delegation. When fellow California representative

Barbara Lee voted against an emergency spending bill against Pelosi's express wishes, she found herself flying commercial. Lee showed up, as usual, at Andrews Air Force Base for the flight back to California. She was informed at the gate that she was not on the list for the flight and, without a word from Pelosi or her staff, the plane took off.

After his election as Speaker, Ohio Republican John Boehner in 2014 punished two members who had voted against him by stripping them of their seats on the powerful Rules Committee, but he eventually allowed them to resume those positions. Pelosi wasn't so forgiving. Former Texas representative Martin Frost waited for years to get on the Appropriations Committee and, after challenging Pelosi for minority leader, then watched fellow Texan Chet Edwards get the coveted committee seat. "If you don't play ball, if you don't participate, she doesn't engage you and that's your stick," said Rep. Mike Thompson, a California Democrat.

John Dingell, the longest-serving member in history, learned the hard way not to cross Pelosi. Dingell tangled with Pelosi over climate-change legislation and his reluctance to cede power to her. That cost the Michigan Democrat his longtime chairmanship of the House Energy Committee. "Trust me, getting on her bad list is an unpleasant experience," said Dingell one afternoon in 2009. Dingell said there were downsides to so much consolidation of power. Pelosi often rushed through legislation that later required correction or, worse, promoted bills that did not pass the Democrat-controlled Senate because they were too rash.

Part of the caucus's unhappiness grew from the fact that not everyone felt consulted. Unlike the women in the West Wing or the Senate, Pelosi wasn't on a team: she was a chief executive and ruled like a man. Continually seeking everyone's opinion would undermine her position. So the group she trusted was small. Indeed, even some of her closest allies said that Pelosi's inner circle of advisers was too small and like-minded. The team was heavily Californian and progressive, with Cardoza as its only moderate, which sometimes resulted in narrow decisions, especially in quick-moving crises. When it was revealed in 2009 that insurer AIG was using taxpayer money to finance lavish executive bonuses, Pelosi quickly pushed through legislation to tax those bonuses. Legal experts criticized the bill as likely unconstitutional—taxes cannot be applied to such a select group—and the measure stalled in the Senate. The move whiplashed against Pelosi in newspaper headlines.

Some said she was too hands-on, micromanaging the process and hip-checking those who interfered. When her former deputy Rahm Emanuel became White House chief of staff, he reached out to House members on his own—only to have his hand slapped by Pelosi: no outsiders were welcome to meddle with her team. And he was no longer on her team.

But often, the strife around Pelosi was theater to assuage liberals while allowing President Obama to seem bipartisan. "It's the old routine of bad-cop Pelosi, good-cop Obama; partisanship versus bipartisanship," Stephen Wayne, a political science professor at Georgetown University, said at the time. "It is also a bargaining tool to limit what the Republicans can expect from the legislation in exchange for their support."

In Obama's first year, Pelosi pushed through an enormous amount of his agenda till reaching the hardest bill of them all: health-care reform. And all the micromanaging, thank-you notes and Ghirardelli chocolate came in handy. Pelosi would need to draw on all her feminine wiles, her masculine game playing, her incredible memory and her political strategizing; it would take everything she had to pass the Affordable Care Act.

In the summer of 2009, the House was waiting for the Senate to finish work on the bill and Republicans were whipping up popular opposition. Former Alaska governor Sarah Palin led the charge with accusations that the legislation would create "death panels," a committee of cost-obsessed bureaucrats who would decide whether granny would get the resources to live or die. Never mind that it wasn't true; the idea sparked mass protests that came to be known as the Summer of Discontent. House Democratic members were burned in effigy. Town halls became screaming matches replete with Nazi allegories.

Members dug in on their positions. Twenty-three moderate Democrats said they would not vote for any of the three versions of the health-care bill on the table. More than 50 progressives signed a pledge not to vote for any bill that did not include a government-run alternative to private insurers, as had been proposed in the Senate. "The question Democrats have to be asking themselves is: How many times is Nancy Pelosi going to make them walk the plank and cast a vote for a fatally flawed bill?" asked Ken Spain, spokesman for the National Republican Congressional Committee, which helps elect GOP candidates to the House. "This kind of overreach would be a policy disaster for middle-class Americans but a dream scenario for any Republican opponent."

By the time the Senate passed a bill on Christmas Eve 2009, more than 218 Democratic House members—the minimum needed for passage—had signed on to one letter or another opposing various pieces of the measure. Pelosi would have to persuade a majority of her party to vote for the bill in spite of their objections. Passage had never seemed harder. Few thought she could do it. Newspapers said health-care reform was dead.

It is a little-known fact of the House that Speakers don't generally vote. But for weeks in February, Pelosi attended every House vote, working her members on the floor. She often sat with Rep. Zach Space, an Ohio Democrat, who was a well-known undecided vote. Slowly, a steady trickle of "yea" votes emerged, including Space, Rep. Tom Perriello of Virginia, Rep. John Boccieri of Ohio and Rep. Chris Murphy of Connecticut.

She tackled members' problems issue by issue. She worked with the New York delegation to iron out changes to the Senate bill, which punished "do-gooder" Medicaid states that already provided the most generous benefits—essentially robbing the rich states to pay for the poor ones. She also met with the Congressional Black Caucus to address concerns about affordability and access. She spent a lot of time with the Hispanic Caucus assuaging their worries about provisions that prevented illegal and some legal immigrants from purchasing plans on new exchanges for the uninsured. All three groups eventually supported the ACA. And for days, Pelosi shuffled back and forth between pro-life Democrats, who were concerned the bill could lead to government-funded abortions, and half a dozen bishops and a group of nuns, hammering out language that allowed healthcare reform to pass.

"She's always better informed about the public policy of the issue," said Rep. Tauscher. "She's always very responsive to constituents. She knows the politics of every district. She knows exactly what the sweet spot is for all 218-plus."

Pelosi's modus operandi wasn't to twist arms and force a vote. She listened in ways few men do. She would then sit and talk for as long as it took. "I can think of three different instances" during a vote that Pelosi resorted to twisting arms, Emanuel said. "But on the other hand, I can think of a thousand different instances where it was never needed because of the work that was done beforehand by listening and hearing and having people understand and finding what was important to people and making that . . . the resolution basically."

Though many studies have demonstrated women's effectiveness in governing by consensus, Pelosi cemented it at the highest levels. She proved that "female" tactics could achieve what many regarded as a male level of success, often even eclipsing what male Speakers had done with their titles and time.

But the hardest negotiations were regional ones. One highly

contentious issue was Medicaid, for which eligibility and spending per beneficiary varied significantly from state to state. Members from low-spending areas felt they should be better compensated because, they claimed, their medical societies and hospital associations had developed higher-quality medicine. Higher-cost areas disputed this. Pelosi would gather three groups, broken down by sub-issues, in separate rooms. She'd get the discussion rolling in one group and then leave it to staff to continue it while she moved on to the next room. She spent weeks like this, like a chess master playing several games at once, rotating rooms all day long. If one started to collapse, she'd come in and redirect, always keeping the conversation going, letting members vent their grievances and explore options.

Toward the end of the negotiations, it was decided to hold a late-night meeting until the high-spending and low-spending Medicaid states agreed. Each group had several representatives. She mulled a critical question: Be the gracious hostess and feed the group? She ultimately decided that a lack of food would get to a resolution quicker, and indeed, a compromise was soon struck resolving one of the last issues holding up the bill.

Despite all of Pelosi's efforts, on March 21, the day of the scheduled vote, after two months of lobbying, she wasn't sure she had enough support to pass it. A Tea Party mob had formed outside the House, jeering and shouting insults at members going in and out of the Capitol—which proved to be a fatal mistake. Among the targets of the jeers was civil rights legend John Lewis, who'd nearly died at the hands of Alabama police on a Selma bridge in 1965. Lewis took to the airwaves denouncing the Tea Party as racist. Pelosi gathered her caucus in Cannon House Office Building on that bitterly cold March day. She didn't speak. After all the hard work gathering the votes, she'd said enough. She knew she couldn't sway her troops any more. She gave Lewis the microphone.

The former Baptist seminary student gave a soaring speech urging members to look at the bigger arc of history and get on the right side of it. "After that, no one wanted to vote against the bill," said Rep. Niki Tsongas, a Massachusetts Democrat who attended the closed-door meeting. The caucus was fired up. The Capitol police urged Pelosi to lead the caucus to the House through an underground tunnel that connects Cannon and the Capitol. But Pelosi knew the power of a mob. Instead, over the panicked protests of her security detail, she led House Democrats outside, through the angry Tea Party crowd and up the Capitol steps to cast the historic vote. To her troops, it signaled that they needed to complete their mission in the face of adversity.

The Affordable Care Act passed 219–212. Democrats celebrated it as a watershed moment. On the House floor during passage, Republicans taunted vulnerable Democrats by waving and singing the Steam song, "Na Na, Hey Hey, Kiss Him Goodbye." They predicted, rightly, that the vote would cost Pelosi the House.

"The word 'afraid' is never anything about me," Pelosi told me in 2009 over dim sum at her favorite Chinese restaurant, Yank Sing, in San Francisco. "I'm not afraid of anything, but I am vigilant about what we do, and it's fun. I enjoy the politics, though I enjoy the policy more."

Pelosi believes women govern differently than men. "People interrupt me, especially women, and say, 'Do you realize how different this meeting would have been if a man was conducting it?' " she later said in our September 2014 interview.

"How so?" I asked.

"We had to listen to what the people had to say, value what they had to say, put a perspective on it: that will work or won't work," she said. "I think women are good consensus builders. I think that there is an intuition of women—and otherwise based on knowledge and judgment and a practicality—of getting something done."

Pelosi "has been pragmatic and effective in unifying her party and building a record of major legislative achievements as Speaker," said Thomas Mann, a congressional scholar at the Brookings Institution. "I think she will be remembered as the most powerful and consequential Speaker in many decades, with a legislative record that compares favorably with her peers in spite of the exceedingly difficult political environment. The 2010 loss of majority status had nothing to do with failures on the Speaker's part."

Indeed, Pelosi spent much of the past five years bailing Boehner out of tough votes. At the start of the 114th session in 2015, Boehner narrowly avoided shutting down the government again thanks to votes Pelosi provided to fund the Department of Homeland Security. After Boehner announced his resignation from Congress in late September 2015, Pelosi delivered the votes to avert another shutdown—this time over Planned Parenthood funding. Pelosi, 74, was as active as ever and still hoping to regain the majority so she can finish her agenda.

In the meantime, she's increased the number of Democratic women in Congress by nearly 50 percent, to 65 in 2015, up from 46 in 2005; women make up 33 percent of the Democratic caucus—a critical mass. And Pelosi has every intention of getting more women elected across the country as she actively recruits them to run.

For Pelosi, that would be her most enduring legacy: a House full of women, changing the way Congress governs, forming coalitions and bringing important new perspectives. Studies show that "female" issues are often dismissed; for example, child care is often marginalized as a female and maternal concern. But access to child care has a huge impact on the American economy and society. It lowers crime rates, increases participation in higher education and even raises the country's GDP by tens of billions of dollars in increased wages for parents and children.

Pelosi says child care is her largest piece of unfinished business. "I do believe child care is the missing link in the evolution of women in a society, in an economy," she said. "Affordable, quality child care—and that makes all the difference in our country and other countries. The most important thing that we can do to grow our economies is to unleash the power of women in our economy."

— 4 —

THE

EXECUTIVE OFFICE

My first indication that Hillary Clinton's 2016 campaign would be different from her last was her arrival in New Hampshire when she began her second presidential bid. In 2007 she had staked her claim on the nomination in January, riding into Concord with a presidential-size motorcade and an aura of incumbency. I remember how she strode out onto the stage at the high school gymnasium in Concord before a cheering crowd of thousands. Women had run for president before, but they'd never gotten close to winning the party nomination. With Clinton's experience, connections, name recognition and fund-raising prowess, many felt she already had the nomination in the bag.

Eight years later, Clinton's announcement came in April, just after a punishing winter that had set records for cold and snow. When I caught up with the Clinton campaign later that month in the quaint New England mill town of Keene, N.H., the evidence of that dark season was just starting to disappear. There were still piles of snow on side streets and on some lawns and vacant lots, but they were melting quickly. Clinton's modest two-vehicle motorcade traveled under branches on the trees on Main Street that had just started to bloom. It included the "Scooby mobile" in which she'd road-tripped to New Hampshire, stopping at gas stations to snap photos with surprised travelers. Clinton's first stop in Keene was the family-owned Whitney Brothers, which had been making wooden furniture and toys for children for more than a century. She was here for a round-table discussion with factory employees, more like an event for a state senate campaign than a presidential one, except for the wall of national media recording every utterance. This campaign Clinton would take nothing for granted. She wasn't arriving triumphant and inevitable, but hat in hand, asking to listen.

Clinton had learned some big lessons from 2008, first among them that nothing is preordained in politics. She may have swept into New Hampshire in 2007 with a feeling of history in the making, but in the end she came up against a force much stronger than inevitability. For women, the executive office, whether for president, governor, mayor or CEO, remains the broadest hurdle to jump.

Only six of the nation's 50 governors are women, and they account for just 12 percent of our cities' mayors. While both major parties have named a female vice presidential candidate, neither has ever nominated a woman for the nation's highest office. Yet when asked, Americans say they are extremely enthusiastic about having a female president. Ninety percent of likely 2016 voters would consider voting for a woman for president, and three out of four believed a female president would be good for the country, according to a May 2013 poll by Emily's List, which helps elect pro-choice women to office. But in polls on individual female candidates for executive offices like governor, mayor or president, voters raise a number of doubts about whether a woman is tough enough to lead.

"Voters will say, 'I would vote for a woman, if she was qualified,' " said pollster Celinda Lake. "But they don't say that about men. What is the code for qualified? In legislative races, people don't think it takes that much to get the job done, so it's solo leadership where women still struggle."

Toughness is a fuzzy metric by which to measure a candidate, particularly a female one. And running for office is a brutal experience, especially for women, whose clothing and demeanor undergo higher levels of scrutiny than those of men. Some female candidates travel with beauticians and makeup artists so that they can be camera ready at all times. For most this is less a sign of vanity than a realistic acknowledgment that if there's a hair out of place, or their outfits are too sexy or too dour, they'll see an unflattering meme of it flying all over the Internet, a big distraction for the campaign. Women are also more likely to be asked about work-life balance and who is raising their children while they are on the campaign trail, and they have to answer those questions carefully.

To endure this, a woman has to be tough and disciplined—but not so tough that the press describe her as bossy or, worse, as a shrew. That line between likability and toughness is the hardest for female executives and candidates to walk, and one that few get right. At her 2007 announcement, Clinton knew polls had confirmed that despite her achievements and name recognition, she too faced the toughness issue. She tried to address it with her campaign slogan: "Ready to Lead on Day One."

Many thought that after her bruising 2008 defeat, Clinton would not want to run again. When she took on the post of Obama's secretary of state, Clinton found an unexpected second wind—or third or fourth or 10th wind, depending how you count up her experience. Her popularity skyrocketed, and President Obama, without an heir apparent given Vice President Joe Biden's age, embraced his former adversary as a potential successor.

This time around, no one is questioning her toughness, and her staff isn't polling to see if voters believe a woman could lead. In this campaign, for perhaps the first time, Clinton will see if she can win by doing something no one has done before: run as a woman.

Clinton has actually campaigned for president four times, the first two as first lady. In 1992, the Clintons ran as a "two for one," saying that, because of her education and skills, the country would be getting two presidents for the price of one vote if Bill Clinton were elected. Almost immediately after her husband took office, Hillary Clinton began to change how things were done in the West Wing. Although it may seem incredible now, it was very bold of her, a Washington woman, to wear pants, said Carol Browner, President Clinton's head of the Environmental Protection Agency. "My entire time at the EPA, I never wore pants to testify. Because you didn't. You wore a dress. And then Hillary started wearing them, and then I started wearing them to work, to the office. We should all thank Hillary for that."

Clinton became the first and thus far only first lady to have an office in the West Wing. Her policy team was key to drafting the president's welfare, tobacco, crime, education and gun-control initiatives. Clinton was part of the budget process, orchestrating a huge expansion of breast cancer funding in, of all places, the Pentagon budget. She also quietly expanded funding for after-school programs to $1 billion annually, from $20 million.

Importantly, Clinton worked to build a critical mass of women, pushing her husband to appoint female Cabinet members and administration officials, fostering a new generation of women in public service who worked their way up the ranks. Janet Napolitano, future Arizona governor and secretary of Homeland Security, got her start in law enforcement in Clinton's Justice Department. President Obama's national security adviser Susan Rice started out as a low-level Africa expert in the Clinton National Security Council. Susan Davies, who as deputy White House counsel was assigned to see Elena Kagan and Sonia Sotomayor confirmed to the Supreme Court for President

Obama, got her start as an associate White House counsel under Clinton. Alice Rivlin, director of Clinton's Office of Management and Budget, went on to become vice chair of the Federal Reserve Board. And Mona Sutphen, Obama's first deputy chief of staff for policy, had worked in the Clinton National Security Council.

Hillary Clinton said in an October 2015 interview, "Both President Obama and my husband contributed to broadening the pool of people who were given the opportunity to serve—some at the very highest positions of government, like I lobbied hard for Madeleine Albright to be secretary of state—but also at the lower positions where they gained important experience and where now they'd be ready for additional responsibilities."

Clinton's interest in women's issues was international as well. She put the treatment of women in Afghanistan and sex trafficking on the president's agenda. Clinton traveled widely for a first lady, visiting 82 countries. After teas and ribbon cuttings, she insisted on meeting with local women and children as well as Peace Corps volunteers.

Clinton's major legislative defeat as first lady was her unsuccessful effort to reform the health-care system. What came to be known as Hillarycare, the precursor to Obamacare, would have mandated health-care coverage for all Americans. Republicans castigated Clinton's involvement in health care as the misguided product of an unelected first lady who was overstepping her bounds. The bill failed after Republicans mocked it as a "top-down," "command and control" plan that restricted personal and business freedom, and Clinton retreated. She joined a Betty Crocker cooking club and wrote a book, *Dear Socks, Dear Buddy: Kids' Letters to the First Pets*, pastimes guaranteed to let the controversy that swirled around her die down.

She emerged from exile in 1995 when she traveled to China for the Fourth World Conference on Women in Beijing. Dressed in a girly pink suit with gold buttons and gold jewelry, Clinton looked like she was about to give a classic first-lady speech about decorum and etiquette. Instead, she took on dowry deaths, in which young Asian women are driven to suicide or are murdered by husbands and their families in the course of attempts to extract more money from the bride's family; and China's one-child policy, which led to the deaths of millions of baby girls. She declared to a fired-up hall of women from around the world, "If there is one message that echoes forth from this conference, let it be that human rights are women's rights, and women's rights are human rights, once and for all."

Buoyed by the international acclaim that followed her powerful speech, Clinton returned to the policy arena to advance an issue she'd been passionate about for decades: child care. She held a summit on the issue in 1997 where she pushed for the biggest increase in child-care funding in 30 years. In the middle of this effort, the Monica Lewinsky scandal erupted. The whole country focused almost exclusively on that fiasco for the rest of her husband's term in office.

Ironically, it was her handling of the president's affair and his subsequent impeachment by the House for perjury that laid the groundwork for her eventual presidential run. Many admired the way she endured the turmoil and stood by her husband, though clearly at a frosty distance. Her reserve in the face of such public humiliation boosted Hillary's approval ratings and led to her successful run for Senate in New York in 2000 and the launch of her own political career. Clinton had already changed the way America viewed first ladies and marriage in the context of work and partnership. She proved that a woman could tackle policy, that a woman could lead. The problem still was getting a woman elected president.

It wasn't that women hadn't tried to run for president; it was that no one took them seriously. There was good reason to dismiss the first candidate, Victoria Claflin Woodhull, who ran for president in 1870. Never mind that women couldn't vote and she wasn't old enough to legally become president; Woodhull won the Equal Rights Party nomination and selected as her running mate Frederick Douglass, the renowned former slave and abolitionist leader. Woodhull, whose open marriage was the talk of New York, traveled the county to promote her platform of suffrage, "free love" and birth control. She even declared marriage to be nothing more than "legalized prostitution." Victoria Woodhull was clearly a woman who would still have a hard time getting elected today.

Thirty-four other women have run since, including Maine Republican senator Margaret Chase Smith in 1964. She received 227,007 votes in the primaries, the most for any woman until Hillary Clinton's candidacy. Smith won 27 delegates at the convention, denying Barry Goldwater a clean sweep.

"The argument contends that I would be pioneering the way for woman in the future—to make her more acceptable—to make the way easier—for her to be elected president of the United States," Smith said in announcing her candidacy. "Perhaps the point that has impressed me the most on this argument is that women before me pioneered and smoothed the way for me to be the first woman to be elected to both the House and the Senate—and that I should give back in the return that which had been given to me."

The Clintons weren't the first husband-and-wife team in which each made a run for the presidency. When Kansas Republican senator Bob Dole unsuccessfully challenged Bill Clinton in 1996, his wife, Elizabeth, was a dogged campaigner with her own plane and staff. The former FTC commissioner and secretary of Transportation and Labor was a power player in her own right. Four years later, Elizabeth Dole launched her own bid for the White House.

Throughout 1998, Dole consistently beat Vice President Al Gore in early polls by wider margins than anyone else in the GOP field, forcing George W. Bush to get into the race earlier than he'd planned. She came in third, after Bush and Steve Forbes, in the Iowa Straw Poll. But prolific and early fund-raising by Bush and Forbes locked down most major donors, leaving Dole scrambling for money. By the time Dole officially got in on Jan. 15, 1999, she had a hard time raising money. After seven months of campaigning, Dole had raised $4.7 million to Bush's $57 million.

What money Dole did raise, 51 percent of it came from female donors—a rarity given that women give far less to political campaigns than men. "As I talked about the joy of leadership—empowering people to believe in themselves, that they can make a difference—I could see women in the audience sit up a little straighter. It's so important for our voices to be heard at every level and in every field. That's why it was so gratifying to welcome thousands of women of all ages to the campaign," Dole recalled. "I truly believe that if we'd started a year earlier, it could've been a different picture."

Raising money has always been a bigger challenge for female candidates. In a 1996 study of political donations, Peter Francia, a political science professor at East Carolina University, found that three fourths of donors who gave at least $200 were men. A 2002 analysis by Barbara Burrell, professor emeritus at Northern Illinois University, found that just 0.14 percent of adult American women gave more than $200, compared with 0.41 percent of adult men. Only six of the top 50 donors in 2014 were women. The disparity is worse for Republican candidates. Francia found that 31 percent of Democratic congressional donors were women, versus only 16 percent of GOP donors. In 2014, only five of the top 20 female donors were Republican. And, notably, there are no female mega–Super PAC donors like Sheldon Adelson, the Koch brothers or George Soros. Women, studies show, tend not to give to politicians because they control the household purse strings and are more inclined to save that money to spend on their kids or more practical items. There also isn't much perceived benefit to political contributions among women who are still on the lower rungs of the economic and professional ladders. Meanwhile, professional men recognize that connections in the halls of power could potentially help their business. Until more women are successful in business, the female donor base will remain relatively small.

Even Dole and Clinton struggled despite the support of their husbands' fund-raising machines. In her 2008 bid for the presidency, Clinton raised more than any other woman—and most men. But Barack Obama consistently outdid her. In the final months of her campaign, she was forced to lend her campaign $13.2 million.

Image has always been a big challenge for female candidates, who receive even closer scrutiny when they run for executive office. "The press portrays female candidates as unviable, unnatural, and incompetent, and often ignores or belittles women instead of reporting their ideas and intent," wrote Erika Falk, author of the book *Women for President: Media Bias in Nine Campaigns*, in which she analyzed the media perceptions of U.S. female candidates from the 1880s to 2008.

The media described Elizabeth Dole as "scripted, robotic, controlled." Hillary Clinton has been plagued for decades by articles about her weight, her hair and her clothes. In the 2008 campaign, she was described by former Fox News host Glenn Beck as a "stereotypical bitch." Conservative pundit Tucker Carlson complained, "When she comes on television, I involuntarily cross my legs." Clinton lamented in her 2014 book *Hard Choices* that during her tenure as secretary of state, the press paid more attention to her "sexy siren red" toenail polish, spotted when she'd doffed her shoes to enter a temple, than to the fact that she was the first U.S. secretary of state to visit Burma in 50 years.

For Minnesota representative Michele Bachmann, who ran for the GOP nomination in 2012, the crowning moment of her presidential bid was not when she advanced a new approach on national policy or foreign affairs but when the *Washington Post* Style section complimented her for setting "a new standard in the race" as "she looked the part" and never made appearance the issue.

Bachmann rose at 4 a.m. every day to perfect her hair, makeup and clothing, and she eschewed naps on long days so as not to disturb them. "There was no moment during my day when I couldn't be camera-ready," she said. One day in 2011 she gave four speeches in South Carolina at the height of summer. "I was completely drenched with perspiration." After every stop she showered in the bus and started over with hair and makeup. "We laughed, because if I was a man I'd take a three-minute shower and be out the door," she said. "I'm not whining about it. It's a fact of life. You have to look the part that you're running for."

Republicans face a different challenge: they are asked more often than men about who's taking care of their children. During the 2012 GOP presidential primaries, a staffer to former Pennsylvania senator Rick Santorum questioned whether Bachmann should be running for president or caring for her five children and 23 foster kids. When I asked Bachmann about this, she rolled her eyes. "That criticism comes from all quarters, not just Rick," she said. "The voters see beyond it."

Voters might see beyond it, but Oklahoma governor Mary Fallin said it took awhile for her male GOP colleagues, and her own mother, to come around. Fallin found out she was three months pregnant with her second child the day after she'd filed the papers to run for the Oklahoma state legislature. "When I told my mother that I was working a full-time job, expecting a baby, parenting a 3-year-old daughter and running for the legislature, she said, 'You can't do that.'"

Fallin was eight months pregnant when she won her primary; 30 days later she gave birth to a nine-pound boy. A week after the delivery, she was out campaigning, and she won the election three weeks later. "A lot of my colleagues said I should stay home and raise my children and not be so ambitious to run for state legislature," she said.

Fallin ignored them.

Yet women tend not to highlight the toughness that motherhood requires; they demonstrate it in more conventional, populist ways. For former Washington State governor Christine Gregoire, Janet Napolitano in Arizona, Jennifer Granholm in Michigan and New Mexico's Susana Martinez, that meant taking what's become a common path to the gubernatorial mansion for a woman: law enforcement.

Gregoire ran for state attorney general against two male prosecutors. Both painted her as unprepared for a law enforcement job, even though she'd worked in the attorney general's office. "Now that wasn't even a point of conversation with respect to my male opponents. They were prosecutors; therefore, they must be tough enough," Gregoire said.

When she ran for governor, the "toughness" question returned—even after serving as Washington's attorney general for three terms. "I can come off as 'intense,' people call it—confident but intense. What our polling showed us was that I was too tough to be governor," she said, laughing. "I don't think anybody would talk about that with respect to a male candidate for governor. Maybe they would say he wasn't friendly enough or he was stiff or something . . . but I've never heard too tough—*too tough*!"

Massachusetts attorney general Martha Coakley encountered the same problem when she ran for the Senate in 2010 and for governor in 2014. She lost both races to Republican men in part because they were considered more likable. But in between she won re-election as attorney general overwhelmingly. "I do think that the woman running for office has to be tough enough and attractive enough, likable enough but competent enough, and I think it's hardest for us to thread that needle," Coakley said. "People thought I'd been a good AG, but did I smile enough? Was I nice enough? Did they want to have a beer with me?" The answer, she said, was they wanted to have a beer with her opponents.

The Barbara Lee Foundation runs what former Kansas governor and Health and Human Services secretary Kathleen Sebelius called "Girl Governor camp," at which former female gubernatorial candidates impart lessons learned—from what experience to highlight to what to say about young children and how to dress.

At camp, Sebelius heard many stories of how the media dismissed candidates, but she never expected to face that back home. The Kansas press had covered her race competently in her successful bid for state insurance commissioner. Things changed after her first debate as the only woman running for governor. "The opening paragraph . . . was my green two-piece [suit], skirt and jacket with open-toe sandals and pink nail polish on my toes." Sebelius was outraged. Her press secretary called up the reporter to point out that he'd written about the male candidates' policy positions and accomplishments—while describing Sebelius's attire. The press secretary asked the reporter how he'd feel if his own daughter were treated differently from her male competitors. The reporter never again described Sebelius's clothing—or that of any other female candidate—a lesson, Sebelius said, she'd never have thought to address without hearing from other candidates about their experiences. Most reporters don't even realize that they are being sexist, the camp teaches, but if you point it out to them, they are often quick to change their stories and learn the lesson to be more aware of their descriptions.

Houston mayor Annise Parker went to a similar boot camp during her first run for mayor. "They had an image coach, a speech coach," she recalled. "I tend to talk with my hands; I do the things that women do when we speak. I say: 'I think,' 'I believe,' 'I feel.' I learned to edit all that out and say: 'We will,' 'we can,' 'we must.' I upped the wardrobe, trying to find that bull's-eye between still looking feminine and conveying authority."

Sometimes focusing on the feminine can actually help. New York City Council speaker Christine Quinn ran for New York mayor in

2013. In the race's Democratic primary, she was characterized as a bitch by the media and judged by many as too tough, an incongruous assertion in a city that has produced such resolute mayors as Ed Koch, Rudy Giuliani and Michael Bloomberg. Members of the media offered to do several feature articles about Quinn's short red bob haircut. "Of course we rejected them outright as sexist," she said. "But in retrospect, I regret not doing them. Now, if it had been features about Hillary [Clinton]'s hair, that wouldn't have worked because she doesn't care about her hair. But for me, I used to have a line in my speeches about how my hair was an economic assistance program because this color doesn't exist in nature. I love getting my hair done, and it would've shown that side of me." Though she was considered an early front-runner in the race, Quinn lost the primary.

The higher women rise, the worse it gets. Though Pelosi had always been a target of the right, she became a punching bag after President Obama was sworn into office. Unable to confront head-on a president with sky-high approval ratings, conservatives went after Pelosi. She was attacked in ways that her Senate counterpart Harry Reid, at least initially, wasn't. Republicans spent millions of dollars running ads mocking her and tying vulnerable swing-state candidates to her liberal persona. Pittsburgh radio host Jim Quinn once referred to Pelosi on his program as "this bitch." Once and future presidential hopeful Mike Huckabee penned a poem that began: "Here's a story about a lady named Nancy / A ruthless politician, but dressed very fancy." The Republican National Committee put out a video called "Democrats Galore," which had a split-screen shot of Pelosi side by side with Bond villainess Pussy Galore. "I think if Speaker Pelosi were still capable of human facial expression, we'd see she'd be embarrassed," Republican strategist Alex Castellanos said on CNN, referring to persistent rumors that Pelosi has had plastic surgery. The onslaught appalled feminists. "If a man gets in a situation about he-said, she-said, or what people knew, you don't go to his maleness as a way to attack him," Marie

Wilson, head of the White House Project, a group seeking to elect the first female president, told the news website Politico.

Even as the number of female political reporters increases, few empathize with female candidates, and many are actually harder on the women they cover so as not to show favoritism. Looking back on my own coverage, I was probably tougher covering Hillary Clinton's campaign in 2007 in part because she was a woman. I discounted her attempts to fairly point out Obama's weaknesses, such as his lack of foreign policy experience. I mocked the Clinton campaign for producing a kindergarten essay of Barack Obama's as evidence that the Illinois senator was not just a political meteor but someone who had plotted his ascent from an early age. Though unconsciously, I gave Obama more leeway.

Female candidates are also too easily caricatured. Sarah Palin is best remembered for her claim that she could "see Russia from my house," even though she never said that; the line was actually spoken by *Saturday Night Live* comic Tina Fey (though Palin did claim, in answering a question about her foreign policy experience, that one could see Russia from an Alaskan island). When Martha Coakley lost a Senate race in 2010 to Republican Scott Brown, costing Democrats a filibuster-proof control of the Senate, *Saturday Night Live* mocked her as Martha Choke-ly. The label haunted her when she ran for governor four years later. Coakley ran a good campaign but lost narrowly, in part hobbled by the perception that she couldn't close the deal, that she would choke at key moments.

A dearth of female reporters covering candidates is another handicap. At less than critical mass, reporters are defensive of their positions and succumb to pressure to be less sympathetic to female candidates. But as female reporters have grown in number, so has their broad influence. Coverage of women's challenges and issues has increased. Appearance is mentioned less and often called out and criticized when it is. When MSNBC host Krystal Ball ran unsuccessfully for

Congress in Virginia in 2010, someone posted photos of her in a sexy costume at a college Halloween party years before. Rather than embarrass her, the photos had the opposite effect: the media declared them youthful folly and not germane. On a national level, female reporters have reached or are beyond the tipping point; women comprise 37 percent of bylines and broadcasters, according to the 2014 *Status of Women in the U.S. Media* study. Fully half the reporters that April morning at Clinton's New Hampshire toy-factory discussion were women. But on a local level, much more progress is needed, as Coakley's plight demonstrated: she was covered by an almost all-male team at the *Boston Globe*.

Part of the problem is that few women run for executive office and there is difficulty in persuading them to do so. Women are more likely to view themselves as less qualified than they actually are. Gregoire, who had served as head of Washington State's ecology department, said she practically had to have her arm twisted by the governor to run for attorney general. "I'd thought if I could apply for the job, great, but running for the job? I just didn't want to," Gregoire said. "But they kept coming to me and encouraging me, and the next thing you know, I'm running."

This is common among female candidates, who need more encouragement than men to run but tend to receive much less. There is a rubric that a woman has to be asked on average seven times to run for office before she agrees.

Once women are elected, they continue to worry about looking weak. Gregoire struggled to hide her tears at funerals for police and National Guardsmen because she thought that was what was expected of a chief executive. Then, in 2006, she lost a longtime family dog, Franz, the day before a big press conference. "I had been consoling my daughter and hadn't thought about it, and I teared up a little bit" when asked about it, Gregoire recalled. She left the press conference furious with herself. "I went into my office. I asked that no one come see me. I wasn't crying. I was angry at myself because to me women are not allowed to cry in public because it would reinforce that we're weak, right?" she said. But polls showed a surge for Gregoire. "The fact that I'd loved an animal like that was very appropriate, and they loved it."

And women do govern differently from men. They are more keenly aware of what it's like to be discriminated against or not listened to, so they often look to empower others. After she was elected insurance commissioner in Kansas in 1994, Sebelius took a tour of the offices. She met the personnel director and asked him why everyone there seemed to be white men. Do you have any women? she asked. Any minorities? Oh yes, he replied, we have two colored girls in the basement. "I kept thinking later, what is it about that answer that he thought would be appealing to me?" she said. "So my first act in the transition was to replace him with an African-American woman."

"Getting women, balancing diversity—I was really pleased that when I was the governor, one of the things that they said was that I appointed more women to the bench than all the other governors combined," Sebelius said. "Changing that balance but certainly always looking for ways to bring women in."

Gregoire pointed to a pension-reform measure that she saw through as governor. At the time, Democrats controlled both chambers of the legislature, but she insisted on bringing in Republicans to pass the bill. "Democrats weren't happy with me. And what I said to them was: I'm not trying to pass a law that's only good so long as Democrats are in charge of the House and Senate and the governor's house. I want something that will stand the test of time, and that only happens when you have all parties at the table," Gregoire said. "They went along with me because they didn't have a choice. Because I refused to negotiate unless I had them in there. But the result of which was, we got a lot done." Indeed, when Obamacare came under attack in most other states, there was no effort to question or repeal it in Washington because Gregoire had built bipartisan support for the state plan.

Oklahoma governor Fallin believes that the multitasking women learn while raising their children helps them to be prepared and calm during emergencies, like the one she faced when 25 people were killed by tornadoes in Moore, Okla., in 2013. "When you're used to multitasking and handling crisis in a family, as a woman you jump on an emergency immediately and not let it [get] out of control. You're more conscientious—you have a mother instinct," she said. "Someone is in trouble, so you go solve the problem."

In Hillary Clinton's 2008 bid for the presidency, members of her inner circle, especially pollster Mark Penn, convinced her she had a "toughness issue," said Neera Tanden, who served on Clinton's staff at the White House and also worked on her 2008 campaign. So the campaign played up endorsements by generals, like former NATO supreme commander Wesley Clark and former chairman of the Joint Chiefs of Staff Hugh Shelton. But compared with Barack Obama's campaign for change, Clinton's experience shtick seemed old, and it backfired. The seemingly inevitable Clinton lost Iowa. By the time she got to New Hampshire, her campaign was nearly bankrupt and her candidacy seemed days away from over. Obama led in Granite State polls by double digits, and an Obama win would end her candidacy. Exhausted and at the end of her rope, Clinton let her emotions show at a campaign stop in a coffee shop in Portsmouth the day before the primary. "How did you get out the door every day?" a woman asked her. "I mean, as a woman, I know how hard it is to get out of the house and get ready. Who does your hair?"

At first, Clinton joked about having "help" on some of the harder days, and then she turned serious. "I just don't want to see us fall backward as a nation," Clinton said, her voice straining, her eyes welling. "I mean, this is very personal for me. Not just political. I see what's happening. We have to reverse it."

Penn feared this lapse in discipline would end not just her candidacy but potentially her career. But voters didn't see it that way. After months of wooden, military Hillary, they saw her as a woman with whom especially female voters could empathize. Her tears were a turning point: primarily thanks to female voters, Clinton won New Hampshire 46 percent to Obama's 34 percent.

Though her campaign survived another five months, she never recovered the lead. Women nationwide urged her to continue to fight, to bring her bid all the way to the Democratic convention in August, even though Obama had enough delegates to lock up the nomination. When she suspended her campaign in June, she said proudly that the glass ceiling "now had 18 million cracks"—the number of people who voted for her in the primaries. It was the first and last time in the campaign that she talked directly about the historic nature of her candidacy as the potential first female president.

"We shouldn't be afraid, like I was, like my generation was . . . of showing emotion," said Gregoire. "I think the electorate has become more sophisticated, and we smell people who are being disingenuous, superficial," she said. "We have to be ourselves." And that is to run like a woman.

Already, Clinton seems a lot more comfortable this time around, talking about women's issues and seemingly unconcerned with proving she's tough. She's running as Hillary Clinton: a woman, a grandmother, a first lady, a senator and a secretary of state. The campaign even began selling pantsuit T-shirts.

Citing her years of service as Obama's secretary of state, Clinton told me, "I'm hoping that when you take all my experiences, and my preparedness to be president, that people will see it as I see it: that I am the best-qualified person to hold the job at this time."

Clinton lost women to Obama in 17 contests in 2008, and while it's impossible to predict any outcomes at this writing, more than a year ahead of Election Day 2016, this is a different time. The rising number of educated and increasingly powerful women and the many voices on social media have created a new level of scrutiny of and intolerance for sexism. Whether it's a viral video of a woman walking for 10 hours in New York and enduring hundreds of catcalls, or the outcry over Baltimore Ravens football player Ray Rice beating his then-fiancée, women are watching, and they're speaking up.

"The sexism is maybe less pronounced, less obvious, but it still is prevalent in our political scene and in our culture," Clinton said, "and as a result people do say things and use language that have implicit biases about women in public life that demonstrate persistent sexism. You just have to grow a thick skin, as one of my favorite Americans, Eleanor Roosevelt, once said, and carry on."

Clinton said she believes that women do govern differently. "Women in general are better listeners, are more collegial, more open to new ideas and how to make things work in a way that looks for win-win outcomes. That has been my experience," she said. Does she feel she would govern differently as the country's first female president? "I do. I do, Jay. I think that my life experiences, what I care about, what I've been through just make me perhaps more aware of and responsive to a lot of the family issues that people are struggling with," she said. "I really do feel that my preparation for being president puts me very strongly on the side of helping American families, and that's at the core of my campaign."

After all, her candidacy rests on it. "At the end of the day, this really comes down to whether I can encourage and mobilize and turn out women to vote for the first woman president, and I'm going to do my best to make that case," she said.

As president, Clinton said, she would hire more women and seek to create a public-private partnership to increase hiring in the private sector and focus on helping women into the workforce by tackling issues like child care.

Certainly this was Clinton's focus at her campaign stop at

Whitney Brothers, the 111-year-old maker of wooden toys in New Hampshire, where half of the six employees in the roundtable were women, as was half of the tiny audience of about a dozen. They sat in folding chairs before Clinton, at the center of three folding tables arranged in a U. Rain pattered on the factory's tin roof, and everyone huddled in coats on the chilly spring morning, their breath still visible in the factory.

Clinton called first on Whitney Brothers president David Stabler, who asked what Clinton would do to address child-care shortfalls since, as a toy company, children were their concern. Clinton recited her résumé on children's issues, starting with her work right out of college for the Children's Defense Fund. "So my whole adult life, both professional and my volunteer work, has been around children and families, and it is to me the most important commitment we can make."

She commiserated over the lack of relevant woodworking classes at the local community college and suggested that she might raise the issue the next day at a similar event, this one hosted at the community college in question. "I want people to know that I'm listening and accessible and that I'm running a campaign that is about them, about the needs of the people of New Hampshire, the families of New Hampshire," she said.

Pat Russell, sitting in her wheelchair listening to Clinton, grew a little teary-eyed. Clinton made her first trip to New Hampshire in 1991 on her birthday to meet Russell, the former mayor of Keene, ahead of Bill Clinton's 1992 presidential bid. "I'm a little more emotional about it now," said Russell, 84. "I never thought I'd live to see the day we elect a woman president. And now I'm so hopeful for my great-grandchildren—my great-granddaughter and great-grandson. The world that those babies will grow up in will be so different. So maybe our struggle meant something, gave them something."

— 5 —

THE

JUDICIARY

When Linda Morrissey first became a county judge in Tulsa, Okla., in 1995, she quickly saw that unpaid child support often sparked domestic violence cases. When one parent did not pay, the other parent refused visitations, and the situation escalated. Morrissey created a "rocket docket" for child support cases to speed resolution and reduce domestic violence. If a defendant failed to pay after arraignment, Morrissey would bring the case to trial within 30 days, "even if I had to stay to midnight to see it done." If the defendant still had not paid by trial, he or she faced up to six months in county jail, had to pay the plaintiff's legal fees and had state-issued licenses, including their driver's license, suspended. Or the defendant could work out a deal to start paying child support.

The court generated $1 million in child support payments in the first year, paid on average in 32 days. The docket is still one of the most effective in the county. "It was so phenomenally successful, it exceeded my expectations," Morrissey said. "Instead of just continuing to do it the same way it had been for 100 years, a woman looked at it and said: What can we do to make it work?" And just as Morrissey had hoped, the rocket docket helped decrease domestic violence cases. With regular child support in place, finances stabilized, and many former partners were allowed regular contact with their children.

But Morrissey didn't stop with domestic violence. She went on to be a divorce court judge and soon found that system was broken. A year later, Morrissey and three female attorneys and another female judge decided there must be a better way to handle divorce as well. Couples' bitter, angry courtroom attacks left families in tatters. She and the other female judges devised a less adversarial system. Instead of assigning blame, the court attempted to view all parties as people in crisis and placed the happiness and well-being of the children as the central goal. They changed the name of the court to the Families in Transition docket and launched a website that provided families with a variety of services: marriage counseling, mediation, employment counseling, food stamps and medical services. Finally, the women redecorated the court lobby, replacing wooden benches with sofas and adding children's books and toys. "I just think that as a woman I have some sensitivity that is very useful when dealing with people's lives," Morrissey said, "especially as a judge."

In short, the courts were desperately in need of a woman's touch.

Morrissey's story is like those of many female judges of her generation: women who became judges in the 1990s, women who were at the cutting edge of critical mass. When the National Association of Women Judges was formed in 1979, it had 100 members; today, it has more than 1,250. Perhaps the biggest impact of that first wave of female judges has been the cases they've kept out of the courts, rather than how they've handled those that appeared before them. It is no coincidence that in the past 35 years, as women's presence on courts has increased dramatically, so too have extracurricular programs designed to prevent people from ending up on trial: employment skills training, counseling, drug rehab, mediation and children's corners. "The rise of problem-solving courts [has] really coincided with the rise of female judges," said former Utah chief justice Christine Durham. "That's not to say there haven't been hundreds of male judges that have taken on these causes and moved them forward, but I really think women judges have taken to those movements very naturally; they make a lot of sense to them, as it's about building consensus."

Indeed, women's biggest contribution to the law thus far has been the explosion of family courts; there are more than a million practicing family law attorneys, according to the National Academy of Family Law Attorneys.

Women have made more progress in the courts than in virtually any other corner of the workforce, which makes the judiciary an apt context to explore the impact of broad influence. The addition of a third female Supreme Court justice, Elena Kagan, in August 2010 brought the court's female ratio up to a third. Women now make up 35 percent of the federal bench, up from 25 percent when President Obama took office, thanks to a record 130 female judicial appointees. Nearly one third of the 2,758 district court judges are female. And those numbers are even bigger in state courts, where women make up 40 percent of all judges. Twenty state chief justices are women.

The rise of a female judiciary doesn't mean that more female defendants go free or get an easier ride. (Indeed, that happens inherently, as studies show men receive 63 percent longer sentences than women on average, and women are twice as likely to avoid incarceration regardless of the judge's gender.) But their presence does bring perspective to arguments that would otherwise go unheard.

Ideally justice should be blind: a judge trained to evaluate the facts within the framework of the law should come to the same conclusion as another judge, whether male or female. In practice, we know that personal history influences whom the judge finds credible and which cases strike him or her as sympathetic and which as frivolous. "Each of us," noted Sandra Day O'Connor, the first female Supreme Court justice, "brings to our job, whatever it is, our lifetime of experience and our values."

For women who entered the legal profession 40 years ago, that experience was of discrimination against women built into law, which viewed women as dependent and judged their rights through the lens of their familial position as daughter, wife and mother. Until the 1930s, women were often seen as their husbands' property, a hangover from British case law. Married women weren't allowed to work without their husband's permission until World War II. And even with women's advances in the workplace in the 1960s, laws prohibiting them from working weren't fully repealed until the early 1970s. Even then, many states did not allow women to work certain jobs: they couldn't be bartenders, for example, unless they were related to the owner of the bar. In most states default custody of children went to the father. And most divorce decrees favored the man.

When O'Connor graduated from Stanford Law School in 1952, more than 40 law firms rejected her, even though she'd been editor in chief of the *Stanford Law Review*. She eventually became a county attorney in San Mateo, Calif., but only after she worked for free, sharing space with the office's secretary. In 1956, when the Supreme Court's second female justice, Ruth Bader Ginsburg, graduated from Harvard Law School, she was one of nine women in a class of 500. Professors rarely called upon women in class unless they were discussing a rape case or a trial with a female defendant. In one of her University of Wisconsin law school classes in 1963, Judith Lichtman was called on only once—to define rape as "penetration, no matter how deep," she recalled. "It was humiliating," she said. "You knew it wasn't right, but at the time you didn't think—didn't know enough to go do something about it." Lichtman, who was one of two women in the class, later became executive director of the Women's Legal Defense Fund, a position she held for decades.

A decade later, in 1973, Brooksley Born, an attorney who went on to chair the Commodity Futures Trading Commission, stood in a swanky hotel ballroom in Georgetown before a lunch meeting of the Junior League. This society club for the young wives of politicians and Washington bigwigs was an unlikely audience for her thundering speech about de jure sex discrimination. "Most people recognize that sex discrimination pervades our society. What might be less clear to many is that sex discrimination also pervades our laws," Born said. "In many ways our legal system perceives women as essentially different from and inferior to men." The club members donated $30,000, seed money for the Women's Legal Defense Fund, which started with pro bono cases and teaching women's-rights law classes to the Junior Leaguers and others. The group remains one of the most influential Washington lobbies for women's issues in the law.

O'Connor, a moderate conservative appointed to the Supreme Court in 1981 by Ronald Reagan, famously scoffed at the idea that her presence on the court would change decisions. Yet as an Arizona state senator from 1969 to 1975, she spent a hefty amount of time undoing centuries of sexist laws. "I care very much about women and their progress," she said. "I didn't go march in the streets, but when I was in the Arizona legislature, one of the things that I did was to examine every single statute in the state of Arizona to pick out the ones that discriminated against women and get them changed."

Throughout the 1970s and 1980s, women worked to make laws foster equal treatment for women. The National Association of Women Judges studied how women, from judges to plaintiffs, were treated by the courts, and it researched women in prison. In the 1990s, as more women became judges, they influenced the issues the courts took up. Female justices, whether on solo courts or in group courts, had sway on what cases they wanted to hear and what decisions they would write. The Conference of Chief Justices tackled foster care. In a 1993 speech to the American Law Institute's annual gathering, New York chief judge Judith Kaye issued a clarion call to better the lives of children. "As a nation, we need nothing short of a Marshall Plan to turn around the lives and life chances of children," she said. "Lawyers and judges can do so much more." The society soon after embarked on a *Principles of Family Law* report that, when finally released in 2002, would be cited in cases in 36 states and the Supreme Court. "There was an enormous amount of education, training and self-awareness that grew out of the women's courts movement," Utah's Durham said.

Latching onto the rising demand for equal treatment under the law for women, President Jimmy Carter appointed a record number of female judges during his administration. "There were always one or two—tokens," said Carter appointee Patricia Wald, former chief judge of the D.C. Circuit Court of Appeals, considered the country's second most powerful court because it adjudicates the majority of challenges to federal legislation. Carter "was the first who, during his campaign, said, I'm going to put lots of women in government on courts. Before him, there were two women judges that I knew in the federal court systems." In all, Carter saw 40 women confirmed to the federal bench.

Even then, not all judges were accepting of female attorneys. As a young lawyer, Wald once went before a male judge who asked for her name. She gave it. And he asked her for it again. "I thought he must be deaf, so I repeated it. And he then said, 'Are you married?' I said yes. He said, 'Tell me what your right name is,' because I wasn't using *Mrs.* before my name," Wald said. "It was humiliating in front of clients."

But once Wald was named to the bench, attorneys learned the hard way not to dismiss her. "Lawyers would talk to male judges, but they learned pretty quickly, especially when you're writing the decision, that they have to pay attention to you," she said.

Even an increase in the number of women entering the legal profession was subject to stereotyping. In the 1970s, the number of women enrolling in law schools had shot up, and it had become fashionable for schools to put together a course on Women and the Law, an elective course of uncertain content. In 1978, Massachusetts senator Elizabeth Warren was hired as the second female faculty member of the University of Houston's law school under legendary dean George Hardy. Warren was brought on board to teach core courses in contracts and commercial law. Hardy "called me into his office and said, 'Elizabeth, I wanted to ask you, if you are teaching next term, would you be willing to teach a course called Women in the Law?' " "And I said, 'Sure, George, if you are going to be teaching Men in the Law.' " Hardy dropped the idea.

Warren is appalled that more women haven't been able to become law firm partners. "What's so shocking is that there aren't more women in that world even a full generation after women are graduating from college at the same pace as men," Warren said. "[Women] don't start those [fast-track] programs, and when they do start those programs, they are washed out very quickly and not making it to the top." And since law is one of the biggest pipeline jobs for politics, women are much less likely than their male peers to take on a race for government even though studying the law well prepares or encourages people to do that.

In the 2012–2013 academic year, women made up 47 percent of law school students. (That number peaked at 50.2 percent in 1992 following Clarence Thomas's confirmation to the Supreme Court.) While women made up 20.2 percent of law firm partners in 2013 according to Catalyst Research, the private law industry is not yet at the critical-mass tipping point because few of those female partners were in leadership positions. Only 17 percent of partners at the nation's 200 largest law firms were women in 2014, according to the National Association of Women Lawyers. It isn't just that there aren't enough senior female partners but also that there aren't enough women on compensation and management committees once they do make partner, according to the American Bar Association's Commission on Women in the Profession. There simply aren't enough critical actors in private practice to bring up the women in the rank and file.

Women also went into the public sector because it offered lower-paying jobs that were eschewed by men. "I think women were able to move ahead in the public sector because salaries were low but they were getting good experience; they were given more responsibility earlier," said former Massachusetts attorney general Martha Coakley, who has served in both the private and public sectors. "Salaries were lower and other rewards might have been lower, but the satisfaction of doing good, important work outweighed the hours . . . It was personally and professionally more rewarding on the public side."

Wald agreed that there is a fair amount of self-selection. More than half of her female former clerks left private practice for the public sector, while the majority of her male former clerks are still at law firms. "The women tend to be more do-gooder types," Wald said. "They question what they want to do with their lives more and how they'll make a difference."

Wald said she believes the courts began to reach critical mass from the 1980s, when there were more female lawyers arguing cases, to the 1990s, when more women began to be appointed judges. There has been a parallel increase in the number of women serving as heads of government agencies. "And, finally, in recent years more women becoming partner," she said.

Though women now make up 33.3 percent of the Supreme Court, Justice Ruth Bader Ginsburg would be the first to say that when issues come to a vote, 33 percent by itself isn't enough to win. Unlike O'Connor, Ginsberg was a full-throated liberal who made her career empowering women. She was co-founder in 1970 of the *Women's Rights Law Reporter*, the first publication to focus exclusively on women's rights in the law. As a professor at Columbia Law School, she co-authored the first textbook on sex discrimination. In 1972, she co-founded the Women's Rights Project at the American Civil Liberties Union, where she won several seminal cases advancing women's rights. In her last case before the Supreme Court in 1978, she argued that Missouri's optional jury duty for women not only was unconstitutional, because women are citizens as much as men, but also denigrated women's service to the state. At the end of Ginsburg's oral presentation, then Associate Justice William Rehnquist asked her, "You won't settle for putting Susan B. Anthony on the new dollar, then?" Ginsburg chose not to respond, but she later said she considered saying, "We won't settle for tokens."

When she was the lone woman on the court, Ginsburg sometimes had to shame her fellow justices into hearing her. In 2009, the Supreme Court considered the case of a strip search of a 13-year-old girl, Savana Redding, at a school in Safford, Ariz. Another girl had accused Redding of giving her prescription-strength Advil, and the school's female nurses strip-searched Redding, asking to search her bra and panties. No pills were found. Redding was humiliated, keeping her head down during the search so that none of the officials would see her cry. Redding and her family sued the school district asserting her Fourth Amendment right against unreasonable search.

In oral arguments before the Supreme Court, several male justices were dismissive of Redding's claim that she had been left scarred by this incident. They said they saw nothing wrong with the search. Justice Steven Breyer compared Redding's experience to his own as a young man in high school. He said this example was not much different than what boys experience changing in the locker room, including that "people did stick things in my underwear," Breyer said, a comment that evoked laughter from Justice Thomas.

Ginsburg, then the only woman on the court since O'Connor's retirement in 2006, told her male colleagues that none understood what it was like to be a 13-year-old girl and how degrading such a search could be. Clearly something about this case engaged Ginsburg deeply. After the arguments, Ginsburg took the unusual step of granting an interview to *USA Today*, discussing how her male colleagues often ignored her comments until someone else—usually another man—made the same point. She said the atmosphere in the Supreme Court chambers resembled what she had faced as a young lawyer when senior men did not take her seriously. As Associate Supreme Court Justice David Souter was preparing to retire at the end of the term, Ginsburg called on President Obama to appoint more women to the court.

"Women belong in all places where decisions are being made," she told *USA Today*. "I don't say [the split] should be 50–50," Ginsburg said. "It could be 60 percent men, 40 percent women, or the other way around. It shouldn't be that women are the exception."

Though they never publicly responded to that interview, the male justices decided for Redding in an 8–1 majority opinion written by Souter. The accusation that Redding was holding drugs, based solely on the word of another student, did not justify an "embarrassing, frightening and humiliating search," Souter wrote, reflecting Ginsburg's point. "Changing for gym is getting ready for play. Exposing for a search is responding to an accusation reserved for suspected wrongdoers and fairly understood as so degrading" that many schools never allow the practice. Thomas was the lone dissenter.

Women's issues are considered more carefully when more women are at the table. Studies show that judges with female relatives are more sympathetic to the challenges women face and that female judges help sway men when making group decisions. Male judges with daughters are 16 percent more likely to decide in favor of women, according to a 2015 study by Adam Glynn, a political science professor at Emory, and Maya Sen, a government professor at Harvard University's Kennedy School. A 2005 study by Jennifer Peresie published in the *Yale Law Journal* found that not only were female judges significantly more likely than male judges to rule for plaintiffs in cases of sex discrimination or sexual harassment, but the presence of female judges on court panels significantly increased the likelihood that a male judge would rule for the plaintiffs in such cases.

The same study also hinted at what happens when the courts reach critical mass. Panels with just male judges ruled for female plaintiffs in 17 percent of sexual harassment and sex discrimination cases. When one female judge was present, that number doubled to 34 percent. And when two female judges were present, it increased to 43 percent. A similar 2008 study by Christina L. Boyd, Lee Epstein and Andrew D. Martin found that male judges were less likely than female judges to decide for plaintiffs in cases of sex discrimination and that male judges are significantly more likely to rule for plaintiffs in such cases when a female judge is on the panel.

"My own personal view is it does make a difference, in that women's experiences are different in the workplace, and in physical life they're different from men," Wald said. "Science in recent years has shown us that women's brains operate in a different way than men's. So, yes, I do think we decide things differently."

Former federal judge Nancy Gertner, who was appointed to the federal bench in 1994 by President Clinton, was a jurist in Ginsburg's mold. Before her appointment, she argued many cases that concerned women's rights, including one in which she sued the state to stop it from shackling inmates while they are giving birth. Gertner, who retired in 2011 and now teaches at Harvard, held a panel of female judges at Harvard Law School in early 2015. The women all agreed: they didn't make decisions any differently than the men. And then they sat down and detailed how they decided things differently than the men. "It's always the same: we don't want to be perceived as different, but the truth is, we are," Gertner said.

"When I first got to the bench, I was keenly aware of this idea of a blank slate, of not imposing myself into the decision," Gertner said. "But then I quickly realized, judges are picked in their 40s and 50s for their wealth of wisdom and experience. I would be wasting mine if I didn't use it."

Gertner discovered that the manner in which higher courts handled cases was creating dangerous bodies of precedent law. The law requires appellate court judges to justify their decisions when they strike down cases brought on appeal, but they are not required to do this when they let the lower-court verdict stand. In discrimination cases this custom tended to hurt women more, because by citing precedent and detailing the reasoning behind striking the case, judges codified and expanded the logic that outlined the weaknesses on the issue of sexual discrimination. When the judge agreed with the discrimination allegation, the agreement was a footnote in the case unless the judge took the extra step of writing why. So all the decisions that formed the body of sexual discrimination law were justifications for striking down cases, a precedent of many well-documented reasons to strike down a case but none on why to let it stand. After she recognized this, Gertner wrote her decisions for every discrimination case she decided, whether she let the verdict stand or overturned it.

Gertner appreciated how easy it is for most judges to just take a glance at the case, look at the precedents in the way other judges ruled on similar cases and follow their judgments. She caught herself about to do this in a case in which a female prisoner alleged that she was raped by a guard. "My own clerk came to me with the case and said: 'This is going to be an easy dismissal. There are 20 cases across the country where it has been dismissed,'" Gertner said. "And I said, hold on a minute. Let's take the time to look at this case on its merits. And we ended up deciding for the prisoner. And she eventually got a small payment. I could've easily just dismissed that. No one would've thought twice, and that would've been one more case to bolster the argument to dismiss the next one. But I took the case and wrote an opposite opinion."

For all the progress that female jurists have made in the lower courts, the presence of three women on the highest court has not led to better outcomes on women's rights. This may have less to do with gender than it does with party affiliation. With only three female votes on the panel, women's issues can't win unless they have the support of at least two male judges with progressive leanings. Presidents tend to select distinguished jurists who reflect their party's political point of view, and five current justices are GOP appointees. In the past few years the Supreme Court has decided against women in cases involving equal pay, medical leave, abortion and contraception. The 2014 *Burwell v. Hobby Lobby* case is, perhaps, the best lens through which to view the challenges women's issues face in the Supreme Court.

When Congress passed Obama's health-care reform in 2010, it allowed the administration to decide whether employers would be required to provide free contraception to female employees under the new insurance plans available through the state health-care exchanges. Almost immediately, several religious groups and faith-based companies, including Hobby Lobby, a chain of craft stores, applied for exemptions from providing the "morning-after pill," which interrupts a suspected pregnancy by preventing the fertilized egg from attaching to the uterine wall. Hard-core right-to-life advocates believe that life begins at the moment of conception and that taking pills to interrupt even a potential pregnancy constitutes murder.

Catholic members of Obama's administration, such as Chief of

Staff Bill Daley and Vice President Joe Biden, argued for a wider exemption that would allow any religious group or entity to opt out. Most of the women in the administration argued for a narrow one, so that as many women as possible could have contraception covered. The issue came up at one of the Cabinet women's regular dinners, a tradition started by Health and Human Services secretary Kathleen Sebelius and Homeland Security secretary Janet Napolitano, who as the respective governors of Kansas and Arizona had dined regularly with the female counterparts from other states. The women decided that they would lobby the president for a narrow exemption through their own channels, bringing it up at the end of unrelated meetings on the environment, economics or foreign policy. The strategy worked. After hearing this message from so many women in the administration, President Obama gathered women from the Cabinet and the West Wing to weigh in. "There were people who were trying to advise the president about strategies that would have limited choices for a lot of women," Sebelius said. "There was a pretty universal belief among the women in the Cabinet and senior White House advisers that was a big mistake." Obama opted for a very narrow exemption.

In March 2012, the Senate took up the matter. Before the vote, Senate minority leader Mitch McConnell lobbied his members to support a much broader exemption. Maine senators Olympia Snowe and Susan Collins, both pro-choice, objected to it, and McConnell threatened to take away future chairmanships if they voted against the measure. The episode was so acrimonious that Snowe, who had been in office 17 years and was weighing another term, abruptly announced she would be retiring. In an angry press conference, she lambasted the "atmosphere of polarization and 'my way or the highway' ideologies" in the Senate. The wider exemption failed 51–48, with both Republican women voting against it. When the GOP took back the Senate in 2015, Collins, the most senior Republican woman in the Senate, did not get a chairmanship.

In June 2014, the Supreme Court had the final verdict when it ruled, by a vote of 5–4 with the male justices in the majority, that employers could deny insurance coverage of certain contraception to female employees on religious grounds; that forcing them to do otherwise would infringe on their freedom of religion. The decision enraged Ginsburg, who wrote a furious 35-page dissent, to which Elena Kagan and Sonia Sotomayor joined.

And yet the court wasn't totally deaf on social liberal issues— just the ones that involved women. A month later, Ginsburg complained to an audience of law school students that while the court, thanks to female jurists, has endorsed "equal dignity" for gays, it has never truly embraced "the ability of women to decide for themselves what their destiny will be." Without the work of female jurists like Margaret Marshall, the former Massachusetts supreme court justice who wrote that state's seminal decision, the cause of gay marriage would not have advanced as it has. Indeed, when same-sex marriage went before the Supreme Court in April 2015, it was Ginsburg who made the clarion argument for the institution.

In the oral arguments when the case was before the court, justices Alito and Roberts said the court should not meddle with the tradition of marriage, saying it had survived for centuries in its current form and didn't need to be adjusted. Ginsburg spoke up, perhaps recalling the battles fought by her and her female colleagues to equalize the laws that applied to women. "Marriage today is not what it was under the common law tradition, under the civil law tradition. Marriage was a relationship of a dominant male to a subordinate female. That ended as a result of this court's decision in 1982, when Louisiana's Head and Master rule was struck down. Would that be a choice that state should be allowed to have? To cling to marriage the way it once was?" Louisiana was the last state to abolish laws giving a husband control over household decisions and joint property without his wife's consent. The women who had worked to equalize the laws for the past 35 years were now helping LGBTQ people in their fight, even as women's progression stalled.

So why is the Supreme Court still so backward on women? "To be frank, it's one person who made the difference: Justice [Anthony] Kennedy," Ginsburg told *Elle* later that year. Kennedy is the court's swing vote and, while he has long had gay friends, most of the women in his life have held traditional roles. This isn't the first time Kennedy and Ginsburg clashed over women's rights. In a 2007 case, *Gonzales v. Planned Parenthood of America*, the court upheld a ban on partial-birth abortion. Kennedy wrote in the majority decision: "Respect for human life finds an ultimate expression in the bond of love the mother has for her child . . . While we find no reliable data to measure the phenomenon, it seems unexceptionable to conclude some women come to regret their choice to abort the infant life they once created and sustained."

Ginsburg's dissent dismissed Kennedy as an artifact, saying that his "way of thinking reflects ancient notions about women's place in the family and under the Constitution—ideas that have long since been discredited." She also wrote that this paternalistic view of women's ability to choose "deprives women of the right to make an autonomous choice, even at the expense of their safety."

Just as women bring their lifetimes of experience to the bench, Kennedy brings his, and it doesn't involve women in positions of power. As David Cohen, a law professor at Drexel University, told the *New York Times*'s Adam Liptak: "Justice Kennedy relies on traditional and paternalistic gender stereotypes about nontraditional fathers, idealized mothers and second-guessing women's decisions."

Despite all the progress that has been made, much remains to be done. If a decision like *Hobby Lobby* or the ban on partial-birth abortions comes down to one justice's life experience, whether that judge is a Kennedy or a Ginsburg, it can spell an enormous difference for women in America.

Yet, Wald argued, the mere presence of female jurists has had a "ripple effect." Half of Wald's clerks on the D.C. appeals court were women, and she made sure to appoint the first female clerk of court and first female chief executive of the court. Seeing women on the nation's highest court not only inspires younger women, she said, but also empowers female attorneys arguing cases before them.

Certainly that was the case for Lisa Blatt. In her 25 years on the Supreme Court Bar—a formal organization of lawyers who are accredited to argue before the highest court in the land—she has seen the court go from one woman to two, back to one and then to three. Blatt, who heads up the Supreme Court practice at D.C. law firm Arnold and Porter and is one of a handful of women on the Supreme Court Bar, has never been more comfortable arguing in that hallowed institution, now that there are three women on the court—what she deems a critical mass.

"I think it does make a difference if there are three of them, as opposed to just one and even when there were two," Blatt said. "It makes a big difference as an advocate, just as it would make a big difference if they were all nine white men and then all of a sudden you have more racial diversity. There's just something unsettling about arguing in front of a monolithic court."

Eventually—and given the momentum, sooner rather than later—the ripple effects of the women on the bench will reach a legal tidal wave.

Sen. Patty Murray told me that she purposefully went to hear the Supreme Court's oral arguments in the *Hobby Lobby* case. "I watched the two men lawyers make their cases, and immediately the lawyer speaking from Hobby Lobby was interrupted by the women on that court asking the questions I would have asked. You know, 'What does this mean?' 'How can an employer decide?' It made a huge difference on that court because it was the women who asked questions,"

Murray told me.

"But the decision still went their way," I noted.

"I know," Murray said. "Guess how many men were in that court?" she said with a wry smile. Murray is resolved to see a fourth woman added to the Supreme Court: in her mind, the work of balancing the bench is far from done.

The *Hobby Lobby* decision energized women's groups to campaign to get more women appointed to the bench. Ultimately, the Obama administration rewrote the law to allow companies to opt out of insuring certain contraceptions; the federal government would instead extend that coverage. As of October 2015, this language had been challenged and upheld in four federal appeals courts and looked likely to withstand a Supreme Court challenge should one emerge. Where there is a will, there is a way.

— 6 —

PUBLIC
VS. PRIVATE

Twenty-nine-year-old tech wunderkind Erie Meyer never dreamed of working for the government. Her goal was to disrupt the world through technology. But that industry's geek-boy culture remains relatively hostile territory for women. After a few years at a tech firm, Meyer quit her job and moved to Ohio to launch a website for the Ohio attorney general's office. She decided to take the huge pay cut involved because she thought working in government would allow her the chance to be effective at work and also make a difference in the world.

"Let's say I went to the private sector or a finance company and worked all day on a product. That's just one product, not a whole chain of products," Meyer said, referring to the government's wider regulatory influence. Her work in Ohio soon drew Washington's attention, and she became a founding member of the United States Digital Service, an innovation hub for the executive branch. In 2014, *Forbes* named Meyer one of the top 30 people under 30 in technology. "Of all the places where I could spend my days, I felt like I could help more people [working in government] than anywhere else."

You can see why Meyer might prefer Washington, D.C., to Palo Alto. At most big tech companies, 30 percent of the employees are women, but only a few of those women are coders or engineers, usually a tech company's most vaunted and influential employees. Most women have jobs in the human resources, communications, accounting or government relations divisions. Only 4 percent of Silicon Valley's venture capitalists are women, and of the more than 6,000 companies that got venture-capital funding between 2001 and 2013, only 3 percent were headed by women. Yet the U.S. Digital Service, where Meyer works, is now more than 50 percent female. "In the CTO office, all the superstar engineers and programmers are women," former White House chief technology officer Todd Park told students at a lecture at Harvard in February 2015.

Meyer is not the only woman in D.C. who abandoned a lucrative tech career. Megan Smith, vice president of Google(x), was named the first female White House chief technology officer in September 2014. Marina Martin, who built the software for Amazon's distribution systems, is now the CTO at the Department of Veterans Affairs. And the CTO on Hillary Clinton's campaign is Stephanie Hannon, who, up until the week Clinton announced her candidacy, was Google's director of product management for civic innovation and social impact.

Almost from its advent, Silicon Valley was a tough place for women. The bursting of the dot-com bubble in 1999–2001 was a setback for women trying to make inroads. More women were laid off after the implosion than men, and fewer women work in tech now than in 1998.

Silicon Valley is a culture that celebrates youth, particularly male youth. Quora, a Silicon Valley chat site, in 2013 famously posed the question: What does one do when they're 35, thus officially over the hill, and haven't made it yet?

It is a notoriously sexist and male-nerd environment where offices are furnished with foosball tables and footballs. In a much-celebrated episode of HBO's *Silicon Valley*, the lead character reaches a mathematical epiphany imagining every man at a conference measuring the distance between his penis and the floor.

Two women in the video game industry, Zoe Quinn and Brianna Wu, were viciously attacked online when they attempted to curb the sexist imagery in the games they were helping to develop. Gamergate, as it was dubbed by the media, launched a prolonged self-examination of the treatment of women in the industry. San Francisco–based Uber Technologies got into trouble when its top executive, responding to reports about women being raped by Uber drivers, threatened to spend millions stalking a female journalist who had written a critical report. He apologized. At one point, a cluster of such incidents inspired *Newsweek* to run a cover story titled "What Silicon Valley Thinks of Women." The cover image depicted a cartoon woman in a red dress with a giant cursor lifting up her skirt from behind.

From this culture a few successes have emerged: Yahoo CEO Marissa Mayer, the "queen of the nerds"; Facebook COO and *Lean In* author Sheryl Sandberg; Google CFO Ruth Porat. But these are the exceptions that prove the rule. For every Mayer, there are a dozen people like Ellen Pao, who unsuccessfully sued venture-capital firm Kleiner Perkins Caufield and Byers for gender discrimination when she was fired from her job as a junior investing partner. Pao then became interim CEO at the online chat site Reddit before being fired in mid-2015—provoking yet another wave of articles about Silicon Valley's mistreatment of women.

"We are going backwards in a field that is meant to be all about moving forward," Hillary Clinton scolded Silicon Valley at a conference of women in tech in February 2015. Yet at that same conference, many female executives expressed a sense of hope: that in an industry that values disruption, there is room for women to rise.

Several female-run and -focused VCs have launched, such as BBR in New York, which invests only in companies run by women. Meyer runs Tech Lady Mafia, one of the most coveted power lists in the industry, where women swap job tips, tech pointers and funding advice. One Silicon Valley start-up run by women, Glassbreakers, trains women on how to succeed despite the odds, helping them to learn everything from coding to pitching VCs for money. Big tech companies have programs to recruit and retain more women. But there are few quick fixes. Perhaps the biggest challenge is getting and keeping girls interested in science, technology, engineering and math, from grade school through grad school. By the eighth grade, half of girls are already turned off these subjects. The falloff has prompted ventures like GoldieBlox, educational toys designed to inspire girls to build things and develop their interest in engineering at a young age. But education will take a generation to bear fruit, and in the meantime, Silicon Valley is one of the most challenging arenas for women.

While Silicon Valley may be the most egregious offender, it is not alone in being tough terrain for women in the private sector. Ambitious women once looked to the world of business to advance their careers, but that is no longer their quickest path to success. In the past decade, mid- and upper-level private-sector job growth for women has stalled, while women have been making amazing gains in public life.

Ten years ago, women held 17 percent of the positions on corporate boards and 20 percent of senior executive posts, while less than 15 percent of the employees in the upper levels of all three government branches—elected members, judges and political appointees—were female. Now Congress is 20 percent female, the administration is at 30 percent, and women hold 35 percent of federal judgeships. Meanwhile the private sector has remained stuck at virtually the same levels.

What's behind the phenomenon of the rise of women in the public sector? Women vote. In 2012, 71.4 million women voted, compared with 61.6 million men. Candidates know that women are paying attention, and if they want to win an election, they must appeal to the female electorate. Presidents increasingly look to appoint more women to senior jobs to demonstrate their commitment to advancing women in leadership. Shelley Moore Capito, a West Virginia Republican who beat a female Democratic opponent to win her Senate seat in 2014, said those numbers drive an increasing focus on "what women want, what are we thinking, what are we doing, how are we phrasing things, how are we legislating."

With women in senior positions in all segments of government, they've created an atmosphere that attracts the next wave of talented women.

Like Meyer, the desire to have an impact leads many women to public service, and it often starts with a local issue they're passionate about. Republican congresswoman Michele Bachmann fostered 23 children, which piqued her interest in public education. She ran for the Minnesota school board because she was appalled at the curriculum in her children's classes. New York representative Carolyn McCarthy, a Democrat, was elected to Congress on a gun-control platform after her husband was killed and her son severely wounded in a mass shooting on a Long Island commuter train. Rep. Louise Slaughter, another New York Democrat, got involved in politics to fight the development of a local forest. Michigan senator Debbie Stabenow ran for the Lansing County board in order to save a nursing home the local commissioner was trying to shut down. She beat the incumbent even though she was just a University of Michigan grad student at the time.

In 40 states, serving in the legislature is a part-time job with flexible hours, making it a good place for women with children. As their children get older and more independent, the women can take on more responsibilities, serving as committee chairs or running for higher office. With women as leaders, policies and practices involving family life start to change. When New Hampshire state legislator Maggie Hassan was approached to run for the state senate in 2002, she was reticent at first. She didn't want to miss more of her kids' lives. A female state senator told her not to worry. A majority of the 24-member senate were women, and when someone's child had to be picked up from soccer, they all took a break and arranged to reconvene later. Hassan decided to run, going on to become a two-term governor, and in 2016 is running for the U.S. Senate. Because New Hampshire has the country's most representative democracy—with more than 400 members representing the state's 3 million people in its lower chamber—a majority of its leaders are women: governor, both senators and one of its two members of Congress.

Elected office may be one of the most family-friendly jobs. Elected officials can set their own schedules: when they come to work, or whom they bring along, is up to them. "I am often asked how do I do it, and one of the keys is that this job does have some flexibility," said Cathy McMorris Rodgers, a Washington congresswoman and the House leadership's top Republican woman. McMorris Rodgers had all three of her children since being elected to Congress in 2005. "People may not look at it immediately and think, 'Oh, there's flexibility being a member of the Congress,' but on any given week there are demands, obviously, but having that flexibility makes all the difference for me."

Being the boss also helps. "When I was running EPA, we were running late one day and a bunch of people were in the room," recalled Carol Browner, the EPA administrator under Clinton. "I remember saying, 'Does anyone have a kid to pick up at day care?' And you can see all these men sitting there thinking, 'I am not gonna put my hand up,' right? And then one said, 'I do.' And then others were also like, 'So do I.' We broke through this taboo. It was OK to bring your family's issues to the workplace, and I did it not just for the women but for the men. They could feel comfortable saying, 'I've got child care duty.' "

The importance of family demands on the lives of professional women gets attention only when they have reached widespread critical mass, as they have in the public sector. But women hold very few senior positions in the private sector, and that culture has yet to change to accommodate their needs.

There is a powerful case to be made for companies to invest in elevating more women. Companies with more women in leadership roles run better and make more money, studies show. Catalyst, a group that researches the impact of women in the workforce, found that in 2004–08, companies that had the highest average percentage of female directors outperformed companies that had the lowest by 26 percent. The management consulting firm McKinsey found that companies with top-quartile representation of women in executive committees saw, on average, 47 percent better returns on equity and 55 percent better average earnings before interest and tax.

When McKinsey wanted to study the differences between male and female bosses, it identified nine leadership behaviors and surveyed companies to ask which behaviors were most used by women and which were more likely to be used by men. Women scored high in people development, expectation and rewards, role models, inspiration and participative decision making. Men were more inclined to use two behaviors, control and corrective action, and to decide things for themselves. The other two behaviors—intellectual stimulation and efficient communication—showed no discernible difference between the sexes. McKinsey then asked business executives worldwide which leadership qualities best prepared companies for the future. The four leading behaviors executives favored were intellectual stimulation, inspiration, participative decision making and expectations and rewards. Women excelled at three out of the four favored leadership qualities, areas that 70 percent of those polled said their companies were deficient in. Clearly these companies need more women in the executive suite; they just don't know it yet.

And there's certainly a large, and largely untapped, number of qualified and credentialed women. In 2012, slightly more than a third of MBAs were awarded to women, according to a Committee for Economic Development study. But the number of women in graduate school started to outpace the number of men starting in 1984; in 2012, women earned 63 percent of all master's degrees and 54 percent of all doctorates, according to the Council of Graduate Schools.

Harvard Business School provides an illustrative look at the challenges women face in entering the private sector. In recent years, the university has done some soul-searching about the women in its midst. From 2006 to 2007, a third of the business school's junior female faculty left. Younger female professors struggled to keep their male pupils' respect and were often mocked and rated, as were female students, for their appearance, according to school staff. That same school year, Harvard president Larry Summers was forced to step down after he lost a faculty no-confidence vote, in part because of a 2005 speech he gave in which he suggested that the underrepresentation of women in science and engineering could be due to a "different availability of aptitude at the high end" rather than to patterns of discrimination and socialization. The woman who succeeded him in 2007, Drew Gilpin Faust, has made a priority of getting a critical mass of female students and professors into science, technology, math, engineering and business. During her tenure, the percentage of female faculty members rose from 24 percent to 40 percent, and the number of female engineering students doubled to 30 percent, twice the national average. She also appointed a woman to be the dean of the engineering school.

Faust said that when she'd first joined the faculty at the Radcliffe

Institute, which houses most of Harvard's professional development programs, another faculty member warned her that she'd be discredited if she talked too loudly about women's issues at Harvard. Faust obliterated that taboo to such a degree that one of her assistants, who'd worked with Summers before her, quipped: "It used to be when you went to a meeting and a woman was in the room, it wasn't an important meeting. Now, if there are no women in the room, it's not an important meeting."

One of Faust's first acts as Harvard president was to appoint a new business school dean, Nitin Nohria, who "took the lid off of simmering discontent over gender disparity at HBS," Faust said. In 2011, the business school began an experiment. Nohria installed stenographers or video cameras in all classes. In part, the transcripts and tapes helped teachers learn how they could do better. But it also evinced how men and women respond differently to seeing themselves on tape. Showing male teachers the tapes helped them improve, but seeing the tapes worsened female teachers' performance. Women were harder on themselves, taking faults personally. When HBS recognized this, it arranged to have others watch the women's tapes and then provide constructive criticism about teaching performance.

One of the other outcomes tracked by recording classes was documentation of which student came up with which idea first. Male teachers tended to overlook female contributions and often misremembered who came up with an idea: a female or male student. At HBS, class participation determines 50 percent of a student's final grade. Among other initiatives, the school assigned students to mixed-gender study groups and provided private coaching for female students and untenured female professors, for some after every class. HBS also diverged from the sacrosanct case-study format, instead creating courses called "Field," in which teams of students, usually mixed-gender, worked together to problem-solve. It also worked to curb the school's alcoholic extracurricular culture.

Though the experiment ended with the class's graduation, many of the reforms were kept in place and have since evolved. A gender initiative was formalized in the spring of 2015, gathering gender research by half a dozen professors and looking at ways to incorporate it at Harvard and in the workforce overall—many of Harvard's faculty in the initiative consult on gender issues for *Fortune* 500 companies, government institutions and other schools. By the end of the project, the students' scoring of the female teachers saw marked improvement, and interviews with female students and staff revealed that women felt more integrated and happier. Some 40 percent of the top 5 percent of the class were women, by far the largest number since women were admitted to the school in 1963. But challenges remained: HBS still has only 17 percent female faculty, well below its unofficial goal of 25 percent.

Harvard Business School's attempt to understand and compensate for the factors holding women back offers a key insight. While women clearly communicate differently than men, the predominant male bias is that the difference proves that women are inferior to men. This led to the marginalization of female students when the women were less than a critical mass of the student body. Understanding the communication differences, Harvard hopes, will lead to better retention of women in the workforce as well as build a work culture that is more female-friendly.

Harvard Business School senior lecturer Amy Schulman, a lawyer and former top executive at Pfizer, said she became keenly aware of how women and men perceive language differently when she saw how her female colleagues in her law firm reacted to their sixth-year reviews, the point at which lawyers often learn if they are on track to become partners. Women comprise only 20.2 percent of law partners but represent 47.2 percent of law students and 45.4 percent of associates. Schulman's experience reflected much of what Harvard found: women listened for different things in a performance review.

Women five years out of law school are generally in their late 20s or early 30s, so the sixth-year review coincides with when they are considering whether to take time off to have children, try to have a career and a child, or have no child at all. Almost a third of women take an average three-year break from their careers, according to a 2009 study by the Center for Work-Life Policy. Though it's a relatively brief interruption in the span of a 40-year career, the timing for women is critical. A *Harvard Business Review* survey found that 37 percent of women stopped working voluntarily at some point in their careers, vs. 24 percent of men. Of the 93 percent of women who chose to leave the workforce and intended to go back, only 74 percent managed to do so and only 40 percent found full-time work.

In the sixth-year review, male bosses would tell associates who were on partner track: everything's OK. "That was it. One word," Schulman recalled. "This woman who's probably in her late 20s, early 30s, feeling the tug of other pressures, thinks, 'Just OK?' And a guy hears that and he thinks: 'Everything's OK, I'm totally on track.' So that same language—'OK'—is actually read and interpreted in profoundly different ways by, I think, men and women," Schulman said. Women generally want more detailed feedback than men; they like to know what they're doing right and what they're doing wrong so that they can correct course. When making a decision, women often seek out more information than men and inevitably perceive a scanty review as negative.

The obvious solution, Harvard discovered, was to provide more feedback to the women and communicate strengths and weaknesses with greater specificity than they would necessarily provide men. Schulman noted that just having diverse teams isn't enough to build diversity and inclusion. "We have to actually change how we lead those teams, how we speak to them," she said. "Corporations are notoriously slow that way."

The basic differences in how men and women communicate is

one reason a lone woman on a corporate board often isn't effective: she is the outsider, or a token, as Rosabeth Moss Kanter, a Harvard Business School professor, found in her seminal 1979 paper.

Former SEC chair Mary Schapiro has been both a lone female director and part of a critical mass. She currently sits on GE's board, where five of the 15 members are women, and also served on the boards of Kraft Foods, which was half female, and Cinergy Corp., the predecessor to Duke Energy, where she was the only woman for many years. "I can tell you from personal experience, my comfort level in an environment where you are the only woman is quite different," Schapiro said. While most people expected Kraft Foods to have women on its board since women were the main purchasers of their products, she noted, "women are consumers of lots of different products, and their intellect, energy, perspective and insight are important for the success of all kinds of businesses."

Schapiro cited studies that have shown that there needs to be at least three women on a board for their voices to be effective. "It takes a certain amount of courage when you come on a corporate board to speak up. The subject matter may be new to you, the dynamics may be new to you, the personalities. It's a pretty daunting thing when you first join," Schapiro said. "And yet you want people on boards to have new perspectives, different experiences and expertise and a range of views. It's empowering for women when there are other women present. It gives you a sense of support and belonging."

A 2006 study by the University of Western Ontario and Wellesley's Centers for Women titled "Critical Mass on Corporate Boards: Why Three or More Women Enhance Governance" found that women who served alone were often ignored and excluded from socializing, and their views were discounted as a "woman's point of view." The situation got better with two women but reached a tipping point with three or more. In interviews with 50 female directors, 12 CEOs and seven corporate secretaries from *Fortune* 1000 companies, the researchers found: "The magic seems to occur when three or more women serve on a board together . . . Women's tendencies to be more collaborative but also to be more active in asking questions and raising different issues start to become the boardroom norm. We find that having three or more women on a board can create a critical mass when women are no longer seen as outsiders and are able to influence the intent and process of board decisions more substantially."

Women's tendency to deeply research issues before making a decision also contributes to their outsider status. "Women, more than men, listen openly to other speakers," the 2006 study's authors found. "Many of our informants believe that women are more likely than men to ask tough questions and demand direct and detailed answers."

Given women's proclivity for deeper detail, men tend to view a lone female board member with suspicion, fearing that she might ask questions that would make them uncomfortable—or worse. One oft-cited reason for the paucity of female representation on corporate boards and the upper levels of management was a spate of high-profile female whistle-blowers. Sherron Watkins, an auditor and former Enron vice president, first raised suspicions of shady accounting practices, which led to the energy company's collapse and its executives' conviction for fraud. And Cynthia Cooper, an auditor at MCI WorldCom, famously exposed that company's $3.8 billion fraud. While these women did the right thing and were celebrated for it, their actions contributed to a perception—however unfair—that women weren't part of the team, that they were outliers and independent actors who couldn't be trusted. Yet there have been plenty of male whistle-blowers, such as Jeffrey Wigand, a former tobacco executive who revealed that tobacco companies knew about the harmful effects of smoking well before the landmark U.S. Surgeon General report on cigarettes.

With greater focus on corporate governance in the post-Enron era, having more women on boards was more important than ever, the 2006 study noted. And it's spurred a concerted effort to make it the norm.

Holding court at the annual gathering at J.P. Morgan's New York offices of the organization WomenCorporateDirectors, WCD founder Susan Stautberg said women raise the bar for their male counterparts. "[Women] ask more questions and they are more prepared. When women come more prepared, men come more prepared, too," she said. "Women address the elephants in the room. They ask the tough questions."

Women bring a diversity of experience and thinking to the table. Retailers, cable television and food companies have realized this, leading the nation in adding women to their boards, but women can help bring new thinking to almost any decision, Stautberg said. "Putting women on the board isn't about doing good or feeling good, it's absolutely great for business," she said.

White House chief technology officer Todd Park agrees, as is evident when one surveys his staff—he's consciously hired to achieve parity. "The more diverse a team is," he said, "the better it is."

WCD's mantra is "One woman is invisible; two is a conspiracy and three is mainstream." WCD's goal is to get at least three women on every corporate board in America.

For Schulman, who left law to become COO of Pfizer, eventually started her own company and now sits on five corporate boards, being the second woman always posed a conundrum. "When a woman is one of two—in a meeting, on a corporate board—walking to the room where there's another woman there, you always make a minute calculation: if I sit next to her, the men are going to roll their eyes and say, 'Women gaggle together.' But if you don't do it, they say, 'They aren't getting along.' Whatever you do, you're judged because you're only two and you're reduced to being a standard-bearer. Once you've reached critical mass, you unselfconsciously own the space the way men do."

It's not as if there isn't a talented pool from which to draw. WCD's membership consists of 3,500 women serving on 6,500 boards globally as members. There are at least 16 organizations that specialize in identifying qualified women for corporate boards in the U.S., including the Financial Women's Association, the National Association of Corporate Directors, the Boston Club (home of Mitt Romney's infamous "binders full of women") and Stanford University's Women on Boards Initiative. Six months out of office, former Washington governor Christine Gregoire had been offered numerous nonprofit board seats—women are well-known do-gooders with a long-proven ability to raise money for charities—but had received no invitations to join a corporate board. Gregoire thought it was an anomaly, given that she had managed a $33 billion budget as governor. Then she spoke on a panel with former Oregon governor Barbara Roberts, who had left office in 1995; though Roberts had served on plenty of nonprofit and volunteer boards, she'd never been offered a seat on a corporate board. "Now I'm going through another glass ceiling that I'm going to have to break through," Gregoire said. "I just find it fascinating that I haven't been asked."

Lynn Schenk, a former Democratic congresswoman from California, in 2004 chaired the search committee to find other directors for a large company. The committee hired an outside headhunter to identify good candidates, but Schenk was shocked to see that there were no women or minorities among them. "I said, You mean to tell me you couldn't find a single qualified woman or person of color? And as soon as I said it, he produced the most incredible people. So it's a matter of pressing people to look outside the norm, challenging them to think outside the box."

Schenk is now one of three women on biotechnology giant Biogen's 10-member board. "When you get three women, it became professional and collegial. It was no longer odd, different or weird. When we got three at Biogen and a female CEO, there was no more questioning. The men just accepted our input as due course."

There are some companies that are ahead of the curve, such as Macy's, Avon, H&M and Estée Lauder, where roughly half or more of the board members are women. But others have few or no top female executives; Sears Holdings has only one woman on its board.

EY, formerly Ernst and Young, is focusing its diversity efforts on changing the criteria upon which board members are selected. "One of the problems with boards is that everyone wants a sitting CEO to be their board member," said Beth Brooke-Marciniak, EY's global vice chair of public policy, who focuses on diversity and inclusiveness. "Well, that narrows the pool of women immediately. Part of the effort is to get the nominating committees to broaden how they're defining the qualifications."

Carly Fiorina, who rose from being a secretary to become CEO of Hewlett-Packard, believes the problem is twofold: men tend to hire people they know, rather than risk hiring the unknown; and women tend to require more support and flexibility, particularly during child-rearing years. Fiorina said the first problem doesn't have an obvious solution beyond encouraging boards to think outside the box. But the second is being addressed "by technology. . . . I can remember pioneering a job-sharing program at HP which women loved and took great advantage of."

A key to change is time: more than half of the current directors of *Fortune* 1000 companies are men over the age of 70. So the public-sector churn seen in regular elections is coming to the private sector as the generation changes guard—which Brooke-Marciniak believes will be more female. Indeed, the rising millennial generation grew up accepting gender equality as the norm. As they age and replace older generations, they carry their standards and beliefs with them. As the workforce turns over, the expectation is that the sexism that exists today will die off.

Some countries have given up on waiting for the sea change to happen naturally. Europe in the wake of the global financial crisis has moved to ensure that more women attain higher levels of power in corporations. In November 2013, the European Commission voted to impose a quota of 40 percent women by 2020 on all non-executive corporate board positions, or those positions not directly involved in the management of the company. A year earlier, Germany enacted a quota of 30 percent women on corporate boards by 2016. The European Central Bank plans to fill 28 percent of its senior management posts with women by 2019, in response to criticism that all 23 members of its governing council are men. Companies that fail to comply will face sanctions or fines. "[The] European Parliament vote is a historic moment for gender equality in Europe," said European Union justice commissioner Viviane Reding, who had pushed for the move. "The Parliament has made the first cracks in the glass ceiling that continues to bar female talent from the top jobs."

Europe is not alone in embracing gender incentives. Other countries have instituted measures to encourage diversification, with varying degrees of success. According to the *Economist*, 32 percent of senior managers in China are women, compared with 23 percent in the U.S. in 2013. Women run 12 percent of the 250 largest companies in both India and Brazil, including energy, hotel and airline giants; in the U.S., women head fewer than 5 percent of *Fortune* 500 companies.

Quotas are controversial: many complain that they promote less-than-qualified individuals, weakening the system and perhaps tarnishing the image of women on the whole. But studies show that after a generation, quotas often prove successful: they offer incentives for women to train and provide roles to which they can aspire.

Europe's bet that having more women on boards will reduce risk and improve its economy isn't one that the U.S. has been willing to make; it's hard to imagine Congress ever passing such a mandate. It is noteworthy that, at least in Europe, there has been a widespread recognition that women must play a larger management role in the private sector, not just for the health of the companies but for the economy as a whole.

But as other countries seek out talented women, they are drawing that talent away from the United States. "I know a lot of female U.S. executives being called and asked to serve on non-U.S. corporate boards," said Brooke-Marciniak. "In my mind, it's a competitiveness issue for America. I mean, we're going to have the competitive brain trust of American women being asked to go serve elsewhere."

— 7 —

LEHMAN
SISTERS

In February 2009, the national climate was one of anger: at Wall Street for the stupid risks that led to the near collapse of the financial system; at George W. Bush, the first MBA president, for his complicity in the mess; and at Washington for its uneven response. Congress was fruitlessly scrambling to figure out how to claw back $169 million in bonuses given by insurance giant AIG to its executives using taxpayer money, an embarrassing episode that only further enflamed populist tensions. And the administration was huddling on how best to rescue Citibank, one of the world's largest banks, for the third time.

In the first and second Citibank bailouts, Federal Deposit Insurance Corporation chair Sheila Bair had argued for imposing tougher conditions on the firm, which she felt hadn't done enough to shore up its messy finances. Bair was scheduled to join an emergency conference call on a Sunday in mid-March with Treasury secretary Tim Geithner and other regulators to decide how to move forward. She wanted Citigroup CEO Vikram Pandit and several of his top aides to go. She'd pushed for this before, noting that Pandit, an investment banker with little commercial banking experience—someone she viewed as a gambler with the bank's money, instead of a protector of its depositors—helped lead to Citibank's weakness. But now she was in her strongest position yet to oust him.

In the lead-up to the financial crisis, Citibank executives knowingly hid extensive problems in the mortgages the bank was securing, which contributed to the financial system's collapse. Citibank would eventually own up to its mistakes, admitting guilt and paying a fine of $7 billion, one of the largest ever levied on a bank, to the Justice Department in July 2014. The cover-up by Citibank and other financial institutions masked the severity of the crisis until it was nearly too late.

Bair had been pushing to downgrade the FDIC's main rating of Citibank, which other regulators worried would spook the market into selling off Citi's stock. In order to avoid the downgrade, Bair was demanding that Citi fire Pandit, along with a laundry list of other conditions. Bair was later "flabbergasted" to learn in Ron Suskind's 2011 book *Confidence Men* that Pandit had gone to Geithner before their scheduled call and asked to make his own deal with the Treasury. But that office, Bair later pointed out, had no say in the FDIC's ratings.

"It was over the top," Bair recalled. "I think they thought that that was going to be the way they could do a backdoor bailout. We just had profoundly different worldviews of how these kinds of problems should be handled. This wasn't just gender; there were also different philosophies. There were a lot of complex things going on there, but I use Vikram going to Tim as an example: if men do not want to accept your position of power, then they will sometimes try to go to another man who they feel may have power over you to avoid having to deal with you."

Bair went into the call thinking that her clampdown on Citibank was going to be successful—only to be blindsided by Geithner with a whole new proposal. "You just need to stand your ground and hope-fully your colleagues will back you up and say, 'No, you need to go talk to Sheila, that's her job,' but it doesn't always happen," Bair said with a sigh. In the end, they compromised. Geithner persuaded Bair to allow Pandit to stay. To address Bair's concerns, Pandit brought in executives with commercial banking expertise to help Citi through the crisis.

The experience was a searing one for Bair, and it prompted her to push Congress to grant the FDIC more power when Congress rewrote banking regulations in the wake of the crisis. She per-suaded President Obama to give the agency "resolution author-ity"—the ability to do whatever it saw fit to resolve the bank's problems, including taking it over or closing it—over "too big to fail" institutions as well as the smaller banks the FDIC was used to dealing with. The Treasury and the Federal Reserve tried to water down the proposal by requiring their sign-off. Bair testi-fied before the House Financial Services Committee that such a move would essentially destroy the FDIC's ability to act on a fail-ing bank. The chairman, Massachusetts Democrat Barney Frank, agreed and left the authority in the FDIC's hands alone. So should there be another bank meltdown, the head of the FDIC won't have to go three rounds with the Treasury on how to bail out a giant. "The markets," Bair said, "must be convinced that there is no such a thing as 'too big to fail,' otherwise they will never stop taking crazy risks."

Bair was one of a class of new regulators put in place to see that the bailout of Wall Street was done responsibly. Notably, the new top cops were women. Though Bair had first been appointed by George W. Bush, she proved so effective that Obama pointedly asked her to stay even after she offered her resignation. Bair was soon joined by other female regulators. Senate majority leader Harry Reid named Harvard Law School professor Elizabeth Warren to head the committee overseeing how Treasury spent the bank bailout funds. Reid also encouraged Arkansas Democrat Blanche Lincoln, a member of the House Banking Committee, to spearhead the reform of derivatives—financial products that derived their value from that of a bundle of underlying assets. A succession of women have led the Securities and Exchange Commission, which regulates the financial sector: Mary Schapiro, Elisse Walter and Mary Jo White. Three of the five SEC commissioners are women. Obama named Christina Romer his first chair of the Council of Economic Advisers and later appointed Janet Yellen to be the first female chair of the Federal Reserve in early 2014. Four of the five federal trade commissioners were women. Christine Varney and Sharis Pozen have headed up the Justice Department's antitrust division. And Obama's second attorney general, Loretta Lynch, took on Wall Street as the U.S. Attorney for the Eastern District of New York and vowed as AG to make the prosecution of white-collar crime her top priority.

The heart of the problem was risk, something mostly male Wall Street seemed to take irresponsibly and something the female regulators were sent in to mitigate. It's a clichéd image: the straying reckless man and a woman at home holding things together. But there is some underlying truth in it. Neuroscience has shown links between risk taking and testosterone, which is 15 times as prevalent in men as in women. Many world leaders, from Bair to International Monetary Fund chief Christine Lagarde to British Labour deputy leader Harriet Harman, who was then Prime Minister Gordon Brown's No. 2, to Japanese prime minister Shinzo Abe, became convinced that if more women had been working in senior Wall Street positions, the global financial crisis probably wouldn't have happened. And many saw the crisis as a wake-up call for Wall Street to diversify its ranks.

"I do believe women have different ways of taking risks, of addressing issues . . . of ruminating a bit more before they jump to conclusions," Lagarde said. "And I think that as a result, particularly on the trading floor, in the financial markets in general, the approach would be different. I'm not suggesting that all key functions and roles should be held by women. But I think that there would have to be a much bigger diversity and a better sharing of those functions and roles." It was a call for critical mass in the global markets.

There's a good deal of evidence that women are inherently risk-averse. Almost all—97 percent—of microlending is done to women in the developing world. Microcredit started in Bangladesh in 1983 and has spread across the developing world since. Development banks give out small loans to individuals or groups to start small businesses. Some men in those cultures were too prone to drinking or gambling away the funds, but women have proved themselves trustworthy enough to use the money for business and family. Most of the world's biggest microfinanciers will lend only to women.

A 2001 study of 35,000 U.S. households' portfolio behaviors found that women's transaction costs were lower—meaning they shifted investments less and so paid fewer fees—leading to higher net returns on investment. A 2009 study by researchers at the University of Hannover in Germany surveyed 649 fund managers in the U.S., Germany, Italy and Thailand and found that female fund managers were "more risk averse and shy away from competition in the tournament scenario"—meaning women didn't like the idea of kill-or-be-killed, zero-sum games. And a 2012 study of 7,000 fund managers worldwide, 36 percent of whom were female, found that women were more cooperative and aimed at "fair play." The study found that women rated higher than men in 12 of 16 leadership competencies, including "displays high integrity and honesty," "develops others" and "builds relationships."

Iceland is an oft-cited lesson in risk and the power of women to mitigate it. Iceland's economy collapsed in the 2008 worldwide financial meltdown. Much like the United States, Iceland invested heavily in bad debt and overleveraged healthy assets, but Iceland's is a small economy. The tiny island nation of just 300,000 with a gross domestic product of less than $20 billion experienced the most drastic bubble of the downturn, with a huge boom followed by a devastating bust. Two women who were appalled by the unhealthy risks their male co-workers were undertaking founded Audur Capital, a financial-services company with the goal of incorporating "feminine" values in the financial sector. They avoided investing in what they knew to be distressed debt and were literally the only Icelandic company to emerge from the crisis unscathed. The crisis led to a wave of women being elected to office, including Premier Jóhanna Sigurdardóttir.

Having more women on the trading floors may even chemically dampen risky behavior. Two University of Cambridge researchers measured the levels of steroids, including testosterone, adrenaline and cortisol, in 17 male traders over an eight-day period at a London bank. The traders with the highest levels of testosterone in tests of their morning saliva were more likely to reap more profitable trades. When a male trader hit a six-day winning streak, making more than double his daily profit, his testosterone levels were up 74 percent. In studies of lab animals, testosterone has been shown to increase risk taking and fearlessness. The risk is that bankers and traders are training their bodies to create financial bubbles, according to researchers John Coates, a former Goldman Sachs and Deutsche Bank trader turned neuroscientist, and Joe Hebert. Biology shows that there is a "winners effect." When two male lions fight for a mate, the winner maintains higher levels of testosterone while the levels in the loser drop, Coates wrote in his book *The Hour Between Dog and Wolf: Risk Taking, Gut Feelings and the Biology of Boom and Bust*. The bankers were compounding the winners effects: with each successful new gamble, their levels rose and they were prone to take bigger risks.

The presence of women—and the absence of other men—tends to reduce the men's testosterone. Men who stay home with their wives and children have markedly less testosterone then men who are single or don't spend much time caring for children, studies show. Coates began his research after observing his fellow traders in the 2001 dot-com bubble. "Normally a sober and prudent lot," Coates told Bloomberg News, "traders were becoming by small steps euphoric and delusional." They were "overconfident in their risk-taking, placing bets of ever-increasing size and ever-worsening risk-reward trade-offs."

Then came the crash, and here too, the researchers found, male hormones compounded the bubble effect. The crash resulted in anxiety, which produces high levels of cortisol in men, leading to "clouded judgment . . . You tend to see danger everywhere rather than opportunity. In that situation you don't do anything. People get paralyzed by that fear. [It] takes over so they are no longer thinking rationally. They are no longer doing the things that they should be doing to make money," Coates said. "I think [testosterone and cortisol are] partly responsible for market instability."

A separate 2012 study found that women's bodies react to high levels of cortisol broadcast by men by secreting more oxytocin. Oxytocin "promotes nurturing and relaxing emotions," the study said, and is "positively correlated with the willingness to cooperate and the expectation that others will cooperate." In other words, it's the antidote to cortisol. More women on the trading floor could bio-chemically end bubbles. They would reduce testosterone and blunt the upswings and mitigate cortisol and the panic freeze that happens in the downswing of bubbles.

In the immediate aftermath of the global financial crisis, a panel of high-powered bankers gathered at the World Economic Forum in

Davos, Switzerland, and debated whether, if Lehman Brothers had been Lehman Sisters, the investment giant would still have failed. In the end, they agreed, Lehman Sisters would've made much less money during boom times but would probably still be around today.

It's impossible to say with certainty that having more women on Wall Street would have averted the crisis. But at least one woman in Washington saw it coming for decades, though few listened to her: Brooksley Born, dubbed the "Cassandra of the derivatives crisis" by the *Washington Post*.

Born, the lawyer who'd given the rousing speech before the Georgetown ladies' society in the 1970s that led to the founding of the National Women's Law Center, was appointed the head of the Commodity Futures Trading Commission by Bill Clinton in 1996. Four years earlier, the CFTC had ruled that it did not need to regulate over-the-counter derivatives. Born argued that many investors might not understand the risk in these complicated financial instruments, whose value was derived from underlying assets—in many cases the subprime mortgages that were at the center of the 2008 financial crisis. Fed chair Alan Greenspan and then deputy Treasury secretary Larry Summers argued against regulation because buyers were savvy enough to distinguish which products were bad bets. And the CFTC had already ruled it didn't have the power to regulate derivatives, they reminded her.

Born then released a white paper filled with her dire predictions. She lost the administration's support and chose not to seek a second term in 1999.

The CFTC was a kind of incubator for many female regulators: Bair, Born and future SEC chair Mary Schapiro all got their start there. It was once considered a backwater—unsexy as far as law enforcement was concerned—but a good place to name a token woman. Except the tokens never seemed to keep their mouths shut. Schapiro started her career in the futures industry, so she had seen both sides. But she quickly moved into government, first as an SEC commissioner and then succeeding Bair as the CFTC commissioner just before Born took the job. Obama named her the head of the SEC in January 2009; there she collected more than $11 billion in fines and fees from Wall Street and returned more than $6 billion to harmed investors.

"I think one of the ways companies get in trouble is they're in an echo chamber," Schapiro said. "They hear from the same people they've always heard from and they don't question conventional wisdom. They don't appreciate that the world and expectations have changed. That echo chamber is so dangerous. It is critical that your team include a few naysayers and skeptics and those who don't subscribe to conventional wisdom. It forces you to understand the world around you. So much of the crisis happened because they didn't see what was happening around them."

After Bair's time at the CFTC, she was appointed the head of another relatively obscure financial oversight agency: the Federal Deposit Insurance Corporation. The FDIC was created during the Depression to stop banking panics. The federal government insures a bank's assets up to $250,000 per depositor so that if there's a run on the bank or the bank goes under, ordinary people won't lose their life's savings. Though few realize it, the FDIC has extraordinary powers to close a struggling bank on a Friday, completely reorganize it, and reopen it on a Monday with new management and an overhauled business plan.

Bair was born in Independence, Kans., and her Depression-era parents raised her to be debt-conscious. "My dad was a doctor. We were quite comfortable, but the community that we lived in was economically depressed. So I had exposure to people who were more vulnerable, and I always viewed government as a tool," Bair said. "I've always thought of government as a source of good, and maybe that's why we reacted so strongly to the bailout. If the government is going to help anybody, it should be helping people who need the help, who are struggling economically, not the very powerful."

Bair, a moderate Republican protégée of former Kansas senator Bob Dole, became an attorney and ran for Congress in 1990 in Kansas as a pro-choice Republican. She lost by 760 votes, but Bair said she learned the valuable lesson of not taking criticisms too personally—experience she'd need in the coming storm. She was appointed by Bush to head the FDIC in 2006. Almost from the get-go, people began drawing comparisons between her and Born: Bair saw the crisis coming and spoke often and forcefully of the need to shore up the banking system. Though regulation of shoddy loans was the purview of the Federal Reserve, Bair insisted on buying an expensive database to confirm her suspicions of systemic weakness. She was "amazed," and not in a good way, by what she found. But her warnings fell mostly on deaf ears in the Bush administration.

When Bair took over the FDIC, it had been years since a bank had failed. In 2008, 25 banks failed, including Washington Mutual, with $330 billion in assets, the largest bank bust in U.S. history. In 2009, another 140 collapsed and were taken over by the FDIC; bank failures peaked in 2010, when 157 institutions went under.

Throughout 2008 as the situation degraded, Bair began to openly quarrel with the Office of the Comptroller of the Currency, which oversees national banks, and the Office of Thrift Supervision, which regulates savings-and-loan associations. She pushed the OCC to issue voluntary guidance on weak subprime loans. She wisely resisted when the OCC and the Federal Reserve wanted to implement the 2004 recommendations of an international banking group known as the Basel Committee on Banking Supervision. Europe had been quick to adopt the measures, which allowed banks with less risky assets—including the infamous credit default swaps that helped fuel the global meltdown—to leverage more against them. They also allowed banks to essentially police their own risk with little supervision. Bair was deeply leery, and in the end, what was called Basel II was never implemented. Had it been, she said, U.S. banks would have been as exposed as their European counterparts. Between 2008 and 2010, the European Commission approved 4.5 trillion euros in aid for European banks—more than six times the $700 billion Congress approved for U.S. banks.

In September 2008, a month before the crisis spiraled, Bair called the CEO of Washington Mutual to warn him that the FDIC would be downgrading one of the bank's benchmark FDIC ratings. When John Reich, the head of the Office of Thrift Supervision, found out, he e-mailed a male colleague: "I can't believe the continuing audacity of this woman." Two years later, Bair quipped to TIME magazine that if she ever wrote a book, it would be called *The Audacity of This Woman*. But in the end, the title of Bair's 2012 autobiography was *Bull by the Horns: Fighting to Save Main Street from Wall Street and Wall Street from Itself*.

Bair said that at the beginning of the crisis she felt lonely, as she was often the only female regulator in a room full of men, though she speaks highly of Hank Paulson and Ben Bernanke, who she says tried to be collaborative. Even so, at times she felt that the men would have conversations along meeting sidelines, from which she was excluded. "So when I would come into a meeting, I felt frequently I had to kind of get them to start over, as they were having all these sidebar conversations," she said.

She was sometimes patronized, particularly in dealing with the finance industry. "It's a weapon," she said. "They treat you like a little girl. It's a way to get you a little off-center, which makes you feel like a subordinate."

Then the Obama administration came in. Though Bair was a Republican from a previous regime, she suddenly had more sway. Sure, she went several rounds with Tim Geithner and Larry Summers, who became director of Obama's National Economic

Council, but now she had other female colleagues, like Elizabeth Warren and Mary Schapiro.

Warren certainly wasn't shy about going 10 rounds with Geithner. Like Bair, Warren was a child of the dust bowl, born the only girl and the youngest of four to working-class parents in Oklahoma City. She grew up arguing with her brothers; she got so good at it that she became Oklahoma's top debater in high school and won a debate scholarship to George Washington University. She dropped out after two years to marry her high school sweetheart, who became a NASA engineer. The two moved to Houston, where she graduated from the University of Houston; later, she earned a law degree at Rutgers.

Warren went on to teach bankruptcy law at several universities before ending up at Harvard, where she began to get more politically motivated. She lobbied Massachusetts senator Edward M. Kennedy to oppose a bankruptcy bill that would have weakened protections for individuals, though it ultimately passed. She became a kind of academic populist celebrity, appearing on Jon Stewart and Bill Maher's shows about her writings, which were often hypercritical of Republicans and Democrats alike for their support of the wealthy to the detriment of the poor and the middle class.

As chair of the board overseeing the Troubled Asset Relief Program—Congress's $770 billion bailout of Wall Street—Warren regularly brought in new Treasury secretary Geithner to grill him in front of the cameras, much to the delight of populists, liberals and Republicans. She issued monthly reports that grated the administration with blunt criticisms. YouTube is crammed with classic Warren moments shaming Geithner for favoring banks over Main Street during the recovery. The Harvard Law professor was so combative that the administration debated internally about whether to appoint her the new head of the Consumer Financial Protection Bureau, an entity she'd pushed to create as Congress was passing bank re-regulation. Ultimately, the administration decided that Warren couldn't get confirmed by the Senate.

So instead, Warren ran for the Senate. She now has a leadership role focusing on banking and pocketbook issues in which she revels in holding fellow senators' feet to the fire, especially free-market Republican colleagues.

Warren subscribes to the idea that having more women in charge would've alleviated the Wall Street mess. "We've seen the data that women are more risk-averse," Warren said. "If those had been the people in charge of doing investments, of pension funds, would they all have gotten wiped out during the crash of 2008? I don't think so. I just think the calculation would have been different."

But taking on an almost monolithically male industry proved a challenge for Schapiro, Warren and Bair—who were hailed by TIME magazine as "the New Sheriffs of Wall Street." What's it like to oversee so many men? "I think," Bair said, "it can be hard for some men to accept a woman who has power or has power over them particularly."

While at that time women made up 40 percent of all financial institution employees, they comprised only 18.2 percent of executive or senior officials, according to data collected by Catalyst from the U.S. Equal Employment Opportunity Commission. And most worked in research, audit and compliance—again, risk mitigators. Very few succeeded as traders or investment bankers; women were 35.4 percent of all investment banking employees but only 16.1 percent of executive or senior officials. Just 3 percent of financial services CEOs were women, according to Catalyst. And women in financial services earned between 55 and 62 cents for every dollar their male colleagues earned—well below the national average of 77 cents to the dollar for women in general.

Warren said Wall Street's culture, particularly in the first years on the trading floor, tended to drive women out of the industry: hazing, alcohol-infused late nights, gambling and games. "They wash out women so early," she said. "I talked to my former students and they just say, 'Who needs this? I just don't need to play this game.' And I think there is real truth in that."

Schapiro, Warren and Bair all agreed that women are naturally more drawn to government than banking, perhaps because the path is easier for women in government, but perhaps also because women are more concerned with the bigger picture. "We have nurturing instincts. We want to help people who need help or protection; that's just kind of wired into us. So it's not surprising that women might be attracted to government or jobs that provide vehicles to achieve the common good," Bair said.

"Women are often not very good at negotiating on their behalf, but they are damn good at negotiating on behalf of others," Warren added. "They are good at negotiating on behalf of those who don't have a voice, who aren't privileged in the game, whether it's children, whether it's seniors, whether it's those who are economically disadvantaged. That tells me that women are often better at seeing the world from multiple perspectives—that they can see their own self-interest, but they can also see other people's points of views and take those into account."

It is that empathy that makes women attractive CEOs for companies in times of distress, a phenomenon known as the glass cliff. First coined by psychology professors Michelle Ryan and Alexander Haslam a decade ago, the term refers to female and minority CEOs who are recruited to turn around struggling companies. For example, Mary Barra at General Motors, Marissa Mayer at Yahoo—who became the first pregnant *Fortune* 500 CEO when she was hired in 2012—and Virginia "Ginni" Rometty at IBM were all hired to turn around those companies.

But the glass cliff can be dangerous. It forced more female CEOs out of their jobs than their male counterparts—38 percent of women, compared with 27 percent of men, in the past 10 years, according to a PriceWaterhouse Coopers study. The theory is that bringing in a woman is a good public-relations move: she isn't really qualified to run the company but is harder to attack and criticize for missteps. NBC's Matt Lauer grilled GM's Barra on the *Today* show in June 2014 regarding a scandal over faulty parts linked to deaths. "There are some people who are speculating that you got this job as a woman and as a mom because people within General Motors knew this company was in for a very tough time, and as a woman and a mom you could present a softer face and a softer image for the company as it goes through the episode," he said.

"Well, that is absolutely not true," she told Lauer. "You know, I believe I was selected for this job based on my qualifications."

Lauer pressed further. "You're a mom, I mentioned, two kids, you said in an interview not long ago that your kids said they're going to hold you accountable for one job, and that is being a mom," he said. "Given the pressure at General Motors, can you do both well?"

"You know, I think I can," Barra responded. "I have a great team, we're on the right path, we're doing the right things, we're taking accountability, and also I have a wonderful family and a supportive husband, and I'm pretty proud of my kids, the way they're supporting me in this."

Lauer's questions sparked a furor. "Would he ever contemplate asking Alan Mulally at Ford, or Sergio Marchionne at Fiat Chrysler, if they could be a good CEO and a good parent at the same time?" business columnist Tom Walsh wrote in the *Detroit Free Press*. Bryce Covert of the website ThinkProgress turned the tables on Lauer. "Lauer himself is a father of three children," she wrote, "but that hasn't stopped him from doing his job, which has included, among other things, traveling to 50 locations for the 'Where in the World Is Matt Lauer' segment or standing in for Bob Costas to host the Sochi Olympics in Russia."

A second glass-cliff study, by Utah State University, found that boards view women as being upbeat and warm enough to motivate employees during tough times. "[A woman's] messaging might be 'We will overcome this,' versus 'Do this because I'm boss,' " said Annette Zimmerman, who became CEO of PrimeWay Federal Credit Union when it merged with a failed credit union. The same study found that in the vast majority of cases, female stewards of struggling companies are ultimately replaced by white men.

Taking the reins of a troubled company is a risk, the studies found, because the tenure is generally short and the chance to shine small. And failure perpetuates the stereotype that women can't lead. "If you do well, it's because of your gender. If you don't do well, it's because of your gender," Elizabeth Dickinson, an assistant professor at the Kenan-Flagler Business School at the University of North Carolina at Chapel Hill, told the *Guardian* newspaper. "The question is: Are those women being judged for the jobs that they do, their skills or their experience? Or are they judged first for being women?"

Sociology has called this the problem of the hyphenate. As a female politician or a female trader, a woman's professional career and history are mapped by external biases and definitions. She is never just a cop but a female cop; never a litigator but a female litigator; never just an employee but a female employee. Often this leads women to shy away from the spotlight, worried that any misstep will have negative implications for their entire gender.

The few highly successful women on Wall Street have worked hard not to be judged as hyphenates. They strive to be traders, not female traders. And in doing so, they often take conspicuous risks in order to prove themselves. The women who choose to go into banking are self-selecting to enter a man's world. One Australian study goes so far as to argue that the thesis of Lehman Sisters wouldn't hold true because the market would just be adding more gung-ho women, not women who would mitigate risk.

Of course, not every woman is risk-averse, but even those most intimately involved in the crisis were clear-eyed about the risks they saw. The credit default swap, involving a financial product so complicated that it effectively hid much of the bad subprime debt, was created by a woman, Blythe Masters, a former executive at J.P. Morgan dubbed "Destroyer of Worlds" by the *Guardian*. Yet even she had warned that her creation was a double-edged sword capable of great harm if wielded indiscriminately.

"Unfortunately, tools that transfer risk can also increase systemic risk," Masters said in a speech to the Securities Industry and Financial Markets Association in October 2008. "It is important to distinguish between tools and their users."

But rather than adding more women to mitigate risk, Wall Street's response to the crisis was to go in the opposite direction and fire many of the top women. Ultimately Citibank's Pandit kept his job, while the FDIC's Sheila Bair won some changes on Citibank's board and executive team and forced them to increase capital reserves. One person who got fired from Citibank after the third bailout? Terri Dial, one of the few women and experienced commercial bankers on the management team.

"It has bothered me that as a result of the crisis, too many management 'improvements' at Citi and elsewhere have really been attempts by weak management teams to circle the wagons, promoting their closest supporters and axing those who are more independent," Bair wrote in her book. "And because women executives are frequently outside top management's inner circle, far too many have lost their jobs."

In the wake of the downturn, some of the highest-profile exits on Wall Street were women: Erin Callan, Lehman Brothers' CFO, was ousted, and four powerful women at J.P. Morgan either left their jobs or were fired. Ina Drew, J.P. Morgan's chief investment officer, was fired over a $6 billion trading loss in her division. Heidi Miller, the former head of J.P. Morgan's international business line;

Masters, head of global commodities—and creator of the credit default swap—and Sallie Krawcheck, who ran the company's wealth management division, left voluntarily.

The crisis led many to call for more diversity on Wall Street. "The time is long past when women were relegated to discussing world events at tea time," then French finance minister Christine Lagarde wrote in a 2010 *International Herald Tribune* op-ed titled "What If It Had Been Lehman Sisters?" "In the economic and political arena they are assuming ever greater power. The current economic crisis affords us an opportunity to impose more responsible, moderate and equitable approaches to finance." A year later Lagarde became the first woman to head the International Monetary Fund. She has spent much of her career advocating that if developing—and even some developed—countries would just give women equal access to their economies, they could increase their GDPs by more than 30 percent in some countries. An IMF study found that bringing women fully into the workforce would raise GDP in the U.S. by 5 percent, in Japan by 9 percent, in the United Arab Emirates by 12 percent and in Egypt by 34 percent.

— 8 —

LAW

ENFORCEMENT

When Janet Napolitano was governor of Arizona, she appointed its first female director of corrections, Dora Schriro. One Sunday morning in 2004, Napolitano got the worst kind of call you can get from the Corrections Department: two prisoners serving life sentences had seized control of a tower in the middle of the maximum-security prison in Lewis, just outside Phoenix. They had taken two corrections officers hostage, one male and one female. The tower was built to be impregnable: a refuge for guards in case of a prison riot. It was also where the armory was kept. "Whenever one of the lifers went up to the roof to smoke a cigarette," Napolitano said, "the other had a gun to the head of one of the hostages."

"Dora and I set up a command center, and she and I began to process a 24-hour-a-day, seven-days-a-week negotiation. The Department of Public Safety and the FBI had SWAT teams lining the prison walls. We had the rest of the prison on lockdown, and this went on. After the first week they sent out the male correction officer, who had been injured when he'd been taken prisoner. And during that second week, particularly on avenues like talk radio, there were a lot of calls on Dora and me just to storm the tower."

While Napolitano, a former Justice Department prosecutor and Arizona attorney general, had law enforcement experience, Schriro did not. Conservative talk-show hosts savaged her, questioning her social work background and, of course, her clothing. "With a penchant for fashionable high heels and frequent hairdo changes, Dora Schriro comes off as more Betty Crocker than Brubaker in photographs adorning the department's newsletter," wrote Bruce Rushton in the *Phoenix New Times*, referring to the Robert Redford movie about a renowned prison warden. Some talk-show hosts even insinuated that the unmarried Napolitano might be listening to and huddling with Schriro because she had a crush on her.

Amid the storm, both women decided it would be better to withhold information from the media and endure the frenzy. They were concerned with what the hostage takers might do if they saw certain details leak out—like the fact that the female correction officer had been raped.

"Our view was that as long as there were talks going on, we were going to try and talk them out," Napolitano said. "Our thoughts were, if we stormed the tower, (a) Lois, the correction officer, would be killed, (b) the lifers would be killed, but (c) also they had enough arms in there they could kill or severely injure those who were storming the tower. So that drumbeat really went on, and Dora and I really kind of took a quiet pact that we were going to stand together on this and hold fast."

They negotiated a deal that released the hostages on Super Bowl Sunday in exchange for a steak dinner and a six-pack of beer. "You know, they wanted to watch the game. I mean seriously," Napolitano said. "That really happened."

After the game was over, the prisoners and their remaining hostage came out of the control tower. Immediately authorities placed the female correction officer in a helicopter and flew her to the hospital. Napolitano and Schriro met her as she exited the chopper on the roof.

"She just grabbed our hands and said, 'Thank you for not storming that tower; they would've killed me,' " Napolitano said. "And they would've, first thing. So I think that was a very good illustration of how you manage a problem and how you hold fast to your conviction in the face of some increasing pressure."

Napolitano's story shows one of the major strengths of women in law enforcement: they tend to use violence as a last resort. Their presence helps lower the temperature of a conflict, and they employ a wider variety of solutions to resolve the conflict with the least harm to all parties involved. They patiently watch the situation evolve and try to talk it through before using force. This is true for both a tense standoff and mundane one-on-one encounters. Of the 117 officers killed in the line of duty in 2014 in the U.S., only four were women—or 3.4 percent, much lower than the 14 percent of women in the overall police force.

The first time Elizabeth Bondurant, the chief of police in Plainsboro, N.J., thought she was in physical danger on the job was as a rookie cop working the night shift alone. After she pulled over a guy for speeding and told him his car would be impounded because of previous violations, she told the *New York Times*, the man was furious. "He was out of his car, and he was really mad. His fists were clenched and his nostrils were flaring, and I thought, 'He's going to hit me!' " said the 5'7" Bondurant. "So I told him, 'What are you going to do now, hit me?' It immediately defused the situation, and the guy calmed down."

Bondurant's response brought him back down to reality. She helped him visualize something that he didn't want to do. She didn't have to wrestle him to the ground and handcuff him to control him. He calmed down on his own.

Both Bondurant and Napolitano demonstrated one of the benefits of having more women on police forces. According to the National

Center for Women and Policing, women rely less on physical force and more on their communication skills to defuse potentially violent situations.

As a result, female officers tend to save their municipalities a substantial amount of money. Lawsuits alleging the use of excessive force by police cost taxpayers millions of dollars every year. Female officers are the defendants far less often than men, and male officers cost between 2.5 and 5.5 times as much to taxpayers because of payouts to settle such suits, according to a study by the Feminist Majority Foundation and the National Center for Women and Policing. For example, the City of Los Angeles paid $63.4 million between 1990 and 1999 in lawsuits for excessive force and other complaints of violence made against male officers. In contrast, it paid $2.8 million for allegations against female officers, but not one of those complaints was for excessive force. Male officer payouts in cases of brutality and misconduct were 23 times the amount paid in cases involving women; in cases involving killings, settlements for male-involved lawsuits were 43 times the amount of those involving women; and male-involved settlements were 32 times the amount paid to settle female-involved assault and battery cases. While this does reflect the fact that there are simply more male cops than female cops, notably, there was no difference in the amount of routine force reported by gender, only in the use of excessive force. Incidents in which suspects are maimed or killed in custody are subject to an excessive-force investigation. Generally, there are substantially fewer public complaints against female police, according to another study, such as for rudeness or other bad behavior.

Size does matter in this regard. The women are more aware that they have to be flexible and inventive in their interactions with the public because their smaller stature places them at a disadvantage. One Arizona female police officer, who requested anonymity so she could speak freely, said she is acutely aware of her size in every encounter: 5'4" and 140 pounds, compared with her husband, also an officer, who is 6'1" and 220 pounds. "Because of this, I have to compensate with how I present myself. I must use my words wisely and exercise 'verbal judo' prior to physical force. This is for my safety and for the safety of my peers," she said. "I also believe women tend to be more self-aware than men. We may trust our gut instinct of healthy fear when presented with a situation in which we have to make a split decision to engage or not engage, more so than male officers."

As with female judges, female cops also tend to consider mitigating factors in crime more than their male counterparts, according to one female NYPD officer, who also spoke on the condition of anonymity. "We tend to be more creative in coming up with solutions to problems—while you may have technically committed a crime, is this more a mental-health issue than a criminal issue?" she said. "Men in policing tend to be more linear in their thinking—you committed a crime, therefore you need to be arrested."

Women's natural communication skills are also an advantage, said the Arizona officer. "We tend to use our words more and, in turn, listen more. When most people call 911, aside from true emergencies, they want to just be heard. Oftentimes there is little we can actually do to remedy their situation. Listening before speaking has helped immensely," she said. "I also feel female officers use their words to de-escalate situations better than males. Perhaps it is patience on top of the listening that helps in 'bringing people down from the ledge,' so to speak."

Women have a long history of social work and community outreach, and female police officers tend to excel at community building—a critical quality in this era of Trayvon Martin, Michael Brown, Eric Garner and the bloody riots in Baltimore following the death in police custody of Freddie Gray in 2015. One of the viral video moments to come out of Baltimore showed a mother who'd gone out into the chaos, found her son and then cuffed him on the side of the head and marched him home, berating him for his recklessness all the way. "Women rarely have the desire to punch someone," noted Sen. Claire McCaskill, a former prosecutor. "Whereas I believe men often have the urge."

Houston mayor Annise Parker, who was elected in 2010, said that early in her tenure, a Houston city audit on police use of Tasers found that female officers were much less likely to use the devices. "What women never think is, 'Can I wrestle this guy to the ground?' She's more likely to control the situation with voice and presence than any kind of physical tool," Parker said.

Baltimore mayor Stephanie Rawlings-Blake came under fire for not being more aggressive with police response to the protests and refusing to call in the National Guard early on. Rawlings-Blake had been considered a rising star in the Democratic Party. She was the youngest person ever elected to the city council, and she became mayor after the previous mayor stepped down under accusations of ethics violations. Rawlings-Blake was lauded for her transparency in cleaning up the city's politics and, until the protests, was considered a front-runner for the nomination to fill Sen. Barbara Mikulski's seat. In her handling of the riots, Rawlings-Blake was particularly criticized for saying she "gave those who wished to destroy space to do that," potentially costing the city $20 million in property damages and untold tourism dollars. She later said she'd misspoke and meant to say she wanted to give protesters the space to air their grievances.

"Nobody died during the riots," Rawlings-Blake told the *Baltimore Sun*. "Out of the two weeks of demonstrations, we only had a few hours of unrest, and then we were able to restore peace and calm . . . If you take a look at the overwhelming amount of officers who responded, they did a masterful job of responding and keeping peace and calm. They showed an amazing amount of restraint. Had they been different, the outcome . . . could have been substantially different." Still, her decision to call for a federal investigation of the officers involved in Gray's death cost her: Rawlings-Blake announced in September 2015 that she would not seek re-election, ending her once-promising political career.

Ever since women started serving on the police force, they have focused on community outreach. The first female police officers, Lola Baldwin in Portland, Ore., in 1908 and Alice Stebbins in Los Angeles in 1910, were former social workers, and most early female officers dealt almost exclusively with women and children. Study after study shows that the tools of social work—an overwhelmingly female occupation—are critical in modern policing, and that women's softer skills may counter the escalation of conflicts.

Yet women remain underrepresented in law enforcement because of "widespread discriminatory hiring and selection practices," according to the National Center for Women and Policing, one of three groups formed in the mid-1990s to help advance women in law enforcement. In 1971, women accounted for just 1.4 percent of police departments; they now account for less than 14 percent of police officers nationwide, according to the National Center. The group tends to survey urban forces, which are more likely to hire women.

There is a surprising dearth of recent research on women in police forces. Most studies are from the 1980s or 1990s, when the first waves of women were integrating. There are no current statistics on women in police academies. Despite the evidence that women help make policing better, little is being done beyond efforts by individual forces, which vary by city and state. Some programs are vigorous. Others, nonexistent. Nationally, next to nothing is being done to change hiring policies, develop training programs or launch recruitment drives. And the Federal Bureau of Investigation remains one of the most challenging workplaces for women in Washington; only 19 percent of agents are women.

But Hollywood, at least, is making it easier for young women to imagine themselves in law enforcement, even if they don't see many women among their local cops. In the 1970s, TV first began featuring sexy, glamorous female cops in *Get Christie Love* and *Police Woman*, which focused on undercover and plainclothes officers. *Cagney and Lacey* in the mid-1980s featured women in uniform and led to such shows as *Hill Street Blues*, *NYPD Blue*, *Third Watch*, *Law and Order: SVU*, *CSI: Special Victims Unit*, *The Closer*, *Major Crimes* and *Blue Bloods*, all of which routinely show the full range of police incidents and often feature women in prominent roles as beat cops, detectives and captains.

An Australian study on women and policing found that attaining a critical mass of women on the force may promote a general cultural change in policing organizations. As with other employment sectors, women in workplaces that haven't reached that tipping point face stereotyped assumptions about their interactions and behavior. "I do see a lot of women in policing who feel they must act more like the men," the NYPD female cop said. "I think it may be a feeling that they need to be just as 'macho' or they will be mistrusted in dangerous situations. Some men still have this mentality, but it is less prevalent now than in the past."

Until there are enough women to make a difference, female officers must also rely on champions to be heard. One of Houston mayor Parker's first acts in office was to order up a uniform option—modified cargo pants, with pockets—that accounted for women's needs. "I came in and talked to women officers," Parker said. "They said, 'You have this big belt, baton, Taser, handcuffs, gun. But no pockets.' So they couldn't stash a feminine product or Kleenex. One of the first things I did was, I sat down with the chief and said, 'You need to fix this.' And it's only because I was aware as a woman about the problem."

There is also hope that an increase in female officers will lead to better response to female victims. Domestic violence is relatively new territory for the police but makes up a considerable portion of police work. The Violence Against Women Act outlawed spousal abuse in 1994. (Its passage was controversial, with many men arguing that the government had little right to legislate what happens at home. Even the American Civil Liberties Union opposed it. Many argued it was impossible to rape a spouse.) In the wake of the act's passage, domestic violence cases fell by more than half between 1993 and 2002, from an estimated 5.4 victims to 2.1 victims per 1,000 U.S. residents over the age of 12, according to the Bureau of Justice Statistics. The act has been reauthorized and updated several times, and in 2013 almost all the women in the House and Senate came together to force an expansion to include Indian reservations, where domestic abuse is a major issue.

Still, domestic abuse remains one of the worst problems facing police today. Some 2 million women a year are victims of domestic abuse, and 1,500 die. Around 40 percent of emergency phone calls are related to domestic abuse, which accounts for the single largest category of calls to police agencies nationwide, according to the National Center for Women and Policing. A 1985 study found that policewomen placed greater importance on domestic violence calls and responding to family fights than male officers did. Studies have shown that female police officers handled these cases with more tact and believed more strongly in the need to show sympathy and understanding for the victims.

Yet despite a lack of critical mass in the ranks, women are becoming increasingly visible as police chiefs, notably Cathy Lanier in Washington, D.C.; Val Demings in Orlando, Fla.; and Sheilah Coley in Newark, N.J. About 3 percent of all chiefs nationwide are women, according to Dorothy Moses Schulz, professor of police studies at John Jay College of Criminal Justice. "It is nice to know that women police chiefs are now flying above—rather than below—the radar screen," Schulz said. As with Nancy Pelosi, CEOs and other critical actors, women at the top both are role models for younger women and, statistics show, tend to bring in more women under them, raising the likelihood of critical mass. For example, D.C.'s female police force has grown to nearly 20 percent under Lanier, its first female police chief. In the wake of the Ferguson protests, Lanier gave a speech at Georgetown criticizing the militarization of police. "I wouldn't bring an armored personnel carrier out . . . for a protest," she said, while also calling for more diversity on police forces. "Different cultures and different races view things very differently."

Once the ceiling is broken, acceptance is easier for subsequent generations. "I'm really lucky because I'm not the first crew who broke the glass; I'm following others," said Nan Whaley, the mayor of Dayton, Ohio. Whaley said she never was questioned if she was tough enough to lead a police force as a mayor. "What that means is, I don't have to be the woman mayor. So I'm super-grateful to the women who came before me because they were the woman mayor, woman executive."

— 9 —

THE

MILITARY

Darlene Iskra never wanted to be a poster child for women's progress. She felt uncomfortable with all the attention that came her way when she became the first woman to command a U.S. Navy ship—the U.S.S. *Opportune*—a salvage vessel anchored off the coast of Italy. Iskra was a good choice for a command. In the 10 years since she'd graduated from the U.S. Naval Academy in 1980, she'd been decorated for her work on salvage ships; she'd served on four, as a diver, an operations officer and then an executive officer. For years, the only thing that stood in the way of her further advancement was the fact that she was a woman.

Even though in 1978 the Supreme Court ruled that the armed services should integrate women into the military at all levels, it was difficult for the first women who served there. Deborah Loewer, one of the first women selected for the Navy's Surface Warfare Officer School in Newport, R.I., said that when she and three other women reported aboard the U.S.S. *Yosemite* in 1979, the executive officer took the women to see the captain. She still remembers the captain's exact words: "I did not ask for women on my ship. . . . find them something to do." Eleven years later, no woman had been given a chance to command.

When after years of resistance, a woman was ordered to take command, it happened suddenly and without ceremony. In December 1990, during the military buildup that preceded the Gulf War, Iskra got the call when the *Opportune*'s commander took ill and the Navy needed to replace him right away. Iskra flew to Naples, Italy, excited to do her best in this new job. When she arrived, she was surprised to see her desk there covered with congratulatory cards from all over the world. The public relations office was fielding dozens of requests to interview her about making history.

Making history, it turned out, would ruin her career.

Darlene Iskra was a little tired of firsts. She'd been in the first class of female graduates from the Naval Academy. She and another female officer were the first women to enroll in the Navy School of Diving and Salvage, the place where the Navy trains divers to repair ships. As the first female commander of a ship, Iskra was again opening a forbidden door. She knew from experience how rough that could be, but this time it was downright brutal.

At the Navy's insistence, she granted as many interviews as she could manage as she prepared to ship out to the eastern Mediterranean Sea. Salvage ships like the *Opportune* patrol the waters waiting to be summoned for rescue or repair missions and to salvage downed aircraft. Lt. Cdr. Iskra's ship would be alone in those waters, which, it only later occurred to the Navy, could make her a high-profile female target sailing through a war zone in the Muslim world. In this heightened state of concern for both her crew and her family, the *Opportune* lifted anchor, Iskra the lone woman—at least for the first nine months of her command—with 100 men to lead.

It was tough enough for Iskra living as the lone woman aboard a ship. She began to doubt herself, torn because she didn't want to be perceived as weak, so she couldn't give her crew the same breaks that a male leader might have. "I felt like I kind of had to be to the letter of the law in the Navy. I didn't have the ability to ignore or look the other way when someone didn't follow the rules," she said. "I felt, especially being the first woman commanding officer, I'd be looked at as soft and not effective." No crewmember, regardless of the infraction, got off with a warning or slap on the wrist: everything went on record.

Compounding matters, her boss was upset by the attention she was getting. In her first evaluation as a commander, Iskra was ranked last in a squadron of five. She was furious—none of the other ships had deployed to a war zone. When she confronted her boss, he told her: You're a woman. It won't hurt you. You'll have other opportunities.

"I knew I was being targeted by my boss, who thought I couldn't do anything right," Iskra recalled. "The stress became so unbearable to me, I'd lash out a little more. I was more hardnosed than normal. When I realized my boss was undermining my authority and command, I went to his boss, which didn't endear me any more towards him, but I felt I had to for the sake of my crew."

When Iskra went to the admiral, he told her, "They call you behind your back 'Attila the Hunette.' "

Iskra never rose any higher, and her reputation haunted her career. She retired from the Navy in 2000 and took a position doing legislative work for Washington senator Maria Cantwell.

In the mid-1990s the Navy began developing a plan to better assimilate women, determining that women should comprise at least 20 percent of a ship's crew. Effectively integrating a ship started with appointing female junior officers, especially Naval Academy graduates, so sailors would become accustomed to having a woman in charge and treating them with respect before they'd have to accept women as peers. The female officers were never alone—usually three or more were assigned together. And Iskra can attest to the importance of numbers. Her experience changed when she was no longer the only female officer. About nine months into her command, the Navy assigned two female junior officers to the *Opportune*, bringing the number of women officers to three of seven. "The dynamics changed. It was much more friendly, open, brother-sister camaraderie kind of thing," Iskra said. "It was the difference between feeling alone and apart to feeling like you are one of the team."

The Navy plans to get all its surface ships to 25 percent women—preferring the terminology "unofficial goal" to "quota," which carries a lot of political baggage. Currently, the Navy is 17 percent female, but the freshman class entering the academy in 2014 was 27 percent women, and it is aggressively recruiting more women for the enlisted ranks: in 2014, 25 percent of new recruits were women, said Chris Servello, special assistant for public affairs for the chief of naval personnel. The Navy is also consulting companies in California and Washington that have successfully recruited and retained diverse workforces, using those lessons to judge how diversity helps improve decision-making. In 1994, women were first allowed to serve on combat vessels, and in 2011 the Navy allowed women onto submarines. Currently there are 6,900 women serving on Navy ships.

With the exception of the Air Force, which is 19 percent female, other branches of the military look upon the Navy with admiration; they have even more catching up to do. The Army is 14 percent female, and women constitute just 7 percent of the Marines, which also has the highest rate of sexual assaults of any military branch. In July 2015, the Marines fired Lt. Col. Kate Germano, commander of the all-women boot camp at Parris Island, in part, according to the *New York Times*, because Germano pushed too aggressively for parity with men's programs in training and funding for her women's program.

Only in the past seven years have women attained the rank of four-star general. In 2008, Army General Ann Dunwoody became the first in history before retiring in 2012; Air Force General Janet

Wolfenbarger was awarded her fourth star in 2010. And Michelle Howard, who ran the carrier group that rescued Capt. Richard Phillips from Somali pirates, was made a four-star admiral on July 1, 2014.

"When I called to order four-star shoulder boards for women, they didn't exist," Howard said at her promotion ceremony in June 2014. "[A] special contract was let, and you folks are seeing the first set in the history of the United States Navy."

Wolfenbarger's career showed the benefits of progress for women and the tough obstacles they face in their everyday lives in the military. Her father was an Air Force pilot whom she wanted to follow into the military; she became a member of the first class of women accepted into the Air Force Academy. Her father worried she might not be tough enough for the rigors of academy life, which hazed the new cadets, and he warned her that the academy would strip away all her rights only to give them back one by one. But for her, it was even more intense.

"I have to tell you, I was a righteous high school senior and I said to my father, 'I am an American citizen and no one can take my rights from me.' So just a few weeks later I enter at the Air Force Academy. I arrived by bus to the academy campus and they drop us off at the base, and at the top of the ramp there was a giant sign that said BRING ME MEN," Wolfenbarger recalled—a relic of a recruitment drive from another era. "So it was very ironic to arrive that very first day and realize that this was a whole new era for this institution, and I have to say that my dad was absolutely right in that description."

Later that first day, Wolfenbarger was walking down the hall when an upperclassman slammed her into a wall and demanded to know what she was doing there. A couple of months later another young male cadet stopped to say that he was going to prove Congress wrong: women weren't equal and didn't belong at the academy. It would take two decades after Wolfenbarger's graduation for the academy to eliminate demeaning language from its marching songs. Though there's no official songbook, a 130-page book labeled "For unofficial use only" was used as evidence in a 2012 sexual assault trial brought by Air Force women. It included songs promoting rape and disparaging homosexuality, with titles like "Pubic Hair," "The Kotex Song," "Will You Suck Me Tomorrow," "The Hair on Her Diki-Di-Doo" and "Bestiality."

"I spent the next year in a state of shock," Wolfenbarger said with pause. "I was not certain after I came out of that experience of serving for four years at the academy whether or not it was something that I would want to spend the whole career at."

Since that time, Wolfenbarger said, the Air Force has worked to open up more opportunities for women. With the integration of the military, now 99 percent of all career fields in all branches of the government permit women to serve, as ordered by former Defense secretary Leon Panetta. The former California Democratic congressman came in as the head of the Central Intelligence Agency in February 2009, and he was impressed by the willingness of female CIA officers to go out to the front lines. Many of the CIA's most senior counterterrorism officials were women: 47 percent of the agency's workforce is female, as well as more than 33 percent of upper management. Northern Virginia is home to numerous soccer moms who by day hunt Al Qaeda or ISIS. Ten months after Panetta's appointment, two of those women, Jennifer Matthews and Liz Hanson, died in an Al Qaeda bombing in the Khost province in Afghanistan. The attack, one of the deadliest in CIA history, killed seven officers. Panetta attended all the funerals, standing graveside at Arlington National Cemetery comforting Matthews's three young children.

In July 2011, Panetta was confirmed as Defense secretary and again saw women as military police guarding convoys and engaging with the enemy as helicopter pilots flew him across war zones. He visited a young woman at a military hospital in San Antonio, Texas, to award her the Purple Heart for her actions in Afghanistan. Flying back from the U.S.S. *Peleliu* to Camp Pendleton in California, he chatted the whole way with a female Osprey pilot. Upon his return to the Pentagon, Panetta started asking his generals why women were barred from forward deployments and combat missions. At first the answer seemed that it was because they couldn't meet the physical standards: for example, the number of pull-ups required. But when he asked about the women who could meet those standards, the generals ran out of answers. "He found it was a gender-based prohibition, not merit- or physical-based prohibition," said Jeremy Bash, who served as Panetta's chief of staff at both the CIA and the Pentagon. "Just, men can and women can't. He thought that was wrong and worked very closely with [chairman of the Joint Chiefs of Staff] Gen. [Martin] Dempsey to make a change."

A month before Panetta left office in 2013, he and Dempsey went to the press briefing room to announce a list of combat positions for which women could begin to compete and serve. Afterward, Bash joined Panetta and Dempsey to reflect on the moment. "That worked out very well. It was a very powerful message. One day, sir, there's going to be a female secretary of Defense, and one day there'll be a female chair of the Joint Chiefs. And then," Bash deadpanned, "we'll have the first unmanned press conference in the briefing room."

By that time, Tulsi Gabbard, who had served on the front lines as a military police officer in Iraq, had been elected to Congress as a Democrat from Hawaii. She found herself educating her male peers about women's roles in the military. Gabbard recalled being "lectured" by an older, long-serving Republican representative that he'd never support women "getting shot at . . . and how he believed that it's just not right for women to go and be in the line of fire."

Gabbard shared her own experiences from the front lines and those of her female colleagues. "I informed him that this has actually been going on for quite some time, that women have been fighting in combat, shoulder to shoulder with their male counterparts. He looked a little confused at the end of the conversation," she said.

What many people don't realize is that as women increasingly joined the ranks during the wars in Iraq and Afghanistan—about 300,000 women served in the two wars, and 150 were killed—many found themselves in the thick of the action. In the era of terrorism and counterinsurgencies, every convoy, every base, every movement is the front line. By simply doing their jobs in war zones—one out of every five convoys in Iraq in 2006 was attacked—women have already been fighting on the front lines for 15 years, even if they weren't formally cleared to do so. And, of course, women have been serving in forward positions as intelligence officers for years, whether with the armed forces, including Navy SEALs and special forces, or with the CIA. When Panetta eliminated the last official restrictions on women in combat positions, he opened nearly 240,000 more jobs to women.

Women are an increasingly important part of the military, even in combat, but the bias against their capability persists. Women aren't necessarily more pacifist than men; Hillary Clinton, Susan Rice and Samantha Power were considered more hawkish than Defense secretary Bob Gates, National Security Advisor Tom Donilon and other men in Obama's first term. Human experience shows that women's protective instincts for their own can make them ferocious fighters. And still others point to the fact that the person responsible for much of the CIA's controversial torture program was a woman, Alfreda Bikowsky.

"You've had plenty of male presidents and male secretaries of Defense who had no military experience. I actually think that I've seen women leaders be extremely tough," said Michèle Flournoy, a former top Pentagon official and, many speculate, a front-runner to become the first female Defense secretary. "We used to sit around the Situation Room advising the president on tough decisions on

Iraq and Afghanistan, and there was no one at that table tougher or more able to make decisions than Hillary [Clinton]. She held her own just fine in that room. So that's a very outdated and uninformed stereotype."

Still, when asked if women command differently than men, Flournoy cites the research of feminist Carol Gilligan. "She looked at the differences between men and women. Men are raised to think about how they fit into the hierarchy, and women are raised to think of their place more in a web of relationships," she said. "If that's true as a premise, many women leaders tend to think more in terms of weaving a network and engaging horizontally as well as vertically."

After training as a military police officer, Gabbard volunteered her platoon to provide security escorts for convoys going from Kuwait to Iraq. They were turned down because the commander objected to having four women—Gabbard and three others under her command—in the mix. Many commanders didn't like having female soldiers in convoys; when women needed to urinate, the convoy had to stop to accommodate them—a dangerous endeavor given that there were often roadside explosive devices and mines. Army psychiatrist Elspeth Ritchie even developed a female urinary cup to avoid stops, but it never caught on. Gabbard appealed, but "there was no opening for negotiating that point; it was that commander's prerogative to be able to make that determination," she said.

In Gabbard's experience, women faced a conundrum: "You are not perceived to be as capable as the male officer standing next to you of the same rank under the same experience," she said. "So to some degree, they automatically dismiss you and expect less of you. To earn the respect, you have to outperform; you are therefore held to a higher standard than someone who is an equal in every other way except for gender."

In basic training, one of her female drill sergeants pulled Gabbard and the other women in her class aside. She told them that she never wanted to see them standing "parade pretty" or joking with the men while at ease in a formation. Men could do it, but for the women, it played into the notion that they're "flirty" and shouldn't be taken seriously. "She said, 'You know basically that you are held to a different standard and you better recognize that and you better hold yourself to the highest standard.'" A few years later, Gabbard would deliver the same message to her fellow female officer candidates.

"I could point to a number of men in history who have been huge pacifists and who have been very hesitant to decide when it's necessary to send our troops into battle. . . . there should not be assumptions based on someone's gender," Gabbard said.

When Air Force officer Annie Kleiman volunteered for a tour in Afghanistan in September 2009, she was among the second team of women to officially serve on the front lines. Her job was to search women and children, instead of having male soldiers do it. To be touched, let alone patted down, by men to whom they were not related distressed the women. "They would start screaming and crying and the soldier would turn off his microphone so the whole team wouldn't have to hear it, which sometimes then proved a security risk," Kleiman said. "When we did it, it became a non-issue. It was no big deal. And the program was really successful."

But it wasn't easy. The first class of women had been assigned to the unit without being consulted, and most hadn't enjoyed it. She said there was a lot more scrutiny of the women. "If a woman accidentally or negligently discharged their weapon, it gets all of us into trouble: Of course, she's a woman," Kleiman said, rolling her eyes. "Whereas if a guy did it, it was just on him."

Despite the challenges—and the debate still rages about fully opening up some elite positions to women—women are integrating most corners of the military and law enforcement. In August 2015, the first two women made it through Army Ranger training. Shortly thereafter, the Navy's top admiral said that women would get their first shot to make it through SEALs training in 2016. And as women become more involved in the frontline operations, it's not hard to imagine them becoming four-star generals in charge of battlefield strategy and force readiness. Wolfenbarger—whose husband is a pilot—hopes that their 16-year-old daughter will attend the Air Force Academy and follow in their footsteps. When Wolfenbarger came up, women advanced only in support roles. The action jobs, like fighter pilots, were reserved for men. She was pleasantly surprised to hear her daughter's ambition: to be a fighter pilot who becomes a four-star general. "It just was a reinforcement for me that through her eyes she sees a different Air Force than those of us who grew up in the Air Force or have been a part of the Air Force, and I love it," Wolfenbarger said.

But for the time being, progress for women in the military is instigated outside its ranks by its civilian overseers, corners of government in which women have broad influence. Certainly, that is already the case for the armed services' congressional overseers, where women in the Senate chaired subcommittees, including those on Emerging Threats, Readiness, Personnel and Seapower. Indeed, these women had a profound impact on the armed forces, particularly on the issue of sexual assault, long considered the main deterrent to women's enlisting.

One of the biggest hurdles to recruiting women to the military is the perception, a thoroughly earned one, that they will be sexually harassed, if not raped. Sen. Joni Ernst, an Iowa Republican, said she was sexually harassed repeatedly during her 20-year career in the military and she had never met a woman in the service who hadn't experienced some kind of harassment. "I had comments, passes, things like that," Ernst said. It is part and parcel of the job and a symptom of the lack of critical mass.

For decades the women of the Senate tried to reform the Pentagon's reporting and prosecution of such crimes, which have been egregious and far too commonplace. Starting in the early 1990s, hardly a year went by when some branch of the military wasn't in the news for awful rapes or sexual assaults aboard ships, at academies or on deployments abroad. After the 1991 Tailhook scandal, when 83 women and seven men were sexually assaulted by Navy and Marine Corps officers at the 35th annual Tailhook Association Symposium, one attendee told media, "Everyone needs to seriously lighten up. What do they expect? This is Vegas, baby! They call this symposium 'Tail' hook for a reason!" Although a number of officers were eventually disciplined in the wake of the scandal, little was done to reform the system.

Rep. Susan Molinari, a New York Republican, was receiving *Glamour* magazine's award for Woman of the Year in 1996 when a sex scandal broke at Aberdeen Proving Ground. Twelve officers had raped a servicewoman at the Maryland base. In the midst of the gala, Molinari met fellow female congresswomen Pat Schroeder and Connie Morella, and the three decided then and there to call Army brass in before the Armed Services Committee to hold them accountable for that and other sexual assaults. They did, but again little came of it.

"I worked on this issue in 1997 and I was the only woman on the Armed Services Committee when there was the Aberdeen Proving Ground scandal," recalled Maine Republican senator Olympia Snowe. Though there had been outrage in the media reports, the Pentagon's response was simply to set up a rape hotline.

Snowe said that change came when women reached a critical mass on the Senate Armed Services Committee. In 2013, seven women sat on the committee of 26.

"It's a major improvement to have seven women on the committee at the time when you're grappling with the reprehensible issue of sexual assault. It's a game changer," Snowe said.

The women hauled generals and admirals before the panel and grilled them about their lack of action. In the previous year, there had been an estimated 26,000 cases of unwanted sexual contact in the armed forces; only 3,000 were officially reported and just 302 prosecuted. The military leaders were asked pointed questions: Why had they allowed the problem to get so bad? The spectacle finally broke through and the issue became the focus of national attention.

The scene was a reversal of the 1991 Clarence Thomas hearings, in which an all-male panel berated Anita Hill. "Going from the visual from where Anita Hill was met with such hostility by almost all the men to the armed-services hearing is just a full arc, and it's an example of the difference a significant number of women senators in very powerful positions can make," said Judith Lichtman, president of the National Partnership for Women and Families, which promotes women's issues on Capitol Hill.

All 20 female senators agreed on 11 policy changes, enacted in December 2013, which would force the Pentagon to address the issue more seriously. They include barring the military from recruiting anyone who was convicted of a sexual offense and the immediate relief from active duty of convicted sex offenders already serving in the armed services; insurance coverage of abortions for servicewomen and family members who are victims of rape; a Special Victims Unit to address sex crimes; and mandatory sexual harassment training.

Yet the female senators remained divided on whether the military could properly bring offenders to justice. New York senator Kirsten Gillibrand, a Democrat, became convinced that the problem could not be handled within the chain of command since all too often the commanding officer sympathized with the offenders or, worse, was the perpetrator. Gillibrand introduced a bill giving the investigation and prosecution of such cases to the Judge Advocate General Corps, a quasi-independent division of the Pentagon responsible for trying military crimes. Sen. Claire McCaskill, a Missouri Democrat who had made her name prosecuting sex crimes, believed that the problem was best left within the chain of command. McCaskill's bill had the support of the Pentagon, the White House, the committee chair (Michigan Democrat Carl Levin) and a majority of the Republicans in the Senate. But most of the female senators were not convinced. Some in the media were already painting McCaskill as a stooge of the generals.

At the end of June 2013, the 20 women gathered under murals depicting the ruin of Pompeii in the ceremonial Appropriations Committee hearing room in the Capitol to privately debate the competing proposals. McCaskill's argument fell flat: 16 of the 20 supported Gillibrand's bill. Suddenly McCaskill's long career championing victims of sexual assault was being called into question by people she had expected to back her.

But the women were sensitive to the optics of McCaskill's situation and decided they would highlight the areas of agreement and downplay the dispute, a rare case of politicians bending over backward to protect the reputation of the author of a bill they disagreed with. "This is an honest disagreement, honest debate, and I believe very much that Kirsten believes this is what's best for the country, as I believe my bill is best for the country," McCaskill said in an August 2013 interview. "There's a list of 12 major reforms. Eleven of those, Kirsten and I worked on together, and they are in the bill. They are huge historic reforms. But all of that work and the nature of that work unfortunately has been overshadowed by one point where we disagree. All the women keep talking about how that's too bad."

Ultimately, McCaskill's bill prevailed; many senators felt it was worth giving the military the time to enact pledged revisions and later reassess to see if those measures worked. But her relationship with Gillibrand and the other women is also an example of critical mass at work. It allows women to break free of their gender identification and disagree with other women, even on "women's issues." At critical mass, the Senate women were no longer tokens or conspiring pairs: they were colleagues with diverse opinions, whose input was valued.

A few months later, McCaskill and Gillibrand teamed up on legislation to battle sexual assaults on college campuses. Gillibrand hasn't given up on her armed-forces legislation and vows to bring it up every year until it passes. If the Pentagon can't demonstrate progress, McCaskill said, she's open to one day supporting Gillibrand's measure. Despite the disagreement, it was a mark of progress that landmark legislation was passed. And the female senators hope that if women feel safer, more will enlist and begin to exert broad influence in the armed services.

— 10 —

ELECTORAL
CHALLENGES

Hours after announcing his presidential bid, Donald Trump stepped off his private jet in Des Moines, Iowa, for his first campaign event. As usual, the billionaire didn't hold back, taking aim at Republican rivals Jeb Bush and Marco Rubio. "How do you beat Hillary?" a man yelled from the back of the old theater, referring to the likely Democratic nominee.

"You know, she's playing the woman card really big," Trump said. "I watched her the other day and all she would talk about was, 'Women! Women! I'm a woman! I'm going to be the youngest woman in the White House! I'm not going to have white hair, I'm going to dye my hair blond!' She could be beaten. She's got a lot of bad things happening."

A few weeks later, after other Republicans accused Clinton of playing the "woman card," she responded with a pithy video of a deck of playing cards criticizing the Republican field for their anti-women stances. The cards flip past, highlighting GOP candidates' positions, including:

[Ohio governor] John Kasich and [Wisconsin governor] Scott Walker signed laws banning abortion after 20 weeks, even in the cases of rape and incest.

Walker repealed an equal-pay law in his state.

Marco Rubio voted against paid sick leave and the Paycheck Fairness Act.

So did Rand Paul.

And Ted Cruz.

And as for Jeb Bush?

"What's the Paycheck Fairness Act?"   —Jeb Bush, Oct. 13, 2014

Women on welfare should "get their life together and find a husband."
—Jeb Bush, September 1994

Under Bush's watch, Florida enacted a law "requiring single women who wanted to put a child up for adoption to publish their sexual histories in a newspaper."   —*Salon*, June 10, 2015

Then, the Joker card appears.

Clinton raised the issue again on July 20 in a Facebook Q&A with supporters. "Wow," Clinton wrote. "There is a gender card being played in this campaign. It's played every time Republicans vote against giving women equal pay, deny families access to affordable child care or family leave, refuse to let women make decisions about their health or have access to free contraception."

Of course, Clinton's was a campaign commercial that left out a lot of context, particularly on the Florida law that required women wanting to put a child up for adoption to publish their sexual histories. Bush immediately moved to amend the law as soon as it was passed and two years later succeeded in replacing it; the new law did not carry those controversial reporting provisions. But Clinton's attacks highlighted a problem for Republicans: even if they have good—or defendable—records on women's issues, they are vulnerable to the perception that they don't support women.

Trump blew the gender question wide open in the first debate among 10 GOP candidates in early August 2015. Fox News moderator Megyn Kelly pressed Trump on his record of calling women "slobs" and "fat pigs." At first Trump said he'd only ever called comedian Rosie O'Donnell such things, but Kelly corrected him, saying he'd said it about many women. Trump then turned to bullying, telling Kelly that he'd been nice to her thus far "but that could change." In comments the following week, Trump seemed to hint that Kelly was menstruating at the time of the debate—a comment he later clarified. He then took to Twitter, retweeting a tweet that called her a "bimbo" and mocking her as "running away" to a long-planned vacation. Two weeks later, polls showed Trump still leading the GOP field but losing ground with women. A Fox News poll three days after the debate saw Trump's support among women slip to 21 percent from 24 percent, and a CBS survey found that 62 percent of women disapproved of him, including 42 percent of Republican women.

The problem for the GOP: the bigger Trump got, the more he put off female voters. This could be a dangerous direction for the Republican Party in the general election: independent and swing female voters have determined every election since 1988. The more damage done in the primary season while courting voters, the more Republicans must atone for when they go up against the likely female Democratic nominee, Hillary Clinton. In the second Republican debate, the 11 candidates on stage finally included a woman, former

Hewlett-Packard CEO Carly Fiorina. But despite Fiorina's commanding performance, and her wry quip that women actually make up the majority of the electorate, all 11 candidates notably fell flat when asked to name which woman should appear on the $10 bill. Three came up with relatives, like mothers or wives; Rosa Parks got three votes (Trump voted twice); Clara Barton, Susan B. Anthony, Abigail Adams, Mother Teresa and Margaret Thatcher each got one vote—never mind that Thatcher and Mother Teresa weren't Americans. Fiorina scoffed at the question and didn't answer.

Women's power and prominence have made the strongest advances in the public sector, but the biggest threat to those advancements is the Republican Party's failure to speak to, champion and elect women. Women are a powerful force, making up 53 percent of the population and turning out to vote at rates 10 percent higher than men. The only times Republicans have won the White House since Reagan are when George H.W. Bush and his son George appealed to security moms and soccer moms; they still lost the women's vote but narrowly enough that their big male turnouts won the day. In recent elections the numbers are moving against the GOP. Even with a female running mate, Republican presidential nominee John McCain lost women to Obama by seven percentage points; four years later, Republican challenger Mitt Romney lost them by 12 percentage points.

To make matters worse, unlike Democrats, Republicans aren't electing many women and have stalled in recruiting women, raising money to back female candidacies and promoting policies and messages that draw women to support the party. While Democratic women increased their presence in the House to 33 percent in 2015 from 18.5 percent in 2005, Republican representation in the same period has actually declined, from 25 seats to 22 seats, or less than 9 percent of the GOP conference. The slippage in electing GOP women to federal office is one of the biggest hurdles to women's advancement in politics. The Republican Party offers few public-sector role models to inspire young conservative women to believe that they too can lead. "It's hard to buck your party when you're 9 percent; it's nigh impossible," said Swanee Hunt, founder of the program Political Parity, which works to bring women to 50 percent of elected offices nationwide. "If Republican women were at 30 percent like Democratic women are, you really would make a difference. You'd create a women's bloc. But if nothing is done, statistics say it'll be 100 years before you reach parity. We'll probably be colonizing the moon by then."

Trump's antics put the party in a hard spot. He was unwittingly drawing attention to some of his rivals' somewhat extreme positions on abortion. Most news stories following the debate not only mentioned Trump's exchange with Kelly but also noted the fact that none of his rivals stepped in to defend her and none condemned Trump's remarks until the following days. The stories also quoted Rubio, Walker, Bush and former Arkansas governor Mike Huckabee's opposition to abortion, even in cases of rape and incest and, for some, when the mother's life is at stake. Six months ahead of the first primary, thanks to Trump, Republicans found themselves in a serious debate about whether their policies advance women—or if they're at war with women, as Clinton and Democrats allege.

'Twas not ever thus. Once upon a time, Republicans were The Party for women. At the request of Susan B. Anthony, it was a Republican, Sen. A.A. Sargent from California, who in 1878 introduced the 19th Amendment granting women the right to vote. Almost 20 years later, in 1896, the GOP became the first party to include equal rights for women in its platform. Twenty years after that, Republican suffragette Jeannette Rankin of Montana became the first woman elected to Congress in 1916—exactly a century ago. Republicans elected the first female speaker of a state legislature (Minnie Davenport Craig of North Dakota, from 1933 to

1935), appointed the first woman to a major ambassadorship (Clare Boothe Luce, to Italy in 1953), had the first serious female presidential candidate (Margaret Chase Smith in 1964) and appointed the first female Supreme Court justice (Sandra Day O'Connor in 1981).

Democrats took over the Party of Women mantle in the 1980s. "Give 'em Hell" Harriet Woods ran for Senate on the Democratic ticket in Missouri in 1982. The race was close, and she went to Washington, hat in hand, looking for $50,000 for a final week of advertising. She went to the party committees and to the labor unions. No one listened. She went back to Missouri, ran out of money and lost by 2 percent. But Woods's loss wasn't for nothing: her plight spurred Democratic women to action. "The women in Washington, in the Democratic Party, saw what happened to Harriet Woods and said, We cannot let this happen again. We need to find other funds for these women," said Stephanie Schriock, who heads Emily's List, which was founded in the wake of Woods's loss.

Emily's List became the force for electing Democratic women. The group trained candidates, helped them raise money, gave them briefing books on every kind of policy imaginable. And, perhaps most important, it helped clear primary fields for female candidates. In other words, it endorsed women against other Democrats and gave them a leg up on fund-raising, sometimes against male candidates handpicked by the Democratic establishment. "For a long time women candidates faced a different set of challenges than male candidates, and we helped level the playing field," Schriock said.

Persuading women to run for office is difficult. Many assume they won't be successful unless they are well informed on every issue and able to handle technical questions with authority. This was why the Emily's List briefing books on policies were so important for first-time candidates. Some women also needed to sort out the potential impact of holding office while raising children: for example, where do the kids go to school, Washington or their home state? Fund-raising is a problem too. Universally, women found it harder to fund-raise for themselves than for charities or causes. Emily's List held training sessions and tutorials to help women learn these skills. Thirty years later, it is a powerhouse, raising more than $60 million for pro-choice female Democrats in the 2014 cycle. It expects to easily top that to help elect Hillary Clinton and other Democratic women in 2016.

In contrast, Republican women had no Rolodexes of devoted donors. While Emily's List grew from Democratic women giving money to elect women, female GOP donors give far less than their Democratic sisters and comprise the smallest percentage of political donations. No one has been asking Republican women to run or briefing them on policies. The impact over the decades is clear: there were 62 Democratic women in the House in the 114th session, compared with 22 Republican women. And there were 15 Democratic senators vs. just 5 GOP female senators. In state legislatures, 59.8 percent of the women elected are Democrats, while 39.4 percent are Republicans.

The Republican Party has had trouble making its message appealing to women. In the 2012 presidential campaign, some Republican women began warning the party that it needed to up its game with female voters. Katie Packer Gage, Mitt Romney's deputy campaign manager, fruitlessly warned her bosses that Romney had a women problem. After Romney's infamous "binders full of women" debate moment, his outreach to women started to look clumsy. In his time as Massachusetts governor, Romney was familiar with the Boston Club, a group that promotes the advancement of women. They maintained, and still maintain, rosters of qualified women that they promote to corporations and public officials looking to add some diversity in their ranks. Romney meant that statement to honor the many qualified women he said he wanted to include in his administration, but the comment was roundly satirized as a sign that he personally knew no qualified women.

Gage was sensitive to this weakness in the campaign and rightly saw that the problem was not just Romney's but reflected in the candidates the party fielded in the Senate races. "I kept saying, pay attention to Missouri, to Indiana," she said. In both states, conservative GOP Senate candidates had falsely asserted that banning abortion in cases of rape would not impact women because their bodies had some sort of natural defense to prevent them from getting pregnant under those circumstances. Democrats seized on these remarks as evidence that Republicans were mounting a "War on Women." Democrats went around the country asking every GOP candidate to condemn or agree with the statements.

Romney ended up losing the women's vote by the largest margin in history: only 44 percent of women voted for him, vs. 56 percent for Obama.

In the months following the 2012 loss, Republican Party leaders—the Republican National Committee, committees overseeing campaigns and fund-raising nationwide, and the House and Senate leadership—began a series of meetings to address the problem. First, they launched sessions with consultants like Kellyanne Conway, a GOP strategist who specializes in the women's vote, and conservative CNN commentator S.E. Cupp to train candidates and members to avoid saying things offensive to women. The Susan B. Anthony List, a group that aspires to be the Emily's List of the right, with a focus on electing pro-life women, produced a 30-minute video for candidates on how to speak about abortion with conviction but without putting off pro-choice voters or moderates.

Female voters actually skew slightly pro-life, 46 percent to 44 percent, according to a Gallup poll, but are put off by some of the extreme language coming out of the right. "We saw our candidates on the defense, caught flatfooted, not knowing what to say," said Marjorie Dannenfelser, founder and head of the Susan B. Anthony List. "The Democrats going on the offense basically silenced Republicans, so the only thing you heard were the bad quotes."

The meetings led to the formation of Women on the Right UNITE, launched in June 2013 to identify women's issues, work on messaging and recruit candidates. UNITE also began to hold training and networking sessions across the country every month. By April 2014, to counter a Democratic push on Equal Pay Day, when Democrats coordinate events across the country to call for equal pay for women, UNITE rolled out the GOP's own equal-pay message, which focused on incentivizing increased transparency and reporting of salaries. That month, the GOP also announced a program targeting suburban women under the age of 40 as volunteers and community captains, empowered to recruit other women. A poll commissioned by UNITE showed that women cared more about everyday economic and security issues than they did about abortion and rape, which they used to show GOP candidates how to talk to women: don't dwell on social issues, but appeal to the pocketbook issues women really care about. In August, UNITE held the first-ever Republican women's summit, which brought together their young community captains as well as female GOP leaders to work-shop ahead of the election on get-out-the-vote efforts and brainstorm new ideas on how to bring more women into the fold.

Several other new women's groups have formed on the right, though efforts remain disparate and halting. The Susan B. Anthony List has been around for decades, but its budget is less than a seventh of Emily's List's and it only supports female candidates after they've won a primary. The National Republican Campaign Committee, which helps elect Republicans to the House, in 2013 launched Project GROW (Growing Republican Opportunities for Women) to encourage more women to run for the House. But the bid fell short, recruiting 13 percent fewer female candidates than in 2012 and holding just one pre-primary fund-raiser for a female candidate; she lost, and GROW withered. Other efforts include ShePAC, launched by former GOP vice presidential candidate Sarah Palin; the Unlocking Potential Project, initiated by 2016 GOP presidential hopeful Carly Fiorina; Right Now, a PAC begun by Brittany Thune, daughter of South Dakota senator John Thune; Women Lead, led by Republican National Committee member Christine Toretti; and the Women2Women listening tour, launched by Sarah Chamberlain at the Republican Main Street Partnership. The groups managed to raise money and back some candidates, but sometimes they backed opposing candidates or ones at odds with candidates picked by Washington.

Fiorina, in a fall 2014 interview, told me that she was sick of Democrats winning the so-called War on Women, which is why she launched the Unlocking Potential Project, which did grassroots outreach to independent and Republican women in six states, including—notably—early-voting states Iowa and New Hampshire. "There's no question that there's a gender gap between the Republican and the Democratic parties," Fiorina said. "Frankly, what the Democrats are engaging on is gestures. So, for example, equal pay for equal work is a political gesture, but it doesn't actually fix anything." She noted that a 1963 law mandated equal pay for equal work, with a means for recourse if violated. "The biggest impediment for equal pay for equal work is the seniority system," she said. "The seniority system is an impediment because women are frequently the last hired or the first fired because they need to cut back on their hours or they drop out from the workforce during childbearing years. Democrats support the seniority system—that's what bureaucracies are about or unions are about." She believes a more meaningful approach is to highlight the existing law and to focus on pay for performance rather than equal work. "But I think Republicans do need to speak to those issues," she said.

In Congress, Republican women of both houses, led by Rep. Cathy McMorris Rodgers and GOP senators Kelly Ayotte from New

Hampshire and Deb Fischer from Nebraska, have authored legislation focused on the economy, introducing bills with Republican plans for equal pay, flexible hours, and expansion of telecommuting and child-care tax credits. But few of them passed the Democrat-controlled Senate. The Republican-controlled House faced a different problem. Without the clout of critical mass to bring the legislation up themselves, the women relied on a champion to help them: Senate majority leader Eric Cantor. When Cantor lost his primary in Virginia in a surprise upset in June, the bill lost its main backer in the House, and the legislation stalled.

Despite the difficulties, the efforts paid off in the 2014 midterm elections. For example, when Democratic senator Mark Udall of Colorado tried to defend his seat by accusing his opponent, Republican representative Cory Gardner, of being anti-women, Gardner called for federally funded contraception for all women. Udall lost his seat to Gardner, 49 percent to 46 percent. The *Denver Post*, in endorsing Gardner, criticized Udall for running an "obnoxious one-issue campaign [that] is an insult to those he seeks to convince." Indeed, while Udall had focused only on abortion, Gardner spent more of his time on the economy. Udall eked out a win with women—52 percent of the vote—but it wasn't nearly enough. By comparison, his Democratic colleague Michael Bennet in 2010 was re-elected to the Senate by winning the women's vote by a margin of 16 percentage points.

GOP efforts like Gardner's worked partly because Democrats failed to significantly turn out single women, one of their strongest voting demographics. Single women turn out in droves in presidential election years but don't tend to vote in midterm and other elections. For example, the only time Republicans have won women since Reagan was in the 2010 midterm elections, when the low turnout of single women allowed Republicans to win women overall 49 percent to 48 percent. In the 2014 midterm elections, single women made up 21 percent of the electorate, compared with 23 percent in 2012. But they also skewed less Democratic in 2014, voting for Democrats 60 percent of the time vs. 67 percent in 2012. That helped cost Democrats control of the Senate and 13 seats in the House.

Female voters are by no means universally Democratic. Married women trend more Republican; 53 percent of them voted for Romney in 2012. But single women went for Obama, 67 percent to 31 percent.

Republicans have not yet come up with a strategy to appeal to single women; indeed, the party seems to have written them off as potential supporters. As Clinton noted in her playing-cards video, Jeb Bush once said single women need to "find a husband." This is a common refrain from conservatives, who believe single women rely on the state much as they would a boyfriend or husband. At a Heritage Foundation panel to mark Women's History Month in March 2014, conservative pundit Mona Charen argued that "it is the decline of marriage that is the lodestar" for single women skewing Democratic.

Quipped fellow panelist Mollie Hemingway: "Everybody go out, right now, go get married if you're not married, and we should be able to solve all these problems . . ." Then she echoed: "[W]e do not have a sex gap here in voting. We have a marriage gap."

Despite the unprecedented push, the GOP in 2014 added only three women to the House and one to the Senate. And the party net lost one female governor, while Democrats gained two. "It remains a problem," Republican representative Elise Stefanik, who in 2014 became the youngest woman ever elected to Congress, said at a Google panel in July 2015 that addressed the Republican Party's efforts to include more women. "We're all aware of it, and we're working on it."

The numbers do not look promising for the Republicans as they assess the future. Millennials—who remember the GOP less for advancing women's right to vote than for the War on Women—are shifting sharply to the Democratic Party, as are Latinos. "I have said a thousand times that it's not identity politics to target women voters; we make up more than half the country," said an exasperated Conway. "It's not a 'special interest group' when it's the majority of the electorate."

Even more troubling, thanks in part to Republican weakness, is that the number of female state legislators from both parties has dropped from a high of 1,809 in 2010 to 1,786 in 2015. The number of female governors has retreated from a high of nine in 2007 to six in 2015. And the number of women elected to statewide offices—such as lieutenant governor, attorney general, secretary of state and comptroller—has dropped from a high of 92 in 2000 to 77 in 2015. The one area where Republican women have an advantage over Democrats is among statewide office holders, the pipeline for future national candidates: of the 77 women in office, 42 are Republicans, 34 are Democrats and one is an Independent.

Several groups, including Swanee Hunt's Political Parity, gathered on a cold winter day in late January 2015 to mull why so few Republican women were getting elected. "We can't win with half of our players on the field, and so we need to make the push and admit that gender does matter," Kerry Healy, Romney's former lieutenant governor in Massachusetts, said at the event at the Capitol Hill Club in Washington, D.C.

Parity introduced a report that found that female Republican candidates were perceived as moderate, even if they weren't any less partisan than the men in the field. As more sharply right-wing Tea Party–infused candidates have become more successful in GOP primaries in the past three election cycles, being considered a moderate was proving an insurmountable challenge to female candidates. Many had simply given up running.

"Women approach Congress a little differently than men," said McMorris Rodgers. "When you ask people what are the qualities that they think a woman brings to elected office, they'll point to things like women being trustworthy and better listeners, willing to work across the aisle, problem solvers, willing to get the job done." The problem is, none of these qualities play especially well in Republican primaries where compromise has become identified as a sign of weakness.

Women's reticence toward leading and calling attention to themselves narrows the field of potential candidates for both parties, especially among Republicans. "There's a pressure that women feel that [running for office] isn't something that they should be away from their kids for, and that's more of a conservative characteristic than a liberal characteristic, and that can make it difficult," said Gage.

Women, especially Republicans, are also more susceptible to stereotyping and caricature. Sarah Palin didn't begin this phenomenon, but she certainly became the poster child for it. In her wake, virtually every female Republican candidate has been labeled "the Sarah Palin" of whatever state she hails from. Many of those have proved patently untrue: Ayotte is as serious and substantive as they come. Texas governor Rick Perry became his party's punch line after his "oops" moment in a 2012 presidential debate when he forgot the third governmental agency he'd have liked to cut if elected. But despite the late-night jokes, no male candidates were caricatured as "the Rick Perry" of their home state.

Republican men haven't exactly been helpful. In January 2015, House Speaker John Boehner was forced to pull an abortion bill off the floor after all 22 female GOP members protested language limiting some abortions only to cases of rape that had been reported to police. The language was changed and the bill eventually passed. In July, Sen. Mitch McConnell accused Hillary Clinton of playing the gender card before he kept the Senate an extra week in a failed attempt to defund Planned Parenthood. "I don't think it's a particularly smart move for the men in our party to be leading the charge on this because it's the gender card," Gage said. "It's better for women to speak out on [gender]." Problem is, there are still so few GOP women in office to speak out.

And then came Trump.

Republicans have never been comfortable with identity politics and until recently have rarely engaged in targeting women, or any other special groups. Conway points to Obamacare as the best example of how Republicans have underestimated the power of speaking to women. The GOP's initial ad campaign against the the Affordable Care Act was analytical and full of data. It resounded with men but left women cold. Then, on Conway's advice, the GOP instead began telling the personal stories of women and men losing their doctors in the midst of cancer treatments, of people being forced into more expensive plans they could ill afford. The narratives resonated with women, and Obamacare began tanking in the polls.

In the days following Trump's scuffle with Megyn Kelly, some Republicans finally came out against his comments. Fiorina tweeted: "Mr. Trump: There. Is. No. Excuse." Bush said, "Do we want to win? Do we want to insult 53 percent of all voters? What Donald Trump said is wrong." Trump himself backtracked, saying he'd be "phenomenal" for women and that he, unlike his rivals, wants "to help the women."

He may have been telling the truth. For all his antics, Trump was the most moderate Republican in the field on social issues and even gender issues. There was a time when Trump was stridently pro-choice. He boasts of hiring and promoting "thousands" of female executives. His daughter Ivanka is one of his closest business partners. And he opened Women for Trump get-out-the-vote chapters in the early states. But he also seemingly couldn't go more than a few weeks without saying something insulting to women. In September 2015, Trump commented on rival Fiorina while watching her on television: "Look at that face. Would anyone vote for that? Can you imagine that, the face of our next president?" When pushed to apologize, Trump simply clarified that he was talking about Fiorina's "persona," not her looks.

At the debate, Fiorina was asked about Trump's comments. She took the high road, calling Trump a "wonderful man" before adding that all of the candidates' capabilities "will be revealed over time and under pressure . . . I think women all over this country heard very clearly what Mr. Trump said," Fiorina said to cheers and applause.

With Clinton the likely nominee, much attention will be paid to Republican efforts with women. If the GOP doesn't find a way to appeal to women, it risks not only losing the 2016 presidential race but permanently alienating female voters, a key to the party's long-term survival. And that hurts all women, because without legislative partners to work with across the aisle, a broad influence of female Democrats is virtually meaningless.

— 11 —

CULTURAL
CHALLENGES

While I was writing this book, Harvard invited me to live for a semester as a resident fellow at the Institute of Politics. As part of my fellowship I held weekly non-graded seminars at the John F. Kennedy School of Government, where I explored with my students much of what I had discovered in researching this book. My students were millennials, born between 1982 and 2003, and most of the regular participants were women. I enjoyed having these fresh young minds as a sounding board for my ideas and was surprised by some of their reactions to the material I presented. The attendance at my seminar and the proportion of the sexes fluctuated from week to week, but the No. 1 lesson I received from the students—male and female—was how shocked they were at how recently society treated women as second-class citizens: good for childbearing but not much else.

I opened most classes with a montage of clips from movies and television shows that illustrated how popular culture 20 or 30 years ago had portrayed women who were trying to break into a man's world. At a seminar about the military, they laughed at video clips of Goldie Hawn in 1980 joining the army as Private Benjamin, who was ditzy and flustered as she protested she'd joined the "wrong army." She thought she was signing up for the one with beachfront condos and spa treatments.

Next up was a clip from *G.I. Jane*, a movie released 16 years later, in which Demi Moore was the lone woman trying to qualify to be a U.S. Navy SEAL. Her master sergeant, portrayed by Viggo Mortensen, beats, brutalizes and nearly drowns her, while telling her SEAL classmates that she is a liability. He says that she doesn't belong there and warns that the squad will all perish if they go into battle with her. They will die protecting her because, as a woman, she is so weak. My students, raised with images of powerful women fighters, from Xena the Warrior Princess to Katniss from *Hunger Games*, were shocked, particularly by the brutality and sexism of the *G.I. Jane* clip. That part of the film seemed so far in the past for these students, many of whom either were toddlers or had not yet been born when it was first released. Their shock grew when I told them that until recently the Army required pregnant women to resign their positions to have their children and that the military still barred women from even applying for some jobs. And they were stunned when I told them that only in 2016, 20 years after *G.I. Jane* hit theaters, would women at last be allowed to try out for the Navy SEALs.

Hollywood was a useful window into women's evolution. Not so long ago, leading ladies were simply the love interests of leading men. In many ways, Hollywood has helped women advance by shattering glass ceilings onscreen long before progress was achieved in real life. Years ago, it imagined the first female president, Defense secretary, nuclear physicists, surgeons and many more roles ahead of their time. But the Hollywood reality has not been so progressive: until E!'s Chelsea Handler, only one woman, Joan Rivers, had broken what she called the "crass ceiling" to helm a late-night talk show. And Handler ended her show in 2013, ceding late night exclusively to men. Feminists have criticized a raft of recent movies such as *Jurassic World*, *Avengers:*

Age of Ultron, *Furious 7* and *Entourage* for their sexist, or nonexistent, depictions of women. *Saturday Night Live* went four years without a black female player in the featured cast until outcry in 2014 over the show's lack of diversity prompted executive producer Lorne Michaels to hire a black woman, Sasheer Zamata. In July 2015, former Disney CEO Michael Eisner was quoted at the Aspen Ideas Festival as saying he'd never met a woman who was gorgeous *and* funny and he wasn't sure such a thing was actually possible, with the exception of Goldie Hawn, with whom he shared the stage. (Perhaps he's never met Tina Fey or Amy Poehler?) He later clarified his remarks, saying that he didn't mean to imply Hawn was the only woman who combined both. "My point was simply that Goldie, unlike many, has not been defined exclusively as one or the other," he said.

Female celebrities are attacked relentlessly for both their appearance and whom they're rumored to be dating. Pop star Ariana Grande recently huffed that she refused to define her self-worth by the man whose arm she's on. Likewise, there's been a push by women in Hollywood to replace those red-carpet questions about their dresses, hair and jewelry with more substantive ones about the work for which they're being honored. Even A-list women are still paid less than men. Powerhouse women like Shonda Rhimes, creator of hit television shows *Grey's Anatomy*, *How to Get Away with Murder* and *Scandal*, and Oscar-winning director Kathryn Bigelow are exceptions to the rule, especially behind the cameras. Only 14 percent of television shows are directed by women, and only 14 percent of the Directors Guild of America is female. Even worse, only 9 percent of films released in 2013 were directed by female DGA members. Indeed, some female directors, as well as the American Civil Liberties Union, are calling on the U.S. Justice Department to investigate the DGA for violating federal law by rejecting the union-membership applications of 1,250 female directors.

Not to mention female actors. "If you think about storytelling," said Madeline Di Nonno, who runs actor Geena Davis's Institute on Gender in Media, which studies women in Hollywood, "people tend to write narrative stories about what they know, things that are authentic. If the ratio behind the camera is 5-to-1 [male], then why is it a surprise there are so few females onscreen?"

Davis spoke to film executives at Disney about the problem nearly a decade ago, when Nina Jacobson was running the studio. "[Davis] pointed out things we never even noticed," said Jacobson, who now produces the *Hunger Games* franchise. "Roles that didn't have to be gender-specific didn't have to be cast as men, even if they weren't even human cartoon characters. She gave me an awareness on that. It definitely influenced the way that I cast things to say: Well, why should this character be a man? This role doesn't need to be one gender or another. You can err on the side of fairness and balance."

In 2004, Halle Berry portrayed the first blockbuster female action lead in *Catwoman*—which flopped, grossing just $82 million on a $100 million budget. Of course, Sigourney Weaver kicked ass in 1986's *Aliens*, but that had a budget of $18 million and was often dismissed as a fluke. The Hollywood establishment saw Berry's *Catwoman* as evidence that females were weak at opening blockbuster movies, which perpetuated the stereotype. Since then, that misconception has been refuted by an array of female leads: Milla Jovovich (*Resident Evil*), Angelina Jolie (*Tomb Raider*), Kate Beckinsale (*Underworld*) and Jennifer Lawrence (*Hunger Games*). "There was a lot of mistaken conventional wisdom that women would identify with a male protagonist and men wouldn't identify with a female protégée. Or women would identify with family films, but men wouldn't," Jacobson said. "These were commonly held assumptions that I don't think have ever been true."

But Jacobson did note that there is a dearth of well-written female roles right now in Hollywood, partly because of the trend in films based on comic books, which historically don't have many strong female characters. Altering the source material would likely alienate a comic book's very large and loyal fan base. The same often holds true for classic works of literature. Fans of J.R.R. Tolkien's *The Hobbit* protested when director Peter Jackson added Evangeline Lilly's Tauriel character, an elf and love interest for Orlando Bloom's Legolas, to his trilogy of films. Without Tauriel, there would have been just one female character, Cate Blanchett's Galadriel, across all three films. "Tolkien was writing in 1937, and the world is a different place today," Lilly told reporters at a 2013 Los Angeles press conference. "I keep repeatedly telling people, 'In this day and age, to put nine hours of cinema in the theaters for young girls to go and watch and not have one female character is subliminally telling them you don't count, you're not important and you're not pivotal to story.' And I just think [the filmmakers] were very brave and very right in saying, 'We won't do that to the young female audience, who will come watch our films.' "

Generally, much less fuss is made over modernizing the classics. Jacobson said that for an upcoming film she is producing based on Homer's *Odyssey*, the hero's wife, Penelope, is written as a modern woman who does more than weave a tapestry while waiting for one of her suitors to marry her. If there are a few fans who want to see Penelope's character depicted as written 13 centuries ago, they'll be out of luck. "Is it for feminist reasons or because it makes a better movie? It makes a better movie! An antiquated woman isn't fun to watch," Jacobson said.

In 2011, only 11 percent of film protagonists and 37 percent of prime-time television characters were women. Women who are 45 or older make up only 15 percent of prime-time characters—a fact comedian Amy Schumer satirized when on her show for Comedy Central she held a wake for Julia Louis-Dreyfus's "last fuckable day"—the day the industry decides that you're no longer attractive enough to be a love interest onscreen. A skit featuring Schumer, Louis-Dreyfus, Tina Fey and Patricia Arquette noted that Sally Field played Tom Hanks's love interest in 1988's *Punchline* at the age of 41 and six years later played his mother in *Forrest Gump*. Of course, they lamented, men don't have a "last fuckable day."

And once they make it to the screen, women are stereotyped. Men on television are portrayed "on the job" 41 percent of the time, while for women it's 28 percent; men are more likely than women to be shown talking about work, 52 percent to 40 percent. Women, on the other hand, are more often seen talking about romantic relationships, 63 percent of the time, vs. men at 40 percent. "Women in Hollywood are valued in their beauty and sexuality," said Jennifer Siebel Newsom, who wrote, produced and directed the documentary *Miss Representation* about female presence onscreen.

Newsom wanted to bring in a prominent female director for the documentary, but the female candidates were remarkably wary. "They loved the idea, but all of them were noncommittal. They said, 'No one will want to hire me afterward,' " Newsom said. "There's tremendous fear because it's such a boys' club. If they challenge it, they will be alienated, ostracized." Newsom ended up directing the film herself and has since made a movement out of it, challenging the media to do substantive red-carpet interviews, cinematographers to ponder gratuitous shots and angles that sexualize female actors and studio chiefs to think of the world they would like their daughters to work in when they are hiring directors.

Jacobson believes things are changing.

A critical mass of female actors, writers and producers is starting to form. In her 2015 Oscars speech accepting the award for Best Actress, Patricia Arquette demanded equal pay for women, with Meryl Streep and Jennifer Lopez whooping her on. Arquette's movie, *Boyhood*, was an independent film, the one arena where women are reaching broad influence in Hollywood. Independent films have smaller casts and budgets, a lower barrier to entry than a project would face as a major studio release. According to a study by the organization Women in Film, 25 percent of all films screened at the Sundance Film Festival in the past 13 years have been directed by women, compared with 4 percent of all films overall in the same time period.

Women now comprise 23 percent of producers, and female producers are more likely than men to hire female writers and directors. There are 6.8 percent more females onscreen in films directed by women, and films written by women feature 7.5 percent more females onscreen globally and 10 percent more in the U.S., studies show.

When Jacobson was producing a movie called *Flightplan* in 2005, Jodie Foster called her to say that she'd do the film if Jacobson made the lead character—which had been written as a man—into a woman. "We didn't even change the name Ryan. It was more interesting with her in it than with a guy," Jacobson said. "But it still takes a woman in a position of power, like Jodie, to pick up the phone to [call] a woman in a position of power—me—for that to make sense."

And an A-plus script featuring a great female character attracts a higher caliber of female actors. Jacobson is producing a movie version of the book *Where'd You Go, Bernadette*, by Maria Semple. "The incoming calls that you get—'I want to play Bernadette'— are extraordinary, the caliber of the women," she said. "If you had *Where'd You Go, Bernie*, you wouldn't get the same caliber of men."

Jacobson has made it a priority to help other women succeed. When Elizabeth Banks was co-starring in the *Hunger Games* series, there was an opportunity for her to produce and direct *Pitch Perfect 2*. Banks had been eager to expand her role behind the camera, but the *Pitch Perfect 2* production schedule clashed with that of *The Hunger Games*. Jacobson rearranged her *Hunger Games* shoots so Banks could direct *Pitch Perfect 2*. "I was highly motived to do it for Liz," Jacobson said. "I definitely felt like it gets us another girl who's a serious player as a director and a producer."

Part of the change is also thanks to the next generation. Lena Dunham, the creator and star of HBO's *Girls*, has been outspoken about Hollywood's gender disparities. In her March 2014 speech at the South by Southwest Conference in Austin, Dunham noted that the career of her co-star Adam Driver had soared after he appeared in *Girls*, with his landing roles in Steven Spielberg and Coen brothers movies, while her three female co-stars had not advanced as quickly. "People are ready to see Adam play a million different guys in one year—from lotharios to villains to nerds. Meanwhile [co-stars] Allison Williams, Jemima Kirke and Zosia Mamet are still waiting for parts they can get interested in."

"There's just no place for me in the studio system," Dunham said, while vowing to keep pushing for change. For her generation, much is already changing.

For my Harvard seminar, I had chosen movie clips to engage students in pop culture's imagery of women but found that the films also stimulated discussions about the history of the women's movement. The women in my classes were surprised by how recently small things that they'd taken for granted had required hard-fought battles to secure. As we discussed the portrayal of women in film, the conversations moved toward the real-life ways society restricted women's clothing and economic freedom. The undergrads were amazed to learn that before Hillary Clinton became first lady, women wearing pants to work was frowned upon, and that in 1993, female senators had to stage a revolt, led by Illinois Democrat Carol Moseley Braun, to wear pants on the Senate floor. The students were also shocked to learn that there were once laws subordinating wives to husbands. A woman had to stop work when she got married? A woman wasn't allowed to have credit without her husband's permission? Most were astounded by how quickly things had changed and how, until recently, women's position in the U.S. was very different than the way these students picture their future today. To hear these millennials talk, one would think that the question of sexual inequality is moot, settled business.

Their reactions were surprising to me; however, after all the women I'd spoken to in the course of researching this book. I wanted to impress on these students that the fight for equality for women was not achieved in some battle won by our distant foremothers in the mists of time. One thing I had found in the year of working on this book is that the battles for significance and access, the struggles to be heard and to be respected, are still being fought daily in the private and public sectors. Indeed, just look closely at Hollywood, and it's easy to see that much work remains to be done.

Then I would think, maybe they're right. I might sound to them like my mother sounded to me when she warned me against choosing a demanding career. Was I, like my mom, fighting the last war? This new generation has a fresh chance to live its own values in the workplace and at home, and perhaps they are about to make a world in which none of these battles will be required.

In many ways, the millennial generation is unique. They are the first generation to grow up in families in which both parents worked and shared in raising kids. In 1972, 53 percent of all married couples were "traditional," in which the men worked and the wives stayed home; by 2009, traditional families accounted for just 26 percent of households. At the same time, the proportion of couples in which both parents work has risen to 52 percent from 32 percent, affording their children—the millennials—a lived experience of equality among the sexes. "The attitude of the millennial generation that will have the most impact on the daily lives of Americans is the distinctive and historically unprecedented belief that there are no inherently male or female roles in society," according to Morley Winograd and Michael D. Hais, co-authors of two books on what is now the largest generation in the U.S.

For millennials, women's equality is more than just that demographic fact. They also are entering the workforce at the time of a generational shift. Neil Howe and William Strauss, the inventors of the theory that identifies generational cycles in American history, defined two types of generations: civil and idealist. They labeled the Founding Fathers and America's so-called Greatest

Generation—those who grew up in the Depression and fought in World War II—as civic generations, which "associated 'effeminacy' with corruption and disruptive passion, 'manliness' with reason and disinterested virtue." In part this was because both were postwar societies, a period of time that venerates the heroes of a recent war and the values that supported it. Idealist generations, meanwhile, like the first feminist movement in the 1840s, the suffragettes of the early 20th century and the baby boomers, are much more feminist. The authors found that millennials are a unique mix of the two: they are a civic generation, with polls showing that nearly three fourths of millennials support more government involvement in Americans' lives, but because of how they were raised, they are also feminist.

For more than 40 years, the American National Election Study has surveyed Americans on their thoughts about women at work. The poll asks respondents: "Some people feel that women should have an equal role with men in running business, industry and government. Others feel that women's place is in the home. Where would you place yourself . . . or haven't you thought much about this?" The first survey, done in 1972 as baby boomers were growing up, found that 29 percent felt a woman belonged at home, 47 percent thought they should have an equal place at work and 24 percent didn't know. In 1990, as Generation X came of age, less than 15 percent thought a woman's place was at home. In 2014, when asked to rate on a scale of 1 to 7 how strongly they agreed with the statement that women should have an equal role with men in business, two thirds of millennials picked 1, the strongest, and 88 percent picked 1, 2 or 3—by far the highest of any generations polled.

As the first half of the millennial generation reaches a decade in the workforce, we can see that they are the lucky beneficiaries of the battles that were fought before them. Millennial women experience a narrower wage gap than their predecessors. In 2012, women ages 25 to 34 were paid 93 percent of their male counterparts' median hourly wages, better than the 84 percent of women overall, according to a 2013 Pew poll. And polls show that 87 percent of millennials support equal pay.

Perhaps, I thought, the reason these students are so shocked by sexism is not just that they have been raised in homes where equality was more the norm, but that sexism is no longer as widespread among elites. They are the first generation for whom women have outpaced men in attaining both undergraduate and graduate degrees. Yet many may be in for a shock when they take their places in the workforce. Young women's careers still suffer because they lack mentors or champions in the workplace. In the Navy, the biggest complaint from women in the ranks is that there aren't enough female role models up the chain of command to which they can aspire. Likewise, the lack of a corporate champion or patron can stall or even truncate women's careers.

Another challenge is that women are much less likely to beat their own drum to promote their advancement. Catalyst, which researches women's advancement in executive offices, studied 200 business school graduates. They found that women were much more hesitant to draw attention to their successes than their male colleagues— which is compounded by a lack of mentors to spotlight women's accomplishments and importance to the team. Part of women's reticence may be old stereotypes about being "ladylike" and how they are supposed to behave. When women in the study did try to promote themselves, their co-workers frequently said that they came off as too aggressive since they lacked champions. "The men had sponsors and women did not," said Catalyst's Debbie Soon. "When they're aggressive about self-promotion . . . they are considered a bitch. It was a Goldilocks effect: some were not strong enough or not aggressive enough. Others were too aggressive. We can be well-liked or competent, but not both."

In its assessment of millennials, the Pew study was quick to note that millennial women were just entering prime childbearing years, a

time when many of their opinions adjust with their new responsibilities. Despite the education and support a woman may have received
while building a career, she finds out just how hard it is to balance
motherhood and career. Society supports her doing the former and
sometimes the latter, but too rarely both. This is when the pay for
women and men starts to diverge markedly, and women's careers
take a pause on the path forward. Not only do women start earn-
ing less than men, but they take four years longer to run for public
office and eight years longer to become CEOs—a lag known as the
"motherhood penalty." The Pew poll found that millennial women
appreciate the difference; they likely observed it as their moms tried
to juggle both. Fifty-nine percent of millennial women said that
being a working parent made it harder to advance in a job or career,
compared with just 19 percent of millennial men.

Millennial women's entry into the workforce during the global
financial crisis helped women overall retain jobs more than men;
by the end of 2009 the unemployment rate for men was 10.7 percent but just 8.4 percent for women. Women under the age of
30 consistently saw unemployment rates lower than their male
counterparts—one to three percentage points during the recession.
And from 2007 to 2012, male unemployment losses amounted to
4.6 million jobs, almost double the number of female job losses,
leading some to dub it the "mancession." Perhaps that's why men
are increasingly entering fields traditionally dominated by women,
such as nursing and teaching; these jobs accounted for 30 percent of
men's job growth between 2000 and 2010, according to an analysis
of census data by the *New York Times*. And as men have turned to
traditionally female jobs, a new trend has emerged known as the
"glass escalator," in which men are promoted more quickly and paid
better than their female counterparts in these industries. So while
men may make up less than 11 percent of all nurses, for example,
proportionately more are in senior management.

This has long been true in post-secondary education. Women comprise 76 percent of the pre-kindergarten through high school teaching force but are only 17 percent of tenured college and university professors. "I actually thought when I came in as president of the university that there'd be a lot of women presidents of universities, and it turns out there aren't," said former Arizona governor Janet Napolitano, who now serves as president of the University of California system and hoped, thus far in vain, to form the same kind of women's club she helped found at the annual Attorneys General conference and National Governors Association meetings. "We're all so busy and so geographically dispersed that I haven't even met most of them, so I don't even have that peer group anymore."

Likewise, though the percentage of female physicians has grown to 32.4 percent in 2010 from 9.7 percent in 1970, most of that progress has come in specialties like pediatrics, primary care and ophthalmology. Very few women have entered the grueling, hypercompetitive world of surgery: only 4.8 percent of thoracic surgeons and 6.5 percent of neurosurgeons in 2010 were women.

As if breaching the final glass ceiling isn't hard enough, sometimes it's also a moving target. "There's a trend: when women penetrate a sector, the money and power leaves it," said Davia Temin, who has served on several corporate boards and cut her teeth on Wall Street. "When women finally got into investment banking, all the money went to private equity. When they got into private equity, it went to hedge funds."

The issue of whether women can have it all has been a topic of national discussion in recent years thanks to books like *Lean In*, by Sheryl Sandberg, and Anne-Marie Slaughter's *Unfinished Business: Women Men Work Family*. Sandberg argued that women haven't attained the highest levels of success because they often aren't confident or ambitious enough. She encourages women to lean into their work, almost literally. Slaughter, meanwhile, said women can lean in all they like, but they are hobbled by a system stacked against them. More support is needed for women to fully succeed.

Both are right: women who seek to break glass ceilings must lean in, and the system needs more support for every woman looking to balance work-life needs.

There is hope here, however. A new generation has the potential to bring fresh solutions to the problems that have tortured ambitious women ever since they entered the workplace in significant numbers in the 1970s. Those women, the first in the successive waves of critical mass, had an even harder time being taken seriously and advancing their careers. But go to human resources conferences, and HR professionals are all abuzz about how different the millennial generation is from any other. "Both women and men are asking for time off for their families," said Gia Colosi, head of human resources at Airbnb, where half the employees are women (though there are no women on its board of directors). "You have to hand it to the millennials, they know exactly what they want and how to ask for it."

Indeed, one day it would be wonderful to imagine large numbers of men choosing to stay home to take care of the kids as their career-minded partners earn the bread. And Hollywood has already tackled this subject. As recently as 1983, the idea of *Mr. Mom* was a Hollywood gag film. In 1993, Hollywood gave us *Mrs. Doubtfire*, a man who had to dress up as an elderly British nanny in order to be considered competent enough to take care of his own children.

But daddy blogs became popular in 2013 to such a degree that the *New York Times* profiled a few of the writers; the blogs inspired a national conference as well as a National At-Home Dad Network. The number of stay-at-home fathers doubled between 2000 and 2010 to 154,000, according to census data. A&E has a reality show called *Modern Dads*, and *The Stay-at-Home Dad* is a popular online series.

A key is to destigmatize stay-at-home fathers and break down children's gender perceptions. "These challenges are not new at all for women, but they are pretty new for men and not yet widely recognized," White House chief of staff Denis McDonough said at the opening of a White House summit on working fathers in June 2014.

Balancing home and work has yet to become a full challenge for men. On an average day, 83 percent of women and 65 percent of men spend some time doing household activities such as housework, cooking, lawn care and financial and other household management, according to a June 2014 Bureau of Labor Statistics report. Women spend an average of 2.6 hours on household activities, while men spend 2.1 hours. On an average day, 19 percent of men do housework—such as cleaning or doing laundry—compared with 49 percent of women. And 42 percent of men do food preparation or cleanup, compared with 68 percent of women. Meanwhile, men are more likely to exercise and on average spend more time at work than women.

I interviewed more than 150 women for this book, and I asked almost all what parity would look like. Many of the answers were strikingly similar. In that world, "Men are writing self-help books about how to balance being a parent and having a life and career that is fulfilling for them—that's parity," said Federal Trade Commissioner Terrell McSweeny.

Echoed the Center for American Progress's Neera Tanden, "I think parity is like, men take paid leave, women take leave," she said. "The reality is, we're not going to get economic parity until we have family parity."

There are signs it's starting to happen. More than 30 percent of primary contacts for kindergartners in 2013 were fathers, not mothers. To my mind critical mass is not only when women reach parity in the workplace but when men reach it in family care, whether caring for elderly parents, children or the home.

And while there have been profound changes in millennials' domestic lives and in young men's perceptions of themselves as caregivers, society's support for work-life balance still lags. The best way to secure a more equal future for women and men is to fight for these reforms in the political arena, but among millennials there is an inherent conflict. Although they are a civic generation, polls show that millennials have next to zero interest in running for office. Their lack of passion for electoral politics strikes me as one of the biggest hurdles to women having more influence in how the country is run. As we've seen in previous chapters, the public sector is where women are making the fastest progress to full equality; as they do, they bring other women up alongside them. If millennials, Democrat or Republican, don't run for office, much of the progress seen in the public sector could stall or, worse, retreat. If the changes they have experienced in their upbringing are to be spread nationwide, millennials will need to start to lead.

In some areas they are already leading. Female artists dominate the pop charts. Aside from Justin Bieber, there has hardly been a male pop star since Justin Timberlake to top the airwaves. Meanwhile, Beyoncé, Ariana Grande, Miley Cyrus, Taylor Swift, Katy Perry, Britney Spears, Lady Gaga, Adele and Rihanna produce hit after hit. The U.S. women's soccer team ruled the spring of 2015, capturing their third World Cup, while Serena Williams dominated the tennis courts, winning the Australian Open, the French Open and Wimbledon. In Hollywood, the first Marvel movie with a female lead, *Wonder Woman*, is in production and due out in 2017. On television, a woman is in the White House in *Veep*, at least for now. I can only hope that the country catches up to Hollywood's imagination and that imagination expands as the industry reaches critical mass.

In 2015, Congress approved a commission to begin the process of building a National Women's History Museum on the National Mall. Why? "A better world awaits the generation that absorbs what women and men have to share about life from a joint perspective," said the museum's founder, Karen Staser. "Together, all things are possible."

—EPILOGUE—

TOWARD

PARITY

"Crikey, it's a girl," an older male Australian tourist exclaimed when he saw that a dump truck hauling 400 tons of rock past our tour bus was driven by a woman.

"Yes, 40 percent of our drivers are female," responded Matt Cook, 39, our guide at the so-called Super Pit, the world's third-largest gold mine. The mine is in Kalgoorlie, some 500 kilometers west of Perth in Western Australia's red desert. The desert is divided into quaint-sounding "shires." Don't let that fool you. This desert is pure Mordor. It's 110 degrees in the winter, and the land is literally sown with salt, leaving large white dots where it pools in the rainy season. Most of the animals here can kill you, from scorpions, deadly snakes and spiders to eight-foot kangaroos that sometimes bat cars with their powerful tails.

This is not exactly a welcoming environment for miners, let alone female miners. And yet the Super Pit, a joint venture of Newmont Mining and Barrick Gold, is ahead of the curve in its efforts to employ a balanced workforce. Women make up 15.5 percent of Australia's miners, and there's a goal to get above 25 percent by 2020. "Our workforce should be representative of the Australian community," said Steve Knott, CEO of the Australian Mines and Metals Association.

The Super Pit has what the miners call nanny shifts. Mothers often want to work part time while their kids are in school. So when the full-time miners take off for a long lunch break, the women arrive to drive the trucks for an hour or two so that those vehicles are never idle. Historically, mining has meant pickaxes and deep, dark holes. Modern mining in Australia is more about pushing a button in a room or driving in the air-conditioned cab of a truck. "The mining industry has a terrible blokey image, whereas we try to promote that it is an environment that women can work in," said Sabina Shugg, founder of the group Women in Mining and Resources Western Australia.

It's part of a larger push in Australia to bring women up to full employment. Necessity is the mother of invention: thanks to an extended minerals boom, Australia has enjoyed more than a quarter century of sustained growth and is now the world's 12th-largest economy. But its tiny population of just over 30 million people, compared with America's 320 million, could not feed the surging labor demand. Though the country welcomed some immigration, economic growth was dependent on harnessing the full potential of its relatively tiny 11.7-million-person workforce. By 2007, Australia faced a choice: increase immigration or bring women up to full employment. By 2012, the gender gap would cost Australia $195 billion, or 13 percent of its GDP annually, Goldman Sachs estimated.

Australia's answer is a program to increase women's participation with an unlikely name—Male Champions of Change, or MCC—but the descriptors are appropriate. When Elizabeth Broderick came into her job as sex-discrimination minister in Australia in September 2007, she wanted to empower women, but she found that there simply weren't enough mid- to high-level women to empower. So she picked up the phone and called a dozen of Australia's most powerful and influential men and made a personal plea to them to use their collective voice and wisdom to create change for women. She found them surprisingly interested. As one responded, "Let's not pretend that there aren't already established norms that advantage men. Men invented the system. Men largely run the system. Men need to change the system." "And that's what the Male Champions of Change strategy is all about—men stepping up beside women to change the system," Broderick told an audience at a Big Ideas conference in November 2014.

The government created a sub-ministerial position for women as well as several reporting and monitoring offices within ministries. It then partnered with Australia's largest companies, which agreed to voluntarily submit annual reports on their progress in hiring, training and retaining women. There are similar federal efforts in the U.S., including the Women's Bureau at the Labor Department, which maintains statistics about women in the workforce and collects voluntary reporting from companies—though few contribute anything that might be construed as embarrassing. Since reporting is not required under U.S. law, companies would have to be willing to suffer the public-relations consequences of candid disclosures when they don't meet goals in hiring women.

MCC has led to astonishing progress for women in the Australian workforce. "We know balanced teams perform better. It follows that, over time, purchasers will increasingly reflect this in their buying decisions. The magic will be when the broader business system works together to make the change. We will share ideas. We will hold each other to account," Stephen Fitzgerald, MCC's non-executive director, said in the group's 2013 report.

MCC developed best practices and set attainable goals. For example, in 2011, Citigroup Australia achieved its goal of a 9 percent annual increase in women in senior vice president roles, and in 2012 continued with a 24 percent increase. And in 2013, 57 percent of

Qantas's class of new hires was female. "We need to get intentional. Now that we have a clear plan, we are less likely to have a discussion about why there are not enough women in our talent pipeline when the time comes to make appointments," said Geoff Wilson, COO of KPMG's Asia Pacific office.

MCC also focused on flexible work in order to help attract women. In September 2013, David Thodey of Telstra, Australia's largest phone company, announced that all roles in Telstra would be advertised as flexible. As a result, the number of female applicants rose, and the number of women accepting offers increased by 13 percent.

Finally, the group tackled the problem of women who don't return to the workforce after having kids. "We need to make parents feel great and want to return, and then ask how they would like to accelerate their careers. I worry when I see so many brilliant young people whose careers plateau after parental leave," said Grant O'Brien, CEO of Woolworths Limited in Australia.

ANZ, one of Australia's largest banks, introduced a child-care allowance. IBM Australia included employees on parental leave on monthly company updates so they could stay informed and engaged. Qantas established a career coaching service, leading to a return rate of 98 percent.

By 2014, Australia's professional workforce was almost evenly split, with women accounting for 53.3 percent of the jobs to men's 46.7 percent. Women chair 12 percent of corporate boards and make up 24 percent of board members, up from 17 percent when the program started. Women make up 17.3 percent of CEOs and 26.1 percent of key management positions, nearly 30 percent of executives or general managers, 32 percent of senior managers and 40 percent of other managers. In 2014, women accounted for more than 30 percent of new board appointments for companies listed on the Australia Stock Exchange. Australia's women were reaching broad influence.

America is about to face the same economic dilemma as Australia.

Retirement of the baby boomer generation will lead to an estimated shortfall of 26 million workers by 2030—that's just 14 years from the publication of this book. That will result in a huge economic loss for the U.S., according to a 2013 International Monetary Fund study. It estimates that the workforce falloff could reduce economic output—the total of goods and services produced—by as much as 27 percent per capita (a country's total output divided per person) in certain regions. But increasing the female labor participation rate to male-participation levels, it found, would lift U.S. overall GDP by 5 percent.

As in Australia, there are two solutions: either increase immigration or bring women up to full employment. Allowing a vast wave of immigration looks unlikely under the current U.S. Congress. What's more possible is the same type of concerted effort that over time will bring women to parity with men.

While women already make up 47 percent of U.S. workers, they account for two thirds of minimum-wage earners and three fourths of shift workers. To achieve full employment and replace the loss of the baby boomer generation, women would also have to fill middle- and upper-management jobs. Women were first brought into the workforce in response to the dire economic need of World War II. And it seems they will only achieve parity when the economy needs them again. When that happens, the country is going to have to rethink work hours, parental leave and domestic arrangements.

Women already have the education and training to do the job: the majority of higher-education degrees are held by women. So getting to parity must involve bringing women back into the workforce after they've left to start families. And that will require changing the way we do business.

Parity isn't a feminist pipe dream or long-term goal: it's an economic imperative.

Australia isn't the only country that has faced this demographic cliff. Europe's response has been, in part, to institute quotas. Canada and the United Kingdom instituted volunteer public-private partnerships aimed at getting women to 30 percent of corporate board memberships. And in Japan, Prime Minister Shinzo Abe has recently launched "womenomics" as a solution to his country's limping economy.

As far back as 1999, Goldman Sachs predicted that Japan could increase its gross domestic product by as much as 15 percent if it brought women more fully into the workforce. But the idea was controversial. Japan's population has been dropping, and officials worried that working women would have even fewer children. But Japan's economy has stalled, and it desperately needs innovation and energy—and sheer numbers. Barring new immigration, an even more controversial idea in the xenophobic Asian nation—less than 2 percent of the country's population is foreign—the only alternative was full employment for women. Abe, who began his second term as prime minister in December 2012, aims to increase women's participation in the labor force from 68 percent to 73 percent by 2020. In 2014, Japan ranked a dismal 104th on the Social Institution and Gender Index and 115th in female parliamentary representation, way behind every other developed nation.

"Womenomics offers a solution with its core tenet that a country that hires and promotes more women grows economically, and no less important, demographically as well," Abe wrote in a *Wall Street Journal* op-ed in September 2013.

To that end, Abe pledged to close Japan's pay equity gap; women now earn 30 percent less than men, compared with 20.1 percent less in the U.S. He has also pledged to invest $3 billion over the next three years into new programs for child care, health and prevention and resolution of conflicts related to women. The early responses were promising. The mayor of Tokyo reported a 16 percent increase in day-care applications. Abe appointed women to seven of his 18

Cabinet positions and set a goal of 30 percent female representation on corporate boards by 2020, a huge leap from the current 10 percent.

"The old way of doing things in Japan made it quite efficient, assuming the environment stayed the same, but those days are over," said Yoko Ishikura, who is on the board of several Japanese companies, including Nissin Foods. "Japan is losing a huge number of workers, and half the population has the education but they don't participate in the labor market as much as they should." Ishikura said she believed that not only would Abe's womenomics work but that it had to work: Japan has no other option.

For Japan, this is a Hail Mary pass: its economy has been in the doldrums since the 1990s. In 2009 it was the world's second-largest economy; by 2050 Goldman Sachs estimates it will be the world's seventh-largest economy, trailing India, Brazil and Russia—that is, unless it can restart its economic engine.

At a forum with Harvard students in May 2015, a student pressed Abe about how realistic his plans were, given how few women serve in leadership positions in the government and in business. Abe said he started with areas under his control: 30 percent of candidates for senior government positions had to be women—which his ministries have achieved; two of the three governing seats of his political party, the Liberal Democrats, are women. Stock-exchange-listed companies took 60 years to have 90 women on their boards; his administration brought in 180 women in two years, he said.

"I must be prepared for a woman rival competing with me," he said, evoking laughter from the audience. "I would hope that the companies have the awareness that they are hiring the women not because of social policy but because women would improve corporate policy . . . I often say that had Lehman Brothers been Lehman Brothers and Sisters, they'd both still be around."

There are other lessons to be learned from abroad. More than 50 countries have had female heads of state; some of them have elected a female head of state more than once. They include Muslim countries such as Bahrain, Pakistan and Turkey. To be fair, though, many of the female heads of state either were hereditary monarchs or were elected in a parliamentary system of governance, which means a woman would only have to win the support of her party, not a popular vote.

Three countries' legislatures have reached parity: Rwanda, Bolivia and Andorra. Another nine have more than 40 percent female representation: Cuba, Seychelles, Sweden, Senegal, Finland, Ecuador, South Africa, Iceland and Spain. And another 80 countries have 20 percent or more women in their parliaments—in other words, the U.S. is behind 92 countries in electing women to Congress.

Some of that has been due to quotas, a system the U.S. is unlikely to adopt. In the past decade, the world average of women in legislatures rose to 18.9 percent of seats in national legislatures from 13.1 percent. Thanks to quotas, female representation in sub-Saharan Africa jumped to 18.8 percent from 11.3 percent. Rwanda leads the world in female parliamentary representation at 67 percent, in part thanks to laws requiring that women make up 30 percent of local councils and reserving 24 of the legislature's 80 seats for women. In 2000, France required that 50 percent of candidates in regional and general elections be women, helping increase female representation in the National Assembly to 26.2 percent in 2015 from 12.3 percent in 2002. France also requires that women comprise 40 percent of board seats of large corporations.

In the Middle East, Morocco stands as the leader in feminist thought, in part because King Mohammed VI was educated in Europe and supports women's rights. In 2002, the North African country adopted an electoral quota of 30 of its 395 seats in parliament for women and expanded it to 60 seats in 2011. In 2004, it revised family code law, or *mundawana*, to allot one husband and one wife per family; abolished requirements that wives obey husbands; raised the minimum marriage age for girls to 18 and granted equal rights to divorce. The feminist leanings are so strong that they inspired Saudi women to push for the right to drive.

Brazil's economic advancement has been coupled with the advancement of its women. The attainment of broad influence in its political leadership has had a direct impact on its female workforce. Brazil's first female president, Dilma Rousseff, was elected in 2011. She appointed women to 10 out of 34 Cabinet positions, and in 2012, all but one in her inner circle of advisers were women. Brazil's female representation in the workforce has increased by more than 15 percentage points to almost 60 percent thanks to programs that helped rural women obtain necessary documentation to access land, credit and government services, Social Security reform, paid maternity leave and microfinancing programs. In 2012, Brazil ranked eighth of 86 countries in the Organization for Economic Cooperation and Development's Social Institution and Gender Index, which comprises five dimensions of social institutions to promote gender equality.

The Scandinavian countries, in particular, lead the world in gender equality thanks to a generous and flexible parental leave policy combined with a high coverage rate for child care, job guarantees and eligibility for reduced working hours. Their political parties also have voluntary so-called zipper quotas—which require that every other candidate on a ballot be a woman—leading to some of the highest rates of female legislative representation in the world. In 2014, Sweden's feminist party fell just 4 percent of the vote short of winning seats in parliament. And Sweden is considering legislation to join its other Scandinavian nations in requiring that women comprise 40 percent of its corporate boards.

So what do these lessons mean for the United States? The political reality is that neither party will ever institute quotas on any level. Americans take pride in their system as a meritocracy, and quotas smack of government meddling. But much can and should be done by the next president. The Australian model is a good one because it's voluntary but very effective. The next president, whether a man or a woman, should start a high-level program engaging male private-sector leaders and challenging them to do better, set goals and be transparent about their progress.

And the tide is starting to shift naturally. Investment funds such as Calpers, the largest public pension fund in the U.S., and Amazone in Europe have begun to include gender diversity as criteria for investments. "I think we're seeing a bigger trend towards the engagement of men in this dialogue," said Beth Brooke-Marciniak, global vice chair of public policy at EY. "You can't just focus on just the women. The men are right now in the positions to make a lot of decisions on who will be on their board. You need to involve men in this, and they need to understand the economic case on why this is in their best interest to not choose people who look, think and act like themselves."

But without leadership from the Oval Office—without the ultimate critical actor to champion women—progress is too slow. At least one would-be president, Hillary Clinton, has said she will make it her top priority to work on these issues if elected to the White House. "I do want to encourage and find a way to incentivize corporations to promote more women, to have more women on their boards of directors," Clinton said. "The private sector is much more impervious to public pressure, and therefore we have to create . . . programs like the Australian program that maybe can provide that push to get more private-sector involvement in hiring and promoting women to positions of responsibility." Without active interaction, estimates of reaching parity in the upper end of the workforce range from 100 to 300 years. But if women can get to a critical mass, as we have seen, that will make all the difference.

I often wonder what my mother would make of this world. At the end of her life, when she and my father retired to Florida, she no longer spoke of her amazing career and the phenomenal and powerful jobs she'd held. It was as if she was embarrassed by how much stress it had caused her and the way it had affected our family life. She made friends with other retired professional women she met at the country club, but they didn't hear her tales of negotiating international business deals in Africa or helping to write the Cambodian constitution. In fact, when her friends read the obituary I wrote for the local newspaper, they were shocked by my mother's past. At her memorial, woman after woman came up to me to say, "I had no idea. Why didn't she tell me?"

Perhaps my mother's sense of her own destiny was grander than the world she lived in would allow. What if she'd been born 30 years later? Would she have been the first female U.N. secretary-general? I think she very well could have. Or, at the very least, she would have found kindred female spirits, allies among the diplomatic ranks, women who could help her smooth out the rough spots of a still oppressively sexist international climate. There is a regular gathering of women in diplomacy in Washington called Diplobabes. I've sometimes imagined my mother at such a gathering: how would it have helped her? Women are not there yet by any means, but reaching broad influence means that we're no longer struggling isolated and alone as my mother had. And I like to think she too would find, as I have, that in numbers comes safety—and power.

—ACKNOWLEDGMENTS—

First of all, thanks to my parents. I wish my mother had lived to see the publication of this book.

Thanks to my editors, Danelle Morton—you are awesome—and Roe D'Angelo, the first person to love the idea, for buying the book, believing in it and me and holding my hand all the way through. Thanks to my agent, Nathaniel Jacks, for going to bat for me, especially toward the end as my energy failed. Thanks to Steve Koepp, the editorial director of Time Books, for always pushing me to do better.

Thanks to my bureau chief, Michael Scherer, for giving me the time and latitude to report and write this book, and to TIME's deputy managing editor, Michael Duffy, for assigning me the story of the women in the Senate that started this whole thing. And thanks to TIME editor Nancy Gibbs for her genius advice to expand the book beyond just politics. Thanks to colleagues Maya Rhodan, who helped me research the House chapter, and readers extraordinaire Haley Sweetland Edwards and Elizabeth Dias. And thanks to Mark Thompson, the best Pentagon reporter ever and a wonderful mentor.

Thanks to Harvard's Institute of Politics, particularly director Maggie Williams for being a surrogate mom, cheerleader, reader and champion. Thanks to fellow program director Eric Andersen. Thanks so much to the best researcher in the world, Amy Friedman.

Thanks to my liaisons Caroline Hunsicker, Andrew O'Donahue, Avika Dua, Erin Shortell, Gabriela Giotti and Aisha Bhoori, who all helped research various chapters. Thanks to my graduate research assistant Eugene Scott, particularly for his reporting on the law enforcement chapter. And, finally, my deepest gratitude to my co-(snow)fellows, some of whom are quoted in the book but all of whom generously gave their thoughts and ideas on the topic over several months: North Carolina senator Kay Hagan; Massachusetts attorney general Martha Coakley; New York Council speaker Christine Quinn; NRSC's Matt Lira; and my favorite comedian and laundry pod hoarder, Bassem Youssef.

A thousand cows for my India posse, Jessica Mayberry and Stalin K., who made me feel like Goa is my second home, and the amazing crew at Video Volunteers, who are fighting on the front lines in citizen journalism in India. Thanks to Richa Ramela, my trusty transcriber, assistant, India smartphone whisperer and scooter guru.

To Rose Styron, thank you for sharing your writing haven in Vineyard Haven and for showing me around Martha's Vineyard. I can't think of a more beautiful place to write.

Thanks to readers Matthew Bigg, Emmy Berning, Terrell McSweeny and Margaret Talev.

Thanks to Davia Temin for helping me navigate the daunting world of the *Fortune* 500 and to Susan Stautberg for so generously giving me access to the hundreds of impressive women at Women on Corporate Boards' annual gathering.

Thanks to former Vermont chief justice Jeff Amestoy for his guidance through the world of the law, insights and connections.

Thanks to Swanee Hunt and everyone at Political Parity. Even though we didn't end up partnering on research, I learned a lot from you.

And finally, thanks to Kimball Stroud, Anu Rangappa, Marty Makary, Pamela Stevens and last—but never least—Juleanna Glover for all your advice and wisdom on how to market a book.

— SOURCES —

I interviewed hundreds of women for this book—more than I can tally. At least 150 of these interviews were substantive, lasting more than 30 minutes; some continued for many hours over multiple sessions. Dozens more were brief encounters at women's conferences or political gatherings. Most of the reporting was specifically for the book, but much of the context and some of the interviews were drawn from my 14 years as a political correspondent. I want to cite and pay homage here to sources who gave me perspective, helped me understand and, in many cases, shared vital information for the book.

An indispensable source, with numerous contributions, is Rutgers University's Center for American Women and Politics at the Eagleton Institute of Politics. The center's resources are voluminous, and its research on women in elected office is unparalleled.

Other key sources: Catalyst's research on women in the private sector, McKinsey's Women Matter series, reports from EY (formerly Ernst & Young) on women, Heidrick and Struggles's research and PriceWaterhouse Coopers's reports on gender in the workplace.

At the beginning of each chapter note that follows, I cite some but not all of the people I interviewed for the chapter. Some may not be quoted, but all named had an impact. Others I have deliberately left out, as they wanted to remain anonymous.

Introduction: Getting to Critical Mass
Sociological sources for definition of "critical mass" on page 5:

Broome, Lissa Lamkin, John M. Conley and Kimberly D. Krawiec. "Does Critical Mass Matter? Views from the Boardroom." *Seattle University Law Review* 34, no. 1 (June 3, 2011): 1049–1080. SSRN-id2383511.

Childs, Sarah, and Mona Lena Krook. "Analysing Women's Substantive Representation: From Critical Mass to Critical Actors." *Government and Opposition* 44, no. 2 (April 2009): 125–145. doi: 10.1111/j.1477-7053.2009.01279.x.

Kanter, Rosabeth Moss. "Some Effects of Proportions on Group Life: Skewed Sex Ratios and Responses to Token Women." *American Journal of Sociology* 82, no. 5 (March 1, 1977): 965–990. Print.

Killewald, Alexandra, and Margaret Gough. "Does Specialization Explain Marriage Penalties and Premiums?" *American Sociological Review* 78, no. 3 (June 2013): 477–502. doi: 10.1177/0003122413484151.

Strack, Rainer, Jens Baier and Jean-Michel Caye. "Stimulating Economies Through Fostering Talent Mobility." *BCG Perspectives*. Web. March 23, 2010.

Chapter 1: The West Wing
INTERVIEWS: VALERIE JARRETT, MONA SUTPHEN, MELODY BARNES, STEPHANIE CUTTER, NANCY-ANN DEPARLE, ALYSSA MASTROMONACO, CAROL BROWNER, LISA BROWN, ELLEN MORAN, ANITA DUNN AND GINA MCCARTHY.

Boone, Ariel. "Short-Changed: White House Women Hired Below White House Men." *Huffington Post*. Web. Sept. 7, 2009.

Bowling, Cynthia J., Christine A. Kelleher, Jennifer Jones and Deil S. Wright. "Cracked Ceilings, Firmer Floors, and Weakening Walls: Trends and Patterns in Gender Representation Among Executives Leading American State Agencies, 1970–2000." *Public Administration Review* 66, no. 6 (November/December 2006): 823–836. doi: 10.1111/j.1540-6210.2006.00651.x.

Kanter, Rosabeth Moss. "Some Effects of Proportions on Group Life: Skewed Sex Ratios and Responses to Token Women." *American Journal of Sociology* 82, no. 5 (March 1, 1977): 965–990. Print.

Kendzior, Sarah. "The Princess Effect." *Politico* magazine. Web. July 2, 2014.

Motavalli, Jim. "California's Quiet But Crucial Role in Shaping Fuel Economy Standards." *New York Times*. Web. Sept. 4, 2012.

Scheiber, Noam. "Exclusive: The Memo That Larry Summers Didn't Want Obama to See." *New Republic*. Web. Feb. 22, 2012.

Suskind, Ron. *Confidence Men: Wall Street, Washington, and the Education of a President*. New York: HarperCollins, 2011. Print.

United States Office of Personnel Management. *Women in Federal Service: A Seat at Every Table*. Rep. March 2015.

Volden, Craig, Alan E. Wiseman and Dana E. Wittmer. *The Legislative Effectiveness of Women in Congress*. Working paper no. 4-2010. Center for the Study of Democratic Institutions/Vanderbilt University, 2010. Print.

Wallsten, Peter and Anne E. Kornblut. "Friction over Women's Role in Obama White House Was Intense." *Washington Post*. Web. Sept. 20, 2011.

Chapter 2: The Senate

INTERVIEWS: PATTY MURRAY, PAUL RYAN, BARBARA BOXER, SUSAN COLLINS, TAMMY BALDWIN, MAZIE HIRONO, DIANNE FEINSTEIN, DEBBIE STABENOW, BARBARA MIKULSKI, AMY KLOBUCHAR, JEANNE SHAHEEN, KAY HAGAN, LISA MURKOWSKI, HEIDI HEITKAMP, MARY LANDRIEU, KAY BAILEY HUTCHISON, OLYMPIA SNOWE, BLANCHE LINCOLN, MICHELLE NUNN AND ALISON LUNDERGAN GRIMES.

Kane, Paul and Ed O'Keefe. "House Passes 2-Year Bipartisan Budget Deal." *Washington Post*. Web. Dec. 12, 2013.

Lawrence, Jill. "Profiles in Negotiation: The Murray-Ryan Budget Deal." *Brookings*. Web. Feb. 26, 2015.

Swers, Michele L. *Women in the Club: Gender and Policy Making in the Senate*. Chicago: University of Chicago Press, April 2013. Print.

Volden, Craig, Alan E. Wiseman and Dana E. Wittmer. *The Legislative Effectiveness of Women in Congress*. Working paper no. 4-2010. Center for the Study of Democratic Institutions/ Vanderbilt University, 2010. Print.

Warner, Judith. *Women's Leadership: What's True, What's False, and Why It Matters*. Rep. Center for American Progress. Web. March 7, 2014.

Wasson, Erik. "Senate Passes First Budget in Four Years." *The Hill*. Web. March 23, 2013.

Whitney, Catherine. *Nine and Counting: The Women of the Senate*. New York: William Morrow, 2000. Print.

Chapter 3: A Critical Actor in the House

INTERVIEWS: NANCY PELOSI, JOHN DINGELL, JOHN SPRATT, GEORGE MILLER, JIM CLYBURN, RON KIND, ELLEN TAUSCHER, MIKE THOMPSON, DENNIS CARDOZA, RAHM EMANUEL, STENY HOYER, CHRIS VAN HOLLEN, ROSA DELAURO, DIANA DEGETTE, ANNA ESHOO, NIKI TSONGAS, MARCY KAPTUR, GAVIN NEWSOM, JOHN BURTON, WILLIE BROWN, TOMMY D'ALESSANDRO, CHRISTINE PELOSI, ALEXANDRA PELOSI AND THOMAS MANN.

Daly, Matthew. "There Are More Women and Minorities in the New Congress Than Ever." *Huffington Post*. Web. Jan. 5, 2015.

Swers, Michele L. *The Difference Women Make: The Policy Impact of Women in Congress*. Chicago: University of Chicago Press, September 2002. Print.

Vekshin, Alison and Laura Litvan. "U.S. House Rejects $700 Billion Financial-Rescue Plan." *Bloomberg*. Web. Sept. 29, 2008.

Volden, Craig, Alan E. Wiseman and Dana E. Wittmer. *The Legislative Effectiveness of Women in Congress*. Working paper no. 4-2010. Center for the Study of Democratic Institutions/ Vanderbilt University, 2010. Print.

Weise, Karen. "Nancy Pelosi on Getting the TARP Votes to Save the Economy." *Bloomberg*. Web. Sept. 12, 2013.

Chapter 4: The Executive Office

INTERVIEWS: MADELEINE ALBRIGHT, MAGGIE WILLIAMS, NEERA TANDEN, KATHLEEN SEBELIUS, JANET NAPOLITANO, CHRISTINE GREGOIRE, MARY FALLIN, ELIZABETH DOLE, MICHELE BACHMANN, MARTHA COAKLEY, CHRISTINE QUINN, SARAH PALIN, BUFFY WICKS, JULIANNA SMOOT, CELINDA LAKE, COKIE ROBERTS, DEBBIE WASSERMAN SCHULTZ, MARIE WILSON AND HILLARY RODHAM CLINTON.

Baker, Peter and Amy Chozick. "Hillary Clinton's History As First Lady: Powerful, but Not Always Deft." *New York Times*. Web. Dec. 5, 2014.

Barbara Lee Family Foundation. *Chronic Challenges: Double Standards Are Alive and Well.* Rep. Web. 2015.

Barbara Lee Family Foundation. *Pitch Perfect: Winning Strategies for Women Candidates.* Rep. Web. Nov. 8, 2012.

Barbara Lee Family Foundation. *Turning Point: The Changing Landscape for Women Candidates.* Rep. Web. 2011.

Burrell, Barbara. "Campaign Financing: Women's Experience in the Modern Era." *Women and Elective Office: Past, Present, and Future*, 2nd ed. Thomas, Sue and Clyde Wilcox, eds. New York: Oxford University Press, 2005: 26–40. Print.

Childs, Sarah, and Mona Lena Krook. "Analysing Women's Substantive Representation: From Critical Mass to Critical Actors." *Government and Opposition* 44, no. 2 (April 2009): 125–145. doi: 10.1111/j.1477-7053.2009.01279.x.

Childs, Sarah and Mona Lena Krook. "Critical Mass Theory and Women's Political Representation." *Political Studies* 56, no. 3 (October 2008): 725–736. doi: 10.1111/j.1467-9248.2007.00712.x.

Chozick, Amy. "Planet Hillary." *New York Times Magazine*. Web. Jan. 24, 2014.

Francia, Peter L. "Early Fundraising by Nonincumbent Female Congressional Candidates: The Importance of Women's PACs." *Women and Politics* 23, no. 1-2 (2001): 7–20. doi:10.1300/J014v23n01_02.

Francia, Peter L., John C. Green, Paul S. Herrnson, Lynda W. Powell and Clyde Wilcox. *The Financiers of Congressional Elections: Investors, Ideologues, and Intimates*. New York: Columbia University Press, 2003. Print.

Friedman, Hilary Levey. "Here She Comes, Miss (Elected) America." *Slate*. Web. June 26, 2012.

Holan, Angie Drobnic. "Hillary's Travels As First Lady." *Politifact*. Web. Dec. 1, 2008.

Kanter, Rosabeth Moss. "Some Effects of Proportions on Group Life: Skewed Sex Ratios and Responses to Token Women." *American Journal of Sociology* 82, no. 5 (March 1, 1977): 965–990. Print.

Krook, Mona Lena. "Empowerment vs. Backlash: Gender Quotas and Critical Mass Theory." *Politics, Groups, and Identities* 3, no. 1 (2015): 184–188. doi:10.1080/21565503.2014.999806.

Lawless, Jennifer L. and Kathryn Pearson. "The Primary Reason for Women's Underrepresentation? Reevaluating the Conventional Wisdom." *Journal of Politics* 70, no. 1 (January 2008): 67–82. doi: 10.1017/S002238160708005X.

Lawless, Jennifer L. and Richard L. Fox. *Girls Just Wanna Not Run: The Gender Gap in Young Americans' Political Ambition*. Rep. American University School of Public Affairs. Web. March 2013.

Merica, Dan. "Clinton Run Charges Up Emily's List Ahead of 2016." *CNN*. Web. Feb. 24, 2015.

Palmer, Anna and Tarini Parti. "Money Gap: Why Don't Women Give?" *Politico*. Web. July 22, 2014.

Palmer, Barbara and Dennis Simon. *Breaking the Political Glass Ceiling: Women and Congressional Elections*. 2nd ed. New York: Routledge, 2008.

Pierce, Meghan. "Hillary Clinton Makes First NH Stop in Keene." *New Hampshire Union Leader*. Web. April 20, 2015.

Political Parity. *Shifting Gears: How Women Navigate the Road to Higher Office.* Rep. May 27, 2014.

Reingold, Beth. *Legislative Women: Getting Elected, Getting Ahead.* Boulder: Lynne Rienner Publishers, 2008. Print.

Sheeler, Kristina Horn and Karrin Vasby Anderson. *Woman President: Confronting Postfeminist Political Culture.* College Station: Texas A&M University Press, 2013. Print.

Traister, Rebecca. "The Best Thing Hillary Could Do for Her Campaign? Ditch Bill." *New Republic.* Web. May 7, 2015.

Traister, Rebecca. "Why Are There No Female Sheldon Adelsons?" *New Republic.* Web. July 23, 2014.

Women's Media Center. *The Status of Women in the U.S. Media 2014.* Rep. Web. 2014.

Zennie, Michael. "Michele Bachmann Claims Sexism After Top Aide to Rick Santorum Questions Whether a Woman Can Be President." *Daily Mail.* Web. Jan. 16, 2012.

Chapter 5: The Judiciary

INTERVIEWS: LINDA MORRISSEY, CHRISTINE DURHAM, NANCY GERTNER, JUDY LICHTMAN, LISA BLATT, PATRICIA WALD, NAN DUFFLY AND MARCIA GREENBERGER.

American Bar Association. *A Current Glance at Women in the Law.* Rep. July 2014.

Applebaum, Binyamin. "What the Hobby Lobby Ruling Means for America." *New York Times.* Web. Jul. 22, 2014.

Biskupic, Joan. "Ginsburg: Court Needs Another Woman." *USA Today.* Web. May 5, 2009.

Black, Eric. "The Notorious R.B.G. (That's Ruth Bader Ginsburg) Comes to Town." *MinnPost.* Web. Sept. 17, 2014.

Boyd, Christina L., Lee Epstein and Andrew D. Martin. "Untangling the Causal Effects of Sex on Judging." *American Journal of Political Science* 54, no. 2 (April 2010): 389–411. doi: 10.1111/j.1540-5907.2010.00437.x.

Clift, Eleanor. "Olympia Snowe Quit Senate to Protest GOP Agenda." *Daily Beast.* Web. March 1, 2012.

Davidson, Amy. "Ruth Bader Ginsburg's Retirement Dissent." *New Yorker.* Web. Sept. 24, 2014.

Enda, Jodi. "Three Audacious Women Before Audacious Was In." *Washington Post.* Web. Feb. 26, 2015.

Freeman, Jo, ed. "The Revolution for Women in Law and Public Policy." *Women: A Feminist Perspective.* Mountain View, California: Mayfield Publishing Company, 1995. 365–404. Print.

Gertner, Nancy. *In Defense of Women; Memoirs of an Unrepentant Advocate.* Boston: Beacon Press, 2012. Print.

Glynn, Adam N. and Maya Sen. "Identifying Judicial Empathy: Does Having Daughters Cause Judges to Rule for Women's Issues?" *American Journal of Political Science* 59, no. 1 (January 2015): 37–54. doi: 10.1111/ajps.12118.

"A Good Compromise on Contraception." *New York Times.* Web. Feb. 1, 2013.

"The History of Divorce Law in the USA." *History Cooperative.* Web. May 29, 2014.

Lewis, Neil A. "Debate on Whether Female Judges Decide Differently Arises Anew." *New York Times.* Web. June 3, 2009.

Liptak, Adam. "Justices' Rulings Advance Gays; Women Less So." *New York Times.* Web. Aug. 4, 2014.

Liptak, Adam. "Supreme Courts Says Child's Rights Violated by Strip Search." *New York Times.* Web. June 25, 2009.

Lithwick, Dahlia. "The Fairer Sex." *Slate.* Web. April 11, 2009.

Miller, Colin. "As Judge Nancy Gertner Retires, We Lose One of Our Greatest Judges but Gain One of Her Greatest Opinions." *Feminist Law Professors.* Web. May 14, 2011.

National Women's Law Center. *Women in the Federal Judiciary: Still a Long Way to Go—Fact Sheet.* Web. Aug. 4, 2015.

Oh, Inae. "Ruth Bader Ginsburg Shuts Down Gay-Marriage Challengers." *Mother Jones.* Web.

April 29, 2015.

Peresie, Jennifer L. "Female Judges Matter: Gender and Collegial Decisionmaking in the Federal Appellate Courts." *Yale Law Journal* 114, no. 7 (May 2005): 1759–1790. Print.

Rosen, Jeffrey. "Ruth Bader Ginsburg Is an American Hero." *New Republic*. Web. Sept. 28, 2014.

Toobin, Jeffrey. "The Obama Brief: The President Considers His Judicial Legacy." *New Yorker*. Web. Oct. 27, 2014.

Torres-Spelliscy, Ciara, Monique Chase, Emma Greenman and Susan M. Liss. *Improving Judicial Diversity*. Rep. Brennan Center for Justice at New York University School of Law. Web. March 3, 2010.

Turnage, James. "Ruth Bader Ginsburg on the Future of the Supreme Court." *Public Slate*. Web. Oct. 20, 2014.

Wald, Patricia M. "Six Not-So-Easy Pieces: One Woman Judge's Journey to the Bench and Beyond." *University of Toledo Law Review* 36, no. 4 (Summer 2005): 979–988. Print.

Wallen, Hannah. "Gender Disparity in Criminal Courts." *A Voice for Men*. Web. July 29, 2013.

Weisberg, Jessica. "Supreme Court Justice Ruth Bader Ginsburg: 'I'm Not Going Anywhere.' " *Elle* magazine. Web. Sept. 23, 2014.

Chapter 6: Public vs. Private

INTERVIEWS: ERIE MEYER, TODD PARK, NICK SINAI, SHELLEY MOORE CAPITO, MAGGIE HASSAN, AMY SCHULMAN, BETH BROOKE-MARCINIAK, KAREN MILLS, TORIE CLARKE, SUSAN STAUTBERG, GIA COLOSI, DARCY HOWE, HENRIETTA FORE, DAVIA TEMIN, LYNN SCHENK AND MINDY MEADS.

Alter, Charlotte. "IMF Chief Christine Lagarde: Female Equality Laws Are Good for the Economy." *Time*. Web. Feb. 24, 2015.

American Express OPEN. *The 2014 State of Women-Owned Businesses Report*. Womenable. Web. Spring 2014.

Beede, David, Tiffany Julian, David Langdon, George McKittrick, Beethika Khan and Mark Doms. *Women in STEM: A Gender Gap to Innovation*. Rep. U.S. Department of Commerce/ Economics and Statistics Administration. Web. August 2011.

Beninger, Anna. *High Potentials on Tech-Intensive Industries: The Gender Divide in Business Roles*. Rep. Catalyst Research. Web. 2014.

Booth, Alison L. and Patrick Nolen. "Gender Differences in Risk Behaviour: Does Nurture Matter?" *Economic Journal* 122, no. 558 (February 2012): 56–78. doi: 10.1111/j.1468-0297.2011.02480.x.

Brooke-Marciniak, Beth. "What's the Difference?" *Huffington Post*. Web. Jan. 28, 2011.

Broome, Lissa Lamkin, John M. Conley and Kimberly D. Krawiec. "Does Critical Mass Matter? Views from the Boardroom." *Seattle University Law Review* 34, no. 1 (June 3, 2011): 1049–1080. SSRN-id2383511.

Burleigh, Nina. "What Silicon Valley Thinks of Women." *Newsweek*. Web. Jan. 28, 2015.

Campbell, Beatrix. "Why We Need a New Women's Revolution." *The Guardian*. Web. May 25, 2014.

Carter, Nancy M., Lois Joy, Harvey M. Wagner and Sriram Narayanan. *The Bottom Line: Corporate Performance and Women's Representation on Boards*. Rep. Catalyst Research. Web. Oct. 15, 2007.

Clark, Dorie. "Why So Few Women and Minorities at the Top? Here's the Real Reason." *Forbes*. Web. Sept. 3, 2013.

Colivariti, Tammie. "Women, IT & the Outrage Machine." *Information Week*. Web. Feb. 20, 2014.

Committee for Economic Development. *Every Other One: More Women on Corporate Boards*. Rep. Washington: November 2014. Print.

Committee for Economic Development. *Fulfilling the Promise: How More Women on Corporate Boards Would Make America and American Companies More Competitive*. Rep. Washington: 2012. Print.

Covert, Bryce. "It's Time to Fix the Very Pale, Very Male Boardroom." *New Republic*. Web. July 9, 2014.

Croson, Rachel and Uri Gneezy. "Gender Differences in Preferences." *Journal of Economic Literature* 47, no. 2 (2009): 448–474. doi: 10.1257/jel.47.2.448.

Dillard, Sarah and Vanessa Lipschitz. "Research: How Female CEOs Actually Get to the Top." Rep. *Harvard Business Review*. Web. Nov. 6, 2014.

European Commission. *Women on Boards—Factsheet 3: Legal Aspects*. Rep. European Institute for Gender Equality. Web. 2012.

Fairchild, Caroline. "Women CEOs in the *Fortune* 1000: By the Numbers." *Fortune*. Web. July 8, 2014.

Flynn, Daniel. "France Sets Quota for Women on Big Companies' Boards." *Reuters*. Web. Jan. 13, 2011.

Full- and Part-Time Legislators. Rep. National Conference of State Legislators. Web. June 1, 2014.

Griswold, Alison. "When It Comes to Diversity in Tech, Companies Find Safety in Numbers." *Slate*. Web. Jun. 27, 2014.

Heller, Laura. "Why Aren't There More Powerful Women in Retail?" *Forbes*. Web. May 31, 2013.

Hill, Catherine, Christianne Corbett and Andresse St. Rose. *Why So Few? Women in Science, Technology, Engineering, and Mathematics*. American Association of University Women. Web. February 2010.

Kanter, Rosabeth Moss. "Some Effects of Proportions on Group Life: Skewed Sex Ratios and Responses to Token Women." *American Journal of Sociology* 82, no. 5 (March 1, 1977): 965–990. Print.

Kantor, Jodi. "A Brand New World in Which Men Ruled." *New York Times*. Web. Dec. 23, 2014.

Kantor, Jodi. "Harvard Business School Case Study: Gender Equity." *New York Times*. Web. Sept. 7, 2013.

Koplovitz, Kay. "Money Talks: Women's Buying Power Starts to Reflect in the Boardroom." *Huffington Post*. Web. Nov. 13, 2013.

Kramer, Vicki W., Alison M. Konrad and Sumru Erkut. *Critical Mass on Corporate Boards: Why Three or More Women Enhance Governance*. Wellesley Centers for Women. Web. 2006.

Mick, Jason. "Uber Exec Threatens to 'Spend Millions' to Stalk Female Reporter and Her Family." *Daily Tech*. Web. Nov. 19, 2014.

Murray, Sarah. "MBA Teaching Urged to Move Away from Focus on Shareholder Primacy Model." *Financial Times*. Web. July 7, 2013.

Nisen, Max. "18 Tech Founders That Bust the Myth of 35 Being 'Over the Hill' in Silicon Valley." *Business Insider*. Web. Oct. 10, 2013.

Petrecca, Laura. "Number of Female 'Fortune' 500 CEOs at Record High." *USA Today*. Web. Oct. 26, 2011.

Planchard, Marie. "The Shortage of Women in STEM Explained." *Fast Company*. Web. Oct. 28, 2014.

Pollack, Eileen. "Why Are There Still So Few Women in Science?" *New York Times*. Web. Oct. 3, 2013.

Sellers, Patricia. "The New Valley Girls." *Fortune*. Web. Jan. 26, 2009.

Sherwin, Bob. "Why Women Are More Effective Leaders Than Men." *Business Insider*. Web. Jan. 24, 2014.

Smale, Alison and Claire Cain Miller. "Germany Sets Gender Quota in Boardrooms." *New York Times*. Web. March 6, 2015.

Soper, Sarah Clatterbuck. "What It's Like As a 'Girl' in the Lab." *New York Times*. Web. June 18, 2015.

Sweeney, Brigid. "Can This Woman Save Sears?" *Chicago Business*. Web. Jul. 13, 2013.

Thorpe, Nicholas. "Retales™: Retailers Set Targets for Women on Boards." *Fieldfisher*. Web. Aug. 2, 2011.

Wallace, Kelly. "No Movement for Women at the Top in Corporate America." *CNN*. Web. Dec. 11, 2013.

Warner, Judith. *The Women's Leadership Gap*. Rep. Center for American Progress. Web. March 7, 2012.

Weiner, Joann. "Diversity Is Good. Why Doesn't Everyone Agree?" *Washington Post*. Web. Nov. 26, 2014.

Women and Girls in Science, Technology, Engineering, and Math (STEM). Rep. Executive Office of the President. Web. June 2013.

Chapter 7: Lehman Sisters

INTERVIEWS: ELIZABETH WARREN, SHEILA BAIR, MARY SCHAPIRO, TERRELL MCSWEENY, MAUREEN K. OHLHAUSEN AND EDITH RAMIREZ.

Adams, Renee B. and Vanitha Ragunathan. *Lehman Sisters*. FIRN Research Paper (Aug. 1, 2015). doi.org/10.2139/ssrn.2380036.

Alden, William. "Scrutiny Falls on a Pioneer at JP Morgan." *New York Times*. Web. May 3, 2013.

Antilla, Susan. "Can Goldman Sachs' Women Make the Cut in 'Extreme Jobs?' " *The Street*. Web. Aug. 18, 2014.

Antilla, Susan. "Goldman Women Say They Make Less Than Men Who Frequent Strip Clubs, Call Them 'Bimbos.' " *The Street*. Web. July 2, 2014.

Bair, Sheila. *Bull by the Horns: Fighting to Save Main Street from Wall Street and Wall Street from Itself*. New York: Free Press/Simon and Schuster, 2012.

Bansal, Paritosh and Megan Davies. "M&A Still Overwhelmingly a Man's Game." *Reuters*. Web. April 12, 2011.

Beckmann, Daniela and Lukas Menkhoff. "Will Women Be Women? Analyzing the Gender Difference Among Financial Experts." *Kyklos* 61, no. 3 (Aug. 2008): 364–384. doi.org/10.1111/j.1467-6435.2008.00406.x.

Bigelow, Lyda S., Leif Lundmark, Judi McLean Parks and Robert Wuebker. "Skirting the Issues? Experimental Evidence of Gender Bias in IPO Prospectus Evaluations." *Journal of Management* 40, no. 6 (September 2014): 1732–1759. doi: 10.1177/0149206312441624.

Buchanan, Mark. "In Traders' Spit, Evidence of an Irrational Wall Street." *Bloomberg View*. Web. June 11, 2012.

Buchanan, Mark. "What Traders' Testosterone Tells Us About Markets." *Bloomberg View*. Web. June 10, 2012.

Calabresi, Massimo. "Why the Banks Should Fear Mary Jo White." *Time*. Web. Jan. 25, 2013.

Carney, John. "The Warning: Brooksley Born's Battle with Alan Greenspan, Robert Rubin, and Larry Summers." *Business Insider*. Web. Oct. 21, 2009.

Clark, Andrew. "Lehman Brothers' Golden Girl, Erin Callan: Through the Glass Ceiling—and Off the Glass Cliff." *The Guardian*. Web. March 19, 2010.

Coates, John. *The Hour Between Dog and Wolf: Risk Taking, Gut Feelings and the Biology of Boom and Bust*. New York: Penguin, 2012. Print.

Cook, Alison and Christy Glass. "Above the Glass Ceiling: When Are Women and Racial/Ethnic Minorities Promoted to CEO?" *Strategic Management Journal* 35, no. 7 (July 2014): 1080–1089. doi: 10.1002/smj.2161.

Craig, Susanne. "Lehman's Straight Shooter: Finance Chief Callan Brings Cool Jolt of Confidence to Credit-Rattled Street." *Wall Street Journal*. Web. May 17, 2008.

Croson, Rachel and Uri Gneezy. "Gender Differences in Preferences." *Journal of Economic Literature* 47, no. 2 (2009): 448–474. doi: 10.1257/jel.47.2.448.

Enrich, David and Deborah Solomon. "Citi, U.S. Reach Accord on a Third Bailout." *Wall Street Journal*. Web. Feb. 28, 2009.

"Full Story of Brooksley Born's Attempts to Regulate the Derivatives Market." *Silver Doctors*. Web. Oct. 20, 2012.

Khimm, Suzy. "Citigroup Pays Up for the Financial Crisis." *MSNBC*. Web. July 14, 2014.

Kolhatkar, Sheelah. "What If Women Ran Wall Street?" *New York* magazine. Web. March 21, 2010.

Kray, Laura J. and Michael P. Haselhuhn. *Male Pragmatism in Ethical Decision Making*. IRLE working paper no. 101-11. University of California, Berkeley, March 2011. Print.

"Lagarde: What If It Had Been Lehman Sisters?" *New York Times*. Web. May 11, 2010.

Leung, Shirley. "Why Do Female CEOs Get Fired More Often Than Male Ones? The Answer May Lie in a Term You've Never Heard: The Glass Cliff." *Boston Globe Magazine*. Web. Oct. 22, 2014.

Liu, Henry C.K. "Financial Reform Warrior Brooksley Born Warns of More Crises to Come." *Roosevelt Institute*. Web. Nov. 24, 2009.

Loosvelt, Derek. "There Are Few Women on Wall Street Because There Are Too Many Weiners." *Vault*. Web. June 8, 2011.

Mattera, Philip. *Citigroup: Corporate Rap Sheet.* Corporate Research Project. Web. July 27, 2015.

McAlvanah, Patrick. "Are People More Risk-Taking in the Presence of the Opposite Sex?" *Journal of Economic Psychology* 30, no. 2 (April 2009): 136–146. doi:10.1016/j.joep.2008.10.002.

McCullough, DG. "Women CEOs: Why Companies in Crisis Hire Minorities—and Then Fire Them." *The Guardian*. Web. Aug. 8, 2014.

Meserve, Myles. "The 'Bros' at Lehman Brothers: Where Are They Now?" *Business Insider*. Web. Aug. 2, 2012.

Morris, Nigel. "Harriet Harman: 'If Only It Had Been Lehman Sisters.' " *The Independent*. Web. Aug. 4, 2009.

Nelson, Julie A. *Would Women Leaders Have Prevented the Global Financial Crisis? Implications for Teaching About Gender, Behavior, and Economics.* Working paper no. 11-03, Global Development and Environment Institute, September 2012. Print.

Nocera, Joe. "Sheila Bair's Bank Shot." *New York Times Magazine*. Web. July 9, 2011.

Orr, Judith. "Lehman Sisters?" *Socialist Review*. Web. March 2009.

Palvia, Ajay A., Emilia Vähämaa, and Sami Vähämaa. "Are Female CEOs and Chairwomen More Conservative and Risk Averse? Evidence from the Banking Industry During the Financial Crisis." *Journal of Business Ethics* (July 5, 2014): 1–18. doi: 10.1007/s10551-014-2288-3.

Roig-Franzia, Manuel. "Brooksley Born, the Cassandra of the Derivatives Crisis." *Washington Post*. Web. May 26, 2009.

Ryan, Michelle K. and S. Alexander Haslam. "The Glass Cliff: Evidence That Women Are Over-Represented in Precarious Leadership Positions." *British Journal of Management* 16, no. 2 (June 2005): 81–99. doi: 10.1111/j.1467-8551.2005.00433.x.

Scherer, Michael. "The New Sheriffs of Wall Street." *Time*. Web. May 13, 2010.

Silver-Greenberg, Jessica. "Commodity Chief Blythe Masters to Leave JPMorgan Chase." *New York Times*. Web. April 2, 2014.

Singh Das, Aman. "Gender vs. Pay: 10 Worst Industries for Women." *Vault Blogs*. Web. April 18, 2011.

Steinberg, Julie. "Heidi Miller: Women on Wall Street Need to Ask for More." *Wall Street Journal*. Web. Sept. 25, 2012.

Stock, Kyle. "Ranks of Women on Wall Street Thin." *Wall Street Journal*. Web. Sept. 20, 2010.

Sunderland, Ruth. "After the Crash, Iceland's Women Lead the Rescue." *The Guardian*. Web. Feb. 21, 2009.

Suskind, Ron. *Confidence Men: Wall Street, Washington, and the Education of a President.* New York: HarperCollins, 2011. Print.

Teather, David. "The Woman Who Built Financial 'Weapon of Mass Destruction.'" *The Guardian*. Sept. 29, 2008.

Torregrosa, Luisita Lopez. "On Wall St., Gender Bias Runs Deep." *New York Times*. Web. July 24, 2012.

Van Staveren, Irene. "The Lehman Sisters Hypothesis." *Cambridge Journal of Economics* 38, no. 5 (2014): 995–1014. doi: 10.1093/cje/beu010.

Viser, Matt. "Geithner Book Details Turmoil with Warren." *Boston Globe*. Web. May 12, 2014.

Walsh, Tom. "Matt Lauer Takes Dopey Route with Mom Questions to Barra." *Detroit Free Press*. Web. June 26, 2014.

"The Weaker Sex: Boys Are Being Outclassed by Girls at Both School and University, and the Gap Is Widening." *Economist*. Web. March 7, 2015.

"Women in Investment Banking: Why Such a Big I-Banking Gender Gap?" *NerdWallet*. Web. Jan. 28, 2013.

Worstall, Tim. "Of Course the Crisis Would Have Been Different If Lehman Brothers Had Been Lehman Sisters." *Forbes.* Web. March 29, 2014.

Zawadzki, Sabina. "Iceland Prepares to Come in from the Financial Cold." *Reuters.* Web. April 2, 2015.

Chapter 8: Law Enforcement

INTERVIEWS: JANET NAPOLITANO, ANNISE PARKER AND NAN WHALEY.

Adams, Kim. *Women in Senior Police Management.* Rep. Australasian Centre for Policing Research. Web. 2001.

Alpert, Geoffrey P., Michael R. Smith, Robert J. Kaminski, Lorie A. Fridell, John MacDonald and Bruce Kubu. *Police Use of Force, Tasers and Other Less-Lethal Weapons.* Rep. National Institute of Justice. Web. May 2011.

Associated Press. "Fifteen-Day Arizona Prison Standoff Ends." *Fox News.* Web. Feb. 2, 2004.

Brereton, David. *Do Women Police Differently? Implications for Police-Community Relations.* Australian Institute of Criminology. Web. n.d.

DeBonis, Mike. "D.C. Police Chief Cathy Lanier: 'I Wouldn't Bring an Armored Personnel Carrier Out . . . for a Protest.' " *Washington Post.* Web. Aug. 27, 2014.

Durose, Matthew R., Caroline Wolf Harlow, Patrick A. Langan, Mark Motivans, Ramona R. Rantala and Erica L. Smith. *Family Violence Statistics Including Statistics on Strangers and Acquaintances.* Rep. Bureau of Justice Statistics. Web. June 2005.

Epler, Patti and Bruce Rushton. "Where's Dora?" *Riverfront Times.* Web. Feb. 18, 2004.

Fenton, Justin. "Police Union Wants Rawlings-Blake Investigated Too." *Baltimore Sun.* Web. May 8, 2015.

Horne, Peter. "Policewomen: Their First Century and the New Era." *Police Chief* magazine. Web. Sept. 2006.

International Association of Chiefs of Police. *The Future of Women in Policing: Mandates for Action.* Rep. Web. November 1998.

Kipnis, Laura. "Why Ferguson Is Also About Gender, Not Just Race." *Time.* Web. Nov. 26, 2014.

Martin, Susan E. "The Effectiveness of Affirmative Action: The Case of Women in Policing." *Justice Quarterly* 8, no. 4 (1991): 489–504. doi:10.1080/07418829100091181.

Martin, Susan E. and Nancy C. Jurik. *Doing Justice, Doing Gender: Women in Law and Criminal Justice Occupations,* 2nd ed. Thousand Oaks, California: SAGE Publications, 2006.

Miller, Michael E. *Examining the Effect of Organizational Policy Change on Taser Utilizations.* Diss. Orlando: University of Central Florida, 2008.

Miller, Jayne. "Baltimore Mayor Stephanie Rawlings-Blake Faces Questions About Her Leadership." *WBAL TV.* Web. May 27, 2015.

Mroz, Jacqueline. "Female Police Chiefs, a Novelty No More." *New York Times.* Web. April 6, 2008.

"Myths and Facts About Women and Policing." *Charlotte Mecklenburg Police Department.* Web. n.d.

National Center for Women and Policing. *Equality Denied: The Status of Women in Policing 2000.* Rep. Women and Policing. Web. April 2001.

National Center for Women and Policing. *Men, Women and Police Excessive Force: A Tale of Two Genders.* Rep. Women and Policing. Web. April 2002.

Price, Barbara Raffel. "Female Police Officers in the United States." *Policing in Central and Eastern Europe: Comparing Firsthand Knowledge with Experience from the West.* Milan Pagon, ed. Ljubljana, Slovenia: College of Police and Security Studies, 1996. Print.

"Read About Women in Law Enforcement." *All Criminal Justice Schools.* Web. n.d.

Ruble, Kayla. "Baltimore Mayor Wants Federal Investigation into Police Abuse in the City." *Vice.* Web. May 6, 2015.

Rushton, Bruce. "Dora's Darlings." *Phoenix New Times*. Web. June 3, 2004.

Sanburn, Josh. "Baltimore Mayor Defends Handling of Riots." *Time*. Web. April 28, 2015.

Spillar, Katherine. "How More Female Police Officers Would Help Stop Police Brutality." *Washington Post*. Web. July 2, 2015.

"FBI Called 'Great Career Choice': Three Female Special Agents Share Their Stories." *Federal Bureau of Investigation*. Web. April 9, 2010.

Wagner, Dennis. "How 2 Inmates Took Hostages, Captured Tower." *Arizona Republic*. Web. Feb. 12, 2004.

Wihbey, John and Leighton Walter Kille. "Excessive or Reasonable Force by Police? Research on Law Enforcement and Racial Conflict." *Journalist's Resource*. Web. July 1, 2015.

Williams, Brandt. "Women's Advocates Say Police Should Hire More Female Officers." *MPR News*. Web. Dec. 14, 2014.

Williams, Clarence; "D.C. Police Chief Cathy L. Lanier Urges Empathy in Policing." *Washington Post*. Web. March 25, 2015.

Worden, Robert E. "The Causes of Police Brutality: Theory and Evidence on Police Use of Force." *And Justice for All: Understanding and Controlling Police Abuse of Force*. William A. Geller and Hans Toch, eds. Washington, D.C.: Police Executive Research Forum, 1995: 31–60.

Chapter 9: The Military

INTERVIEWS: DARLENE ISKRA, JANET WOLFENBARGER, TULSI GABBARD, JONI ERNST, MICHÈLE FLOURNOY, KIRSTEN GILLIBRAND, CLAIRE MCCASKILL, JEREMY BASH AND ANNIE KLEIMAN.

"Air Force Personnel Center—Air Force Personnel Demographics." *Air Force Personnel Center/ Air Force Personnel Demographics*. Web. June 30, 2015.

Callahan, Sheree. "Navy Celebrates 25 Years of Women at Sea." *Military Sealift Command*. Web. December 2003.

Clark, Meredith. "Gillibrand's Tireless Fight Against Military Sex Assault." *MSNBC*. Web. Jan. 26, 2014.

Department of Defense. *2013 Demographics Profile of the Military Community*. Rep. Web. 2014.

Dooley, Erin. "Meet the U.S. Military's Three Four-Star Women." *ABC News*. Web. July 2, 2014.

Iskra, Darlene. *Breaking Through the 'Brass' Ceiling: Elite Military Women's Strategies for Success*. Diss. Web. College Park: University of Maryland, 2007.

Jennings, Erin. "Officer and a Gentlewoman: Darlene Iskra Made History As First Female Commander of a U.S. Navy Ship." *North Kitsap Herald*. Web. March 18, 2011.

Kageyama, Yuri and Richard Lardner. "Documents: Judgments Random in Military Sex-Crimes." *Associated Press*. Web. Feb. 10, 2014.

Leed, Maren. "Will Infantry Men Accept Women As Peers?" *CNN*. Web. Jan. 26, 2013.

Lemmon, Gayle Tzemach and Kevin Baron. "Meet the Women Who Survived Army's Ranger School." *Defense One*. Web. Aug. 19, 2015.

McDermott, Jennifer. "Navy to Gauge Interest Among Female Sailors in Serving on Subs." *The Day*. Web. Feb. 25, 2014.

Phillips, Dave. "Marine Commander's Firing Stirs Debate on Integration of Women in Corps." *New York Times*. Web. July 12, 2015.

Putko, Michele M. and Douglas V. Johnson II. "Women in Combat Compendium." *Strategic Studies Institute*. Web. January 2008.

Shapira, Ian. "For CIA Family, A Deadly Suicide Bombing Leads to Painful Divisions." *Washington Post*. Web. Jan. 28, 2012.

Thomas, Patricia J. *Women in the Military: Gender Integration at Sea*. Rep. Defense Technical Information Center. Web. May 1981.

Thompson, Mark. "The Woman Is in Command." *Chicago Tribune*. Web. Nov. 9, 1992.

Thompson, Mark. "Female Generals: The Pentagon's First Pair of Four-Star Women." *Time*. Web. Aug. 13, 2012.

Thompson, Mark. "Navy Names First 4-Star Admiral." *Time*. Web. Dec. 13, 2013.

Tritten, Travis J. "Air Force Songbook Again Cited, This Time in Sex Assault Lawsuit." *Stars and Stripes*. Web. March 31, 2015.

Voorhees, Josh. "The U.S. Could Have Its First Female Navy SEALs by 2016." *Slate*. Web. June 18, 2013.

Yuhas, Alan. "US Navy Seals Plan to Accept Women After Female Soldiers Graduate As Rangers." *The Guardian*. Web. Aug. 19, 2015.

Chapter 10: Electoral Challenges

INTERVIEWS: CATHY MCMORRIS RODGERS, DEB FISCHER, KELLY AYOTTE, CARLY FIORINA, DANA PERINO, ELAINE CHAO, ILEANA ROS-LEHTINEN, SUSAN MOLINARI, KELLYANNE CONWAY, S.E. CUPP, KATIE PACKER GAGE, KRISTI NOEM, MARILINDA GARCIA, SWANEE HUNT, MARSHA BLACKBURN, MARTHA ROBY, SARAH CHAMBERLAIN, MARJORIE DANNENFELSER, CHRISTINE TERRETTI AND STEPHANIE SCHRIOCK.

Bassett, Laura. "Senate Republicans Propose Stripped-Down Equal Pay Bill." *Huffington Post*. Web. April 14, 2015.

Borger, Gloria. "Donald Trump Loves Women but Do They Love Him?" *CNN*. Web. Aug. 8, 2015.

Brennan, Christopher. "Trump Stays in the Lead in First Post-Debate Fox Poll As He Boasts He'll Spend $1 BILLION of His Own Money to be the Next President." *Daily Mail*. Web. Aug. 16, 2015.

Bresnahan, John and Anna Palmer. "GOP Men Told How to Talk to Women." *Politico*. Web. Dec. 5, 2013.

Carmon, Irin. "How the Women's Vote Failed to Save the Democrats." *MSNBC*. Web. Nov. 7, 2014.

Chinni, Dante. "Women Are Not a Unified Voting Bloc." *The Atlantic*. Web. Nov. 9, 2014.

Clift, Eleanor. "The Republican War on Women Continues, Just More Quietly." *Newsweek*. Web. Oct. 13, 2014.

Denver Post Editorial Board. "Cory Gardner for U.S. Senate." *Denver Post*. Web. Oct. 10, 2014.

Fox, Lauren and Daniel Newhauser. "How the House GOP's Abortion Bill Fell Apart." *National Journal*. Web. Jan. 23, 2015.

Fuller, Jaime. "Women Are Winning Senate Primaries This Year—but Not Many of Them Are Running." *Washington Post*. Web. May 22, 2014.

Garber, Kent. "Behind Obama's Victory: Women Open Up a Record Marriage Gap." *US News*. Web. Nov. 5, 2008.

Goldfarb, Zachary A. "Democrats Target Unmarried Female Voters." *Washington Post*. Web. April 2, 2014.

Goldfarb, Zachary A. and Juliet Eilperin. "Child-Care Issues Move to Political Forefront As Both Parties Position for Midterms." *Washington Post*. Web. June 23, 2014.

Green, Stephanie. "Republican Women Challenging Gender Gap: 2014, 2016 Targeted." *Bloomberg News*. Web. Jan. 15, 2014.

Hafner, Josh. "Trump Riffs on Policy, Slams Hilary Clinton in Iowa." *Des Moines Register*. Web. June 17, 2015.

Healy, Patrick and Jeremy W. Peters. "Fear That Debate Could Hurt G.O.P. in Women's Eyes." *New York Times*. Web. Aug. 7, 2015.

Hunt, Darnell. *The 2014 Hollywood Writers Report: Turning Missed Opportunities into Realized Ones*. Rep. Writers Guild of America West. Web. July 2014.

Hunter, Kathleen. "Paycheck Issues Top Senate Agenda in Bid for Women's Vote." *Bloomberg News.* Web. April 4, 2014.

Jones, Jeffrey M. "Gender Gap in 2012 Vote Is Largest in Gallup's History." *Gallup.* Web. Nov. 9, 2012.

Kucinich, Jackie. "Fiorina to Head New PAC Aimed at Recruiting More Women to the GOP." *Washington Post.* Web. June 30, 2014.

Lake, Celinda, Kellyanne Conway and Catherine Whitney. *What Women Really Want: How American Women Are Quietly Erasing Political, Racial, Class, and Religious Lines to Change the Way We Live.* New York: Free Press/Simon and Schuster, 2005. Print.

Martin, Jonathan. "Glass Ceilings in Statehouses in the Northeast." *New York Times.* Web. May 18, 2014.

Milbank, Dana. "Conservatives to Women: Lean Back." *Washington Post.* Web. March 31, 2014.

Mundy, Liza. "100 Women in Congress? So What." *Politico.* Web. Nov. 6, 2014.

Paulson, Amanda. "In Colorado Race, Mark Udall Painted Cory Gardner as Anti-Woman. Did It Backfire?" *Christian Science Monitor.* Web. Oct. 22, 2014.

Political Parity. *Shifting Gears: How Women Navigate the Road to Higher Office.* Rep. May 27, 2014.

Political Parity. *3:1: Right the Ratio.* Rep. Web. January 2015.

Rich, Frank. "Stag Party: The GOP's Woman Problem Is That It Has a Serious Problem with Women." *New York* magazine. Web. March 25, 2012.

Chapter 11: Cultural Challenges

INTERVIEWS: MADELINE DI NONNO, NINA JACOBSON, JENNIFER SIEBEL NEWSOM AND DEBBIE SOON.

Alfonsi, Sharyn and Claire Pederson. "Is Dad the New Mom? The Rise of Stay-at-Home Fathers." *ABC News.* Web. Jun. 18, 2012.

American College of Surgeons Health Policy Research Institute. *The Surgical Workforce in the United States: Profile and Recent Trends.* Rep. Web. April 2010.

Appelbaum, Eileen, Heather Boushey and John Schmitt. "The Economic Importance of Women's Rising Hours of Work." *American Progress.* Web. Apr. 15, 2014.

Belkin, Lisa. "Calling Mr. Mom." *New York Times Magazine.* Web. Oct. 21, 2010.

Bureau of Labor Statistics. *Women in the Labor Force: A Databook.* BLS Reports. Web. May 2014.

Bureau of Labor Statistics, U.S. Department of Labor. *Changes in Men's and Women's Labor Force Participation Rates.* Rep. BLS Reports. Web. Jan. 10, 2007.

Butler, Karen. "Lilly Explains Why 'Smaug' Needed a New Female Elf Character." *United Press International.* Web. Dec. 31, 2013.

Callan, Erin. "Is There Life After Work?" *New York Times.* Web. March 9, 2013.

Chemaly, Soraya. "10 Words Every Girl Should Learn." *Huffington Post.* Web. June 30, 2014.

Council of Economic Advisers. *The Economics of Fatherhood and Work.* Rep. White House. Web. June 9, 2014.

Council of Economic Advisers. *15 Economic Facts About Millennials.* White House. Web. October 2014.

Dawes, Amy. "Women's Movement?" *Directors Guild of America.* Web. Summer 2014.

DeWan, Shaila and Robert Gebeloff. "More Men Enter Fields Dominated by Women." *New York Times.* Web. May 20, 2012.

"DGA Five-Year Study of First-Time Directors in Episodic Television Shows Women and Minority Directors Face Significant Hiring Disadvantage at Entry Level." *Directors Guild of America.* Web. Jan. 8, 2015.

Dickler, Jessica. "Stay-at-Home Dads: More Men Choosing Kids Over Career." *CNN Money.* Web. April 30, 2012.

Dockterman, Eliana. "Lena Dunham Has a Point: New Research Documents Hollywood's Sexism." *Time*. Web. March 11, 2014.

Drexler, Peggy. "Don't Call Him Mr. Mom: The Rise/Reign of the Stay-at-Home Dad." *Huffington Post*. Web. June 6, 2012.

Drexler, Peggy. "Our Gender, Ourselves: The Changing American Family." *Psychology Today*. Web. n.d.

Furman, Jason and Betsy Stevenson. "The Changing Role of Fathers in the Workforce and Family." *White House*. Web. June 9, 2014.

Goudreau, Jenna. "A New Obstacle for Professional Women: The Glass Escalator." *Forbes*. Web. May 21, 2012.

Grow, Kory. "SNL Hires Sasheer Zamata, First Black Female Member in Years." *Rolling Stone*. Web. Jan. 6, 2014.

Hais, Michael D. and Morley Winograd. "Race? No, Millennials Care Most About Gender Equality." *National Journal*. Web. Oct. 25, 2013.

Hare, Breeanna. "Once More, with Feeling: Where Are the Women in Late-Night TV?" *CNN*. Web. April 10, 2013.

Howe, Neil and William Strauss. *Millennials Rising: The Next Greatest Generation*. New York: Vintage, 2000. Print.

Kearney, Melissa S. and Lesley Turner. "Giving Secondary Earners a Tax Break: A Proposal to Help Low- and Middle-Income Families." *Brookings*. Web. Dec. 4, 2013.

Kesler, Jennifer. "If Audiences Don't Want Women As Leads, Why Did *Aliens* Succeed?" *The Hathor Legacy*. Web. Jan. 5, 2011.

Killewald, Alexandra. "A Reconsideration of the Fatherhood Premium: Marriage, Coresidence, Biology, and Fathers' Wages." *American Sociological Review* 78, no. 1 (February 2013): 96–116. doi: 10.1177/0003122412469204.

Killewald, Alexandra and Margaret Gough. "Money Isn't Everything: Wives' Earnings and Housework Time." *Social Science Research* 39, no. 6 (November 2010): 987–1003. doi: 10.1016/j.ssresearch.2010.08.005.

Killewald, Alexandra, and Margaret Gough. "Does Specialization Explain Marriage Penalties and Premiums?" *American Sociological Review* 78, no. 3 (June 2013): 477–502. doi: 10.1177/0003122413484151.

Kutner, Jenny. "A Majority of Americans Support Gender Equality—So Why Don't They Identify As Feminists?" *Salon*. Web. April 29, 2015.

Lawless, Jennifer L. and Richard L. Fox. *Girls Just Wanna Not Run: The Gender Gap in Young Americans' Political Ambition*. Rep. American University School of Public Affairs. Web. March 2013.

Madland, David and Ruy Teixeira. "New Progressive America: The Millennial Generation." Center for American Progress. Web. May 13, 2009.

Marcotte, Amanda. "Even When They Don't Have Jobs, Men Do Less Housework Than Women." *Slate*. Web. Jan. 6, 2015.

Marcotte, Amanda. "Michael Eisner's Comment That Beautiful Women Aren't Funny Says More About Eisner Than Women." *Slate*. Web. July 6, 2015.

Martosko, David and Wills Robinson. "Donald's New Woman Trouble: Trump Refuses to Back Down Over 'Look at That Face' Attack on Carly Fiorina—and Claims it Was a 'Jocular' Remark About 'Her Persona.' " *Daily Mail*. Web. Sept. 10, 2015.

"Michael Eisner Clarifies 'Beautiful, Funny Women' Comment: They're 'Hard to Come By in Hollywood.' " *Hollywood Reporter*. Web. July 6, 2015.

Millennials at Work: Perspectives of a New Generation. Rep. PriceWaterhouse Coopers. Web. 2008.

Millennials at Work: Reshaping the Workforce. Rep. PriceWaterhouse Coopers. Web. 2011.

O'Keefe, Meghan. "Heroine Chic: 10 Essential Female-Led Action Movies." *Decider*. Web. Nov. 19, 2014.

"On Pay Gap, Millennial Women Near Parity—for Now." *Pew Research Center*. Web. Dec. 11, 2013.

PwC's NextGen: A Global Generational Study. Rep. PriceWaterhouse Coopers. Web. 2013.

Robb, David. "Martha Coolidge: Blaming DGA for Lack of Female Directors Is 'Dangerous Side-Path.' " *Deadline Hollywood*. Web. May 22, 2015.

Rovner, Julie. "Even in Nursing, Men Earn More Than Women." NPR. Web. March 24, 2015.

Sager, Jeanne. "10 of the Best Dad Bloggers Out There: Read 'Em & Weep (or Laugh)." *The Stir*. Web. June 13, 2013.

Sandberg, Sheryl. *Lean In: Women, Work, and the Will to Lead*. New York: Knopf, 2013. Print.

Sifferlin, Alexandra. "Women Are Still Doing Most of the Housework." *Time*. Web. June 18, 2014.

Slaughter, Anne-Marie. "Why Women Still Can't Have It All." *Atlantic*. Web. July/August 2012.

Smith, Stacey L., Marc Choueiti and Katherine Pieper. *Gender Bias Without Borders: An Investigation of Female Characters in Popular Films Across 11 Countries*. Rep. Media, Diversity, and Social Change Initiative–University of Southern California. Web. 2015.

Stout, Hilary. "Real-Life Stay-at-Home Husbands." *Marie Claire*. Web. Aug. 9, 2010.

Tanden, Neera. "Working Mother, Washington Powerhouse? Good Luck." *National Journal*. Web. July 25, 2014.

Tierney, John. "How to Win Millennials: Equality, Climate Change, and Gay Marriage." *The Atlantic*. Web. May 17, 2014.

Bureau of Labor Statistics. *Unemployment by Sex and Age, January 2014*. Rep. Web. Feb. 11, 2014.

Williams, Alex. "Just Wait Until Your Mother Gets Home." *New York Times*. Web. Aug. 10, 2012.

Wilson Hunt, Stacey and Michael O'Connell. "Lena Dunham, Amy Schumer and Comedy Actress A-List in Raunchy, R-Rated Roundtable." *Hollywood Reporter*. Web. May 27, 2015.

Winograd, Morley and Michael D. Hais. *Millennial Momentum: How a New Generation Is Remaking America*. New Brunswick: Rutgers University Press, 2011.

Epilogue: Toward Parity

INTERVIEWS: STEVE KNOTT, SABINA SHUGG, REBECCA MCGRATH, YOKO ISHIKURA AND HILLARY RODHAM CLINTON.

Aon. "Responding to the Needs of an Aging Workforce: An Aon White Paper." *Aon*. Web. April 2014.

Barsh, Joanna and Lareina Yee. "Unlocking the Full Potential of Women in the US Economy." McKinsey Consulting. Web. April 2011.

Broderick, Elizabeth. "Towards a Gender Equal Australia." Australian Human Rights Commission. Web. Nov. 18, 2014.

Casselman, Ben. "What Baby Boomers' Retirement Means for the U.S. Economy." *Five Thirty Eight*. Web. May 7, 2014.

Clements, Benedict, Katrin Elborgh-Woytek, Stefania Fabrizio, Kalpana Kochhar, Kangni Kpodar, Monique Newiak, Gerd Schwartz and Philippe Wingender. "Women, Work, and the Economy: Macroeconomic Gains from Gender Equity." International Monetary Fund. Web. September 2013.

Committee for Economic Development of Australia. *Women in Leadership: Looking Below the Surface*. Rep. Web. September 2011.

Costello, Cynthia B. and Anne J. Stone, eds. *The American Woman 2001–2002: Getting to the Top*. New York: W.W. Norton & Company, Inc., 2001.

Dent, Georgia. "The Blokes of Business Agree: Intervention Needed on Female Leaders." *Crikey*. Web. Nov. 7, 2013.

D.M. "The Incredible Shrinking Country." *The Economist*. Web. March 25, 2014.

Ewing, Walter A. *The Future of a Generation: How New Americans Will Help Support Retiring Baby Boomers.* Rep. Immigration Policy Center. Web. February 2012.

Flanders, Stephanie. "China Overtakes Japan As World's Second-biggest Economy." BBC Business. Web. Feb. 14, 2011.

Heber, Alex. "Women to Make Up 25% of Mining Workforce by 2020." *Australian Mining.* Web. Feb. 26, 2013.

"Japan PM Shinzo Abe Boosts Women in Cabinet." BBC News. Web. Sept. 3, 2014.

Kantor, Jodi. "Working Anything But 9 to 5." *New York Times Magazine.* Web. Aug. 13, 2014.

Laden, Greg. "How Many Countries Have Ever Had a Woman Leader?" *ScienceBlogs.* Web. June 3, 2012.

Lobo, Rita. "Japan Leans In: Shinzo Abe's Push for Womenomics." *World Finance.* Web. Jan. 21, 2014.

Lockwood, Nancy R. *The Aging Workforce: The Reality of the Impact of Older Workers and Eldercare in the Workplace.* Rep. Society for Human Resource Management. Web. 2003.

Lundin, Emma. "Feminist Initiative's Strong Showing in the Swedish Elections Puts Pressure on Mainstream Parties." *The Guardian.* Web. Sept. 15, 2014.

Male Champions of Change. *Progress Report 2014.* Rep. Australian Human Rights Commission. Web. 2015.

Marston, Ama. "Are Women in the West Being Left Behind on Leadership?" *The Guardian.* Web. Oct. 23, 2013.

"Morocco." Rep. The Quota Project. Web. April 4, 2014.

"New Survey Reveals Shocking Mining Stats About Women in Mining." *Mining Oil and Gas Jobs.* Web. Jan. 4, 2014.

OECD Development Centre. *2012 Social Institutions and Gender Index: Understanding the Drivers of Gender Inequality.* Rep. Web. 2012.

Ramli, David. "Updated: IBM Boss, Glen Boreham, Quits Post." *ARN.* Web. Jan. 5, 2011.

Reeves, Scott. "An Aging Workforce's Effect on U.S. Employers." *Forbes.* Web. Sept. 29, 2005.

Reuters. "New Swedish Government Mulls Quotas for Women on Company Boards." *Euractiv.* Web. Oct. 1, 2014.

Sekiguchi, Toko. "Abe Wants to Get Japan's Women Working." *Wall Street Journal.* Web. Sept. 11, 2014.

Strack, Rainer, Jens Baier and Jean-Michel Caye. *Stimulating Economies Through Fostering Talent Mobility.* Rep. BCG Perspectives. Web. March 23, 2010.

Stupnytska, Anna, Kathryn Koch, Amy MacBeath, Sandra Lawson and Kathy Matsui. *Giving Credit Where It Is Due: How Closing the Credit Gap for Women-Owned SMEs Can Drive Global Growth.* Rep. Goldman Sachs Global Markets Institute. Web. Feb. 28, 2014.

Workplace Gender Equality Agency. *Gender Workplace Statistics at a Glance.* Rep. Web. August 2015.

—ABOUT THE AUTHOR—

JAY NEWTON-SMALL has been covering Washington for 14 years, nine of them for TIME magazine. She's reported on the White House, Congress and the 2004, 2008, 2012 and 2016 presidential campaigns. She's been embedded with the Pesh Merga in Iraq, been detained in Iran and witnessed the police shootout with Dzhokhar Tsarnaev in Boston. She's covered myriad national and international events, including Hurricane Katrina; the Moore, Okla., tornadoes; the earthquake in Haiti; the *Charlie Hebdo* attack in Paris; and the Emanuel 9 massacre in Charleston, S.C. *Broad Influence*, her first book, grew out of her TIME story in October 2013 about the women of the Senate coming together during the government shutdown to restart negotiations when the men wouldn't speak to one another. Newton-Small lives in Washington, D.C.

—INDEX—